WORD OF GOD SPEAK: UNDERSTANDING THE BIBLE, HEARING GOD'S VOICE

DR. TODD PYLANT

2011

toddpylant.com

To the Creator,

Sustainer,

Redeemer,

Savior,

Deliverer,

Lord of Lords,

and Kings of Kings.

Who chose me.

And to my incredible family:

My wonderful wife, Kelli

My delightful children: Bailey, Cade, and Ainsley

TABLE OF CONTENTS

1 | TERMS AND CONDITIONS

"I agree with these terms and conditions."

How many times have you seen that statement? How many times have you actually read the terms and conditions that preceded it?

Whenever I make on online purchase, or pay a utility bill online, or download a software update, I am always asked to check a box that says, "I agree with these terms and conditions." Has anyone actually ever read the terms and conditions? I personally think the lawyers don't want us to read them or they would have written them in plain English with cute pictures. I have agreed to all sorts of terms and conditions that I have never read. How crazy is that?

Who knows what was buried inside the mountain of fine print. I might have agreed to surrender my first born child should the Rangers win the pennant next year. Perhaps, when I signed all of those papers when I bought my house, I agreed to allow the realtor's grandmother to stay at my house during the Thanksgiving holidays. When I upgraded Microsoft Office last year, did I agree to donate all of my next year's salary to Bill Gates' foundation. I sure hope not, but how would I know?

I am assuming that you don't read those terms and conditions for pretty much the same reasons I don't. Other than the fact that it would probably kill the better part of a day, I don't read them because they are full of legal phrases that I don't understand. Most likely, the fine print describes situations that don't apply to me, and they certainly won't hold my attention or keep me from falling asleep.

And really, I don't need to read them because common sense tells me what I am agreeing to, right? Common sense is enough to purchase a song at the iTunes store or to order a book from Amazon.

In short, I don't read terms and conditions because I believe nothing in there is really going to hurt me, nothing in there is really going to impact my life, and nothing in there is of interest to me. So I skip the reading and just check, "agree."

Terms and Conditions of Faith

Most of us agree to terms and conditions that not only impact us for 30 years like a mortgage, but also for eternity. I suspect you are reading this book because you are a follower of Christ. What exactly are the terms and conditions of professing Jesus as Lord? What will this Lord expect of me? What can I expect of Him? How will following Jesus change my life?

To keep the analogy going, the terms of following Christ cover everything from behaviors to beliefs. They impact how I relate to my children, my spouse, my friends, my co-workers, and even my enemies. There are expectations on how I spend my money and what I do with my possessions. In fact, the terms of following Christ describe a complete personal makeover. Following Christ means loving Him above all other relationships in my life, making Him my highest priority. That is quite a term.

But the conditions to following Christ are equally amazing. While the terms are what Christ expects of us, the conditions describe what we can expect of Christ. Peace, joy, hope, love, comfort, guidance, counsel, encouragement, companionship, and wisdom are just a few of the promises offered to the believer described in the "conditions" clause. And unlike making a purchase from the Apple store, the conditions of following Christ are more than just an initial transaction. The conditions continue to change our heart, mind, and soul until we become like Christ.

So with such great expectations upon those who would follow Jesus and with such great promises, why do so many Christians ignore the terms and conditions of following Christ as described in the Bible?

Legalese

One of the reasons I don't read the terms and conditions for common purchases is that I expect it to be filled with legalese. Legalese is the way that lawyers talk so that no one else can understand them. They use big words and fancy phrases, mostly to make sure they have continued job security since lawyers are the only ones who can translate it.

One time, I tried to be a responsible adult and read the terms and conditions before I installed Turbo Tax. That lasted all of five minutes. If they don't want me to understand it, then I don't want to read it. That will show them.

Many Christians feel the same about the Bible. The language itself might not be legalese because most English translations are written on a seventh or eighth grade reading level. But the contents can be just as confusing. If legalese is language meant to confuse rather than clarify, then much of the Bible seems to fall into that category.

I remember the first time I decided to read the Bible from cover to cover. I fell headfirst into legalese around the third chapter of Leviticus. What in the world is a grain offering, and why should I care? Irrelevant information that is over my head. Not a good combination for compelling reading.

Common Sense

Another reason I don't read the terms and conditions is because I think I already know what is in there. Or to put it another way, I believe I have enough common sense to know what is expected of me.

When I pay a utility bill online, common sense tells me that I am agreeing to have a set amount deducted from my checking account. I don't really need to read thirty pages of fine print to agree to that. I know what is expected when I bought my house: pay the mortgage payment on time. We all know that we can't sell pirated copies of software. Why read the details?

For many, the same is true of what it means to follow Christ. Surely, we all have enough common sense to know what God expects of us. God wants us to be good, be moral, go to church, be kind, and help others. Surely we don't need to wade through the book of Jeremiah to discover what common sense already tells us, right?

Reasonable Expectations

Another reason I don't read the terms and conditions is that I assume, and trust, that the people I am making the agreement with have reasonable expectations. The bank expects me to pay my bill on time, but they won't expect me to weed the flower bed in front of the bank building. Amazon expects me to agree to pay for the book, but they won't expect me to make a donation to the Salvation Army. Microsoft expects me not to sell unauthorized copies of Microsoft Office, but they won't expect me to move to Seattle and work for them at minimum wage. Common sense tells us that the expectations will be reasonable.

But what are the reasonable expectations of following Christ? Be good? What does it mean to be good? Who defines good? Would it make a difference if the fine print says that Christ expects us to bless our enemies, to forgive those who abuse us, or to give financially to help the poor? What if the fine print contains clauses about Christ entering into our hearts and souls and changing us from the inside out? What if the fine print speaks of God working through us? What if the fine print describes a good work that God created us to do? What if Christ expects us to quit our jobs and move to the other side of the globe to share the good news of God's love?

What if the expectations are anything *but* reasonable?

Relevance

Another reason I don't read the fine print is because I seriously doubt the fine print contains anything of relevance to my life. The song I purchased is relevant; the fine print is certainly not. There is nothing in the fine print that will either change my life for the better or worse. Really, what is missing from my life because I did not read the terms and conditions when I made my last hotel reservation? Absolutely nothing.

And many feel the same about the Bible. Christ rocks, but the details in the Bible are irrelevant. And what is really missing from our lives because we have not been reading the Bible? And what could be added to our lives if we suddenly started to read it?

What If It Could Be More?

But what if the Bible could be more than just confusing and irrelevant terms and conditions? Or better question, what if it was meant to be more?

What if the Scriptures hold the key to living into the fullness of all that God created you to be? What if God actually intended His words to be life changing, impacting, and personally profitable to you?

Wouldn't that be a game changer?

Profitable. Now that is a powerful word. Profitable means "yielding advantageous results" (*Merriam-Webster*). If the Bible were profitable, or could be profitable, it would certainly be more than terms and conditions that we would want to ignore. If it were profitable, if I experienced the positive results of Scripture, then that would be something different entirely.

2 | MAKE IT PROFITABLE

Before any of us take on a project, whether it is repainting the living room or going to graduate school, most of us do some kind of cost benefit analysis. Basically, we analyze whether the benefit of doing something is worth the cost of getting it done. Any project takes resources and effort, and the return on investment must be of value on some level to the one putting forth the effort. The value may be objective (this degree will increase my earning potential) or subjective (learning photography will be fun to me), but for us to put forth continued effort towards a project, there must be some degree of perceived value.

Reading the Bible, and pursuing spiritual growth, is no different. We all do a cost/benefit analysis in our heads before making a commitment to attend church, join a small group, or read the Bible.

I am assuming since you have made it this far into a book about understanding the Bible, that you are at least considering putting forth more effort in your spiritual growth. On some level, you have done some degree of cost benefit analysis. But before we jump off into trying to understand the Bible, into putting forth the effort, let's make sure that we understand the benefits first.

Going back to those annoying terms and conditions, in what way is the Bible different, or should be different, or *could* be different, than just a list of terms and conditions?

Is The Bible Relevant?

I said earlier that I don't read the terms and conditions because there is nothing in there that is going to really impact my life. Or another way of saying it is that I don't think anything is missing from my life because I have not been reading them. My life seems to have been going along just fine. The bills get paid. The software gets updated. Hotel rooms get reserved.

But this is where we need to stop and ask a very simple question: what exactly is the Bible? Is the Bible a theological textbook? Is the Bible a rule book? Is the Bible a love letter from God? Is the Bible the opinions of ancient philosophers?

If the Bible is a theological textbook, then normal people can ignore it just like normal people don't read medical textbooks. If the Bible is a rule book, then normal people can ignore it just like most players have never read the rule book for the sport they play. Trust me, I officiated high school football games for four years. Not even the coaches have read the rule book.

And if the Bible is a love letter from God, as some preachers call it, then how often do we need to read it? No offense, but once you know God loves you, what else is there to know? And if it is just the opinion of people who lived a long time ago, then it can stay on the shelf right next to Plato and Socrates.

But the Bible is different, or at least claims to be different. It is more than a book. It is more than ink on a page. And it is that something more that transforms the Bible from irrelevant "terms and conditions" into something relevant and life giving.

The Breath of God

Consider one of the most significant verses in the Bible about the nature of Scripture.

> *But as for you, continue in what you have learned and have firmly believed, knowing from whom you learned it and how from childhood you have been acquainted with the sacred writings, which are able to make you wise for salvation through faith in Christ Jesus. All Scripture is breathed out by God and profitable for teaching, for reproof, for correction, and for training in righteousness, that the man of God may be competent, equipped for every good work. (2 Timothy 3.14-17)*

The apostle Paul wrote these words to young Timothy to encourage him to stay faithful to Christ despite the growing godlessness around him. But I want you to notice how he described the Scriptures to Timothy.

The sacred writings, or the Scriptures, are "breathed out by God." In the original Greek, that phrase is one compound word, combining the two words

"God" and "to breathe." That word is often translated as "inspired" (as the *New American Standard Bible* does), meaning that God breathed out the Scriptures. The Scriptures come from deep within God Himself.

But "God breathed" means more than just the origination of the Scriptures. It speaks to the current nature of the Scriptures. Because it is the breath of God, God's continued presence is found in the Scriptures, which is why the Word of God is described as living and active.

> *For the word of God is living and active, sharper than any two-edged sword, piercing to the division of soul and of spirit, of joints and of marrow, and discerning the thoughts and intentions of the heart. And no creature is hidden from his sight, but all are naked and exposed to the eyes of him to whom we must give account.(Hebrews 4.12-13)*

Rule books don't discern the thoughts and intentions of the heart. Rule books don't pierce to the division of soul and spirit. Rule books are not a person "to whom we must give an account."

The Bible is the very breath of living God. It is a living book. The Bible is not a text book. The Bible is not a rule book. The Bible is not a theology book. The Bible is the very breath of God.

And this is the reason why the Bible is relevant to our lives. God speaks through the Bible. Present tense. He continues to breath through the sacred text and into our souls. The Bible is relevant because we are in relationship with a living God who is relevant because He is alive and He continues to speak.

If you get nothing else out of this book, then I hope this one truth will be etched in your soul: **the primary reason we read the written Word is so that we can hear the Living Word speak into our souls**. We don't read the written Word to learn Bible facts, though they are useful and important. We don't read the written Word to impress our friends in our small group. We don't read the written Word to earn brownie points with God. We read the written Word so that we can hear the Living Word speak.

Breathless Scripture

That may sound like a simple concept, but not everybody gets that. If you can embrace that one simple truth, that the reason you read the written Word is so that you can hear the Living Word speak to you, that alone will liberate your spiritual walk from the abyss of terms and conditions.

For some reason, the people of God are always tempted to turn the living, breathing, active Word of God into a lifeless collection of spiritual truisms.

This was exactly what happened during the days of Jesus. The Scriptures were held in high regard and were the object of intense study. Whole religious communities existed for no other purpose than to study the content of the Scriptures. The Pharisees, Sadducees, Scribes, and religious lawyers professionally studied, taught, and copied the Scriptures. From the outside, it looked like they were on the right track.

Yet, despite all of their study, they missed the point. Jesus said about them,

> *You search the Scriptures because you think that in them you have eternal life; and it is they that bear witness about me, yet you refuse to come to me that you may have life. (John 5.39-40)*

According to Jesus, the Scriptures bear witness to Him so that we might find life. But the religious leaders of His day missed that. They studied the contents of Scripture but missed the God of Scripture. And they missed Jesus. And they missed life.

So, the goal of our experience with the Scriptures is to hear God speaking through the Scriptures, to be pointed to Jesus, to find life.

Experience with the Scriptures

Let me take a moment to introduce a new phrase: experience with the Scriptures. I don't know that I am the first person to use that phrase, but this is the first time I have used it in this book.

It is my hope that you will move from "reading the Bible" to "experiencing the Word of God." Reading the Bible can be more like reading a religious textbook

Dr. Todd Pylant 17

while experiencing the Bible has more to do with interacting with Christ, the Living Word, who is experienced through the Bible.

All of our efforts to regularly read the Bible, or to meditate on the Bible, or to memorize Scripture are part of our journey to experience the Christ of the Bible. If our experience with the Bible is less than this, then it *will* seem irrelevant and lifeless. Until we get to the point in our faith journey where God is speaking to us through the Scriptures, where we are experiencing the Living Word, the Bible will never be profitable.

If we can get to that point, to the point where we hear God speak to us through the Bible, then how could our life be changed? What would be the benefits? How could that be profitable to us?

Don't We Already Know What Is In The Bible?

Back to the pesky terms and conditions, the ones I never read. I don't read them because I already know what is in them. Of course, that is not exactly true. I don't know what indemnity clauses might be in subsection 24 of the first part of the second part. I don't even know what that previous sentence means. What I am saying is that generally speaking, I think I know what is basically in the terms and conditions. The general knowledge that I already have, combined with a little common sense, will tell me all I need to know.

The rest is just unimportant details.

Right.

Think about whatever it is that you love. Do you love fantasy football, or photography, or working on cars, or painting, or economics? Do you have a passion about cooking, or running half-marathons, or politics, or history? Regardless of what your "thing" is, I bet that you take great delight in the "unimportant details" that others around you ignore.

When you get into conversations with your friends about your hobbies, don't you see that as you begin to talk about your hobby in great detail that your friends begin to lose interest or roll their eyes? When you talk about F stops, or fantasy points, or carburetor settings, you get all excited because you know that the real joy about what you love is experienced in the details. You cannot be passionate about photography or painting or cooking and not find some excitement in the details.

The love of something is in the details.

I would say that our love for Christ is no different. Remember, we are not talking about developing a love for the Bible. We are talking about experiencing the Christ, the Living Word, through the Bible. And just like you love to know the intimate details of your spouse or child, you will want to know the intimate details of the Christ who gave Himself up for your salvation.

The truth is we really do *not* know what is in the Bible. Generally speaking, we might have a vague idea, but we don't really know what the Bible teaches.

George Barna may be the king of religious pollsters, but I did a little survey in my own church. I surveyed the Sunday night crowd in a Baptist church, which means these were the hard core, committed, mostly mature believers. What did I discover?

Only 8% of them could name all Ten Commandments. Less than half had a plan to regularly read the Bible. Less than a third were able to write down one verse from memory from the gospels. About half could arrange nine major biblical characters in chronological order. Sure, generally speaking, we "know what's in there," but in reality, we don't.

But there needs to be some reason for us to dive into the details of the Bible, to put forth serious effort to understand the Scriptures. Since I train for half-marathons, I read the details about training plans because I think they will help me to improve my time. Since I am a writer, I attend writing conferences and focus on the details of publishing because I believe it will make me a better writer. If you are a photographer, you continue to hone your craft because you think there is a practical benefit.

Which is why the apostle Paul described in detail the potential benefits of pursuing a life changing experience with Scripture. When we combine our confession that we don't know what is in the Bible and our desire to experience the Christ of the Bible, and add to that an expectation of the benefits of experiencing the Bible, then we are ready to jump into Scriptures.

Teaching

According to Paul, the Bible is profitable for teaching, for reproof, for correction, and for training in righteousness, that the man of God may be competent, equipped for every good work. I think if we take a closer look at each of those categories, we might see that common sense might not take us as far as we think.

The first advantageous result of investing time and energy into the Word of God is that it is profitable for teaching. The word translated "teaching" can also be translated as "instruction or doctrine" (*Thayer's*). While some may consider doctrine as the irrelevant study of spiritual minutia, orthodoxy (correct doctrine) has always been vitally important to the health of the people of God. How we understand basic issues like the nature of God, the way of salvation, the problem of pain and suffering, life after death, assurance of salvation, the person of Jesus, the role of the Holy Spirit, and a myriad of other religious questions significantly shapes our religious experience and practice.

What we believe to be true about spiritual things is extremely important. And the fine points are extremely important. Is there a hell? What happens after we die? Does prayer work? The truth behind these questions are significant, and life altering.

God's people have always wrestled with false teachings, and always will. Theological discussions are not just a part of our history, they are a part of our present. Listen to the words of Peter.

> *But false prophets also arose among the people, just as there will be false teachers among you, who will secretly bring in destructive heresies, even denying the Master who bought them, bringing upon themselves swift destruction. And many will follow their sensuality, and because of them the way of truth will be blasphemed. And in their greed they will exploit you with false words. Their condemnation from long ago is not idle, and their destruction is not asleep. (2 Peter 2.1-3)*

False teachers will secretly bring in destructive heresies that deny Christ, and many will follow them. Their motivations will be greed, and their appeal will be sensuality. And the result of following these false teachers is swift destruction.

The church today continues to battle false teachings. The Scriptures, while easily accessible to almost every believer, remain ignored and forgotten. False teachers peddle the gospel to the masses by distorting its basic message, and yet they sell huge numbers of books and attract crowds by the thousands.

While debates over the number of angels who can dance on the head of a pin are useless, it is imperative that we have a good understanding of the doctrinal content of Scripture. Without this basic building block, a life cannot be transformed into the image of Christ. A believer must first be transformed by the renewing of the mind (see Romans 12.1-2).

The Word of God is profitable because it teaches us what is true about spiritual things.

Correction

The Scriptures are also profitable because God uses them to correct us. One aspect of correction is the other side of the teaching coin, correcting a person's false beliefs. But it also goes beyond our understanding and reaches into our actions.

The Scriptures impact far more than just our mind. The apostle John was very clear: "For this is the love of God, that we keep his commandments. And his commandments are not burdensome" (1 John 5.3). God expects His people to be obedient to His commands. His first revelations were commands (the Ten Commandments), Jesus gave His followers a new command (to love one another), and the seven churches in Revelation were either affirmed or condemned by their obedience or disobedience to the Lord's commands.

God instructed His people to be careful to obey "all" His commands (Deuteronomy 6.2). In other words, it is not enough for followers of Christ to be devoted to "being good." We must know the practical definitions of godliness as described in the Scriptures. The law was very specific in describing righteousness, and the New Testament is equally specific in describing unrighteousness.

Now the works of the flesh are evident: sexual immorality, impurity, sensuality, idolatry, sorcery, enmity, strife, jealousy, fits of anger, rivalries, dissensions, divisions, envy, drunkenness, orgies, and things like these. I warn you, as I warned you before, that those who do such things will not inherit the kingdom of God. But the fruit of the Spirit is love, joy, peace, patience, kindness, goodness, faithfulness, gentleness, self-control; against such things there is no law. (Galatians 5.19-23)

In order for a Christian to be able to obey "all" the Lord's commands, we must know the specific instructions in Scripture regarding righteousness.

Which is why we speak of experiencing the Scriptures more than just reading the Bible. Speaking of the Holy Spirit, Jesus said,

And when he comes, he will convict the world concerning sin and righteousness and judgment. (John 16.8)

When we experience the Living Word, the Spirit of God will convict us of our sins and correct our behaviors and attitudes. And this Living Word is experienced through the Scriptures, which is living and active, and through which, the Spirit judges our thoughts and intentions (see Hebrews 4.12-13).

We may think we know what it means to be good, but the specific correction by the Spirit comes through experiencing the exact descriptions of holiness as revealed in the Bible.

For the grace of God has appeared, bringing salvation for all people, training us to renounce ungodliness and worldly passions, and to live self-controlled, upright, and godly lives in the present age. (Titus 2.11-12)

For the Bible to be profitable, we must submit our thoughts, attitudes, and behaviors to the Living Word. We must confess when convicted, and repent (change directions).

The correcting ministry of the Word of God is part of what makes it profitable and fruit bearing for Christians. But this only happens when we submit ourselves to it.

Training in Righteousness

The third advantageous result of Scripture is that God uses it to train us in righteousness. The word translated "training" is one of those Greek words that is so rich in meaning that it is almost impossible to carry it over into the English language.

The Greek word is *paideia* and refers to the whole training and education of a child. It involves everything from mental development, moral development, and even physical development. The wealthy class in first century Rome would often enlist the services of a *paidagogos* to oversee the development of their children. This tutor, or guardian, was charged with the duty of supervising the mental, moral, and physical development of the children under their charge. This person supervised the training and education and development of the child.

Paul was using this image as he talks about the ways that God uses the Scriptures in our lives. The Scriptures, the very breath of God, oversee our development into righteousness. Righteousness definitely involves spiritual truth, and it surely involves our morality, but righteousness is so much more. A simple definition of righteousness is a right relationship with God. So God uses the Scriptures to mature us into Christlikeness.

The writer of Hebrews talked about developing into righteousness. His concern was that some were not progressing in their development.

> *About this we have much to say, and it is hard to explain, since you have become dull of hearing. For though by this time you ought to be teachers, you need someone to teach you again the basic principles of the oracles of God. You need milk, not solid food, for everyone who lives on milk is unskilled in the word of righteousness, since he is a child. But solid food is for the mature, for those who have their powers of discernment trained by constant practice to distinguish good from evil. (Hebrews 5.11-14)*

There were some in the church who should have been maturing, who should have become skilled in the word of righteousness, whose powers of discernment should be trained through practice to distinguish good from evil. But their growth was stunted.

If we ignore the Scriptures because common sense teaches us all we need to know, then we will remain immature with undeveloped powers of discernment.

The Scriptures are profitable because they oversee our spiritual development.

Equipping for Every Good Work

Finally, the Scriptures are profitable because God uses them to equip us for good works.

Let me share with you two remarkable truths from the Bible that help me to understand what the divine author of the Bible wants to do with the Bible in my life. The first truth comes from the book of Ephesians.

> *For we are his workmanship, created in Christ Jesus for good works, which God prepared beforehand, that we should walk in them. (Ephesians 2.10)*

I think this is one of the most incredible truths in the New Testament. According to this promise, each one of us has been created by God to do something special, something uniquely designed by our Creator. We are His workmanship. We don't have to go find something to do for God! God has already prepared what He wants us to do, and has created us uniquely to walk in those good works. What an amazing truth! God created you and me with a purpose in mind, and He has already prepared the good works He wants us to do.

But how will we ever be prepared to live into and fulfill those good works? How will you and I become the person God created us to be, doing the good works He created us to do?

The answer is that God uses the Scriptures to equip us for every good work.

> *All Scripture is breathed out by God and profitable for teaching, for reproof, for correction, and for training in righteousness, that the man of God may be competent, equipped for every good work. (2 Timothy 3.16)*

God's breath is profitable because it makes us "competent," a word that speaks about maturity or completeness. God's breath is profitable because it "equips" us, a word which means to furnish completely.

Do you want to be mature? Do you want to be fully furnished? Do you want to be equipped to do the very thing God created you to do? One of the primary ways that will happen in your life is through experiencing the Scriptures.

Legalese

Back to those annoying terms and conditions. Even when we try to be responsible and read them, we get lost in the complicated language and legal terms. While written in English, they sure seem like a foreign language.

Most of us own a Bible translated into our native language. And since you are reading this book and this book is written in English, I am assuming you are reading a Bible translated into English. Most English Bible translations are written on a seventh grade reading level because that is the average reading level of the American adult. That means that the problem is not that we cannot understand the vocabulary or grammar of the Bible. I think the problem is that we don't understand how all the pieces of the Bible fit together into one story.

The One Story of the Bible

For many believers, the Bible seems to be a collection of disconnected stories much like a collection of fairy tales. They know the stories of David and Goliath, Elijah on Mount Carmel, the woman at the well, but they don't know how these individual stories connect to the big picture.

The Bible is really the one long story of God's relationship with His people. The story began in creation and ends in glory. I believe that we understand the Bible more completely when we see the one big story and then understand how each individual story fits into the larger story.

One of the reasons I have written this book is because this was a significant part of the Bible coming to life in my personal faith journey. As a college student, I served a church as a youth minister. I wanted to teach the seven people in my youth group the Bible, but I could see they weren't getting the big picture. So I started to tell the one long story of God's relationship with His people. And as I prepared to teach them, the Bible came to life for me. When I understood how each individual story related to the whole, I experienced Christ in a whole new way.

I have written this book is to help you understand the one large story of God's relationship with His people. I hope to translate the "legalese" of the Bible into the simple language of a story. To that end, the main portion of this book will tell the story of the Bible by dividing the story into nine acts. Each act has a primary character and plot theme. My hope is that when you see how each individual story relates the one story of the Bible, then you will be better equipped to encounter the Christ of the Bible.

New Covenant Eyes

Understanding the one story of the Bible and how each individual story fits into that one large story does more for us than give us an "ahah" moment. It enables us to read the Bible through new covenant eyes.

As you know, the Bible is divided into two testaments. But more importantly, the story of God's relationship with His people is divided into two covenants: the old covenant of law and the new covenant of grace. Those under the new covenant of grace have a difficult time understanding and applying the story of the Bible that took place under the previous covenant of law. But the promise of 2 Timothy 3.16, that all Scripture is profitable, is a promise about the Old Testament, too.

Believers tend to ignore Leviticus and the Old Testament minor prophets. We dismiss them as part of the old covenant of law. But the promise of 2 Timothy 3.16 is that God still speaks through the Old Testament to us today. And if we ignore that portion of His breath, then there are teachings and corrections and trainings and equipping that we are missing out on.

I understand how you might wonder how the book of Leviticus could be profitable today. After all, that is a book that describes sacrifices, offerings, and dietary codes, things that have passed away under the new covenant of grace. But it is a book about worship, a book where God describes the way we are to approach Him. Worship in Leviticus was personal, costly, sacrificial, and confessional. While our worship today is through the once and for all sacrifice of Christ, God still speaks to us today about worship through the book of Leviticus. He still desires worship where the worshipper is personally involved, where confession and repentance takes place, and where we take up our cross and follow Him.

I hope God is able to use this book to equip new covenant believers to read the Old Testament through new covenant eyes. With each act of the story, I will attempt to explain how followers of Christ can still hear God speak to them through these seemingly irrelevant portions. My hope is that you will be pleasantly surprised to hear God's voice through books like Amos, Haggai, and Ezra.

Developing Basic Spiritual Disciplines

But even if we come to understand the one major story of God's relationship with His people, and even if we develop new covenant eyes, the Bible will never become profitable unless we develop some basic spiritual disciplines. The truth is that it does not matter how much you know about the Bible, if you do not mature in the practice of four basic spiritual disciplines, the Bible will never be profitable to you.

You may not be familiar with the term "spiritual disciplines." Spiritual discipline are those activities that we do to put ourselves in the path way of God's grace. In and of themselves, these spiritual activities will not bring about spiritual growth. But they put ourselves in the pathway of God's grace so that God can do something in and through our lives.

Another way to look at spiritual disciplines is through the eyes of a farmer. A farmer cannot cause his seed to grow. He can prepare the soil, plant the seed, and pull the weeds, but God alone causes the growth. Spiritual disciplines are a way that we prepare the field so that God can cause the growth.

Without these basic spiritual disciplines, the Bible will never be profitable to you. You can understand it. You can get a doctorate in theology. You can study the original languages. But if you never develop these basic disciplines, it will never be profitable for you. God will never be able to use it to teach, correct, train, or equip you.

What are those four basic disciplines? For the Bible to be profitable, you must read it on a regular basis. For the Bible to be profitable, you must be meditating on the Word of God. For the Bible to be profitable, you must be regularly memorizing the Word of God and hiding it in your heart. For the Bible to be profitable to you, you must be dialoguing with God about it through prayer.

<u>Regularly Reading Scripture</u>

Many believers never read the Bible outside of church. If you only read the Bible at church, it will never become useful to you in your pursuit of living into the good works God has planned for you to do. Never. You must read it regularly, and you must have a plan, which most believers simply do not have.

To encourage you to develop the spiritual discipline of regularly reading the Bible, I have included suggested daily readings that coincide with each act of the story. I will intentionally expose you to different Bible reading plans through these daily readings, and in the last chapter I will give you some more Bible reading plan resources.

But you will never get anywhere in your spiritual life without a plan to regularly read Scripture.

I want to challenge you to use this book as a study guide more than a text book. While you could read this book from cover to cover in a few days, the most beneficial way to read this book is to read one act a week. Take the week to digest the content of that act, and take the week to complete the daily readings. Not only will you be learning the story of the Bible, but you will be developing the disciplines necessary to hear God speak through the Bible.

<u>Meditation</u>

The second basic spiritual discipline that every believer should practice is meditation.

Meditation is not mumbling some phrase over and over while sitting in an uncomfortable position. Meditation is not emptying the mind as some eastern false religions teach. Meditation is to think deeply about the meaning of God's Word. Meditation is to chew on a truth. Meditation is talking with God about how to apply a biblical truth to your life. If you know how to worry, then you know how to meditate because worry is just meditation in reverse.

One of the best ways to meditate is through the practice of journaling. Journaling is capturing what God is saying to you through His Word by writing it down. A journal does not have to be fancy nor expensive to be effective. A simple spiral bound notebook will do.

The method of meditation and journaling that has been most effective for me personally is the SOAP method. I first discovered this method when I was given a *Life Journal, First Steps* by a friend. It is a very simple journaling method that can be used with any Bible reading plan.

There is a journal page in this book for each daily Bible reading. As you read these suggested daily readings, pay attention to the verse of Scripture from that reading that jumps out at you. This is Spirit of God pricking your spirit. Write that verse in your journal (Scripture is the S of SOAP).

Then take some time to make a few observations about that verse (observation is the O of SOAP). Is there a significant word of truth or correction? What did you see? Observations can also include questions. Is there something in the Scripture that you don't understand that you would like to learn more about?

Then, take some time to ask God how He wishes to apply that verse to your life today (application is the A of SOAP). Why is God illuminating this verse to you today, of all days? What is God saying to you? How will you be different today because of what you just read?

Pay attention to the four areas of profitability. What is God teaching you? How is God correcting you? How can God use this to train you in righteousness? How can God use this to equip you for the good works He created you to do?

Then, write out a prayer in which you talk back to God about what He is saying to you (prayer is the P of SOAP).

This is a very simple, yet effective method that leads you to meditate on the Word each day.

Unfortunately, most of you will skip right over the meditation discipline because you don't like to write or because you have never kept a journal before. Beware, you are missing out on something that can radically change your life.

Scripture Memory

Another necessary basic spiritual discipline is Scripture memory. The psalmist said it well,

> *I have stored up your word in my heart, that I might not sin against you. (Psalm 119.11)*

We store God's words in our heart by memorizing them.

Many believers practice the "somewhere in the Bible it says something like" theory of Scripture memory. This is not Scripture memory. We memorize Scripture when we can quote it word for word *and* remember the reference. The exact words of Scripture have power, and one day, the Spirit of God will bring to your memory a truth from Scripture that you memorized years before. The practice of Scripture memory will change your Christian walk.

With each act of the story, I suggest several possible verses to commit to memory. Take the week to do the work of memorizing one of those verses. Write it out daily. Write it on a note card and tape it to your bathroom mirror. Tape it to your visor in your car. Read it every morning on your phone. Do whatever it takes to store that word in your heart and soul.

Prayer

The fourth spiritual discipline is prayer. Prayer is nothing more than talking to God, and most of us don't have any problem bringing our problems and needs to God in prayer.

But the type of prayer that matures the believer is more than "God help me" prayers. We need to develop the discipline of dialoguing with God about life. Prayer is a two way conversation. God's Spirit speaks to us through His Word, and we speak back to Him through prayer. If you are not dialoguing with God about your life and His words, then your spiritual life will never mature into the fullness of Christ.

Now We Are Ready

If you are convinced that the Bible is more than a textbook, if you are convinced that the Bible is the very breath of God, if you want to experience Christ through the Bible, if you want the Bible to become profitable to you so that God can teach you, correct you, train you, and equip you, if you are ready to add to your faith journey the basic spiritual disciplines to put yourself in the pathway of God's grace, then we are ready to take a deeper look at the Bible.

Before we look at the nine acts of the one story of the Bible, let's take a few moments to ask the question, "Where did the Bible come from?" How did God's breath get from His heart to our hands?

3 | FROM GOD'S HEART TO OUR HANDS

When the first Christians quoted Scripture, they described Scripture with an incredible phrase.

> *Sovereign Lord, who made the heaven and the earth and the sea and everything in them, who through the mouth of our father David, your servant, said by the Holy Spirit, "Why did the Gentiles rage, and the peoples plot in vain? The kings of the earth set themselves, and the rulers were gathered together, against the Lord and against his Anointed." (Acts 4.24-26)*

The church understood these words from Psalm 21, written by King David almost 1000 years beforehand, to be spoken by the Spirit through the mouth of David. God's breath came through the Scripture writer and onto the page of sacred text.

How did the Bible get from God's heart to our hands?

It is an interesting process to see how God's revelation of Himself developed from the pens of the authors and now sits in a nice leather bound book in our hands. It took a period of over 1500 years and more than 40 different authors from all across the Middle East to write 66 books that deal with a variety of subjects.

God was not only at work revealing Himself to the Scripture writers, but He was also at work preserving that revelation so that it continues to be profitable to you and me today. So before we jump into the one story of God's relationship with His people as told through the Scriptures, let us take some time to appreciate the work of God in bringing His Word into our lives.

A Fair Warning

Let me offer you a fair warning before you get too far into this chapter.

I remember when my father first started reading the Tom Clancy novels. While my father loved them, my mother was not the biggest fan. But since they are both avid readers, mom agreed to give it a try. Her first Clancy book was *The Hunt For Red October* which is about a rogue Russian submarine commander who wants to defect to the USA and take the new, top secret submarine with him. Like so many Clancy novels, he went into great detail about the submarine, prompting my mom to say, "I didn't want to know how to build a nuclear submarine; I just wanted to read about one."

Have you have ever asked someone for the time, and they told you how to build a watch? Some of you might have the same reaction to this chapter. You asked a few questions about the Bible, and I am going to tell you how it was built.

This chapter explores how God inspired the Scripture writers with His words, and how those written words were transmitted through history to you and me. I have tried to give you enough historical information to explain that process, but I understand that it might be more information than you are interested in at this particular point of your faith journey. But before you skip this chapter because you don't want to know how the submarine was built, let me encourage you to reconsider.

Some of these issues are absolutely critical in understanding the Bible and learning how to hear God speak to you through His words. For instance, what you believe about the inspiration of the Scriptures will pretty much determine the role the Bible will play in your life. And unfortunately, so many believers have never given that issue much thought, and yet their relationship with God's Word is completely impacted by that one belief.

So, please don't skip this chapter. It's worth knowing how the Bible was built.

Why Think About How The Bible Was Built?

Why take the time to look at the formation of the Bible?

First, we really ought to have some foundation behind the assumptions of our faith. Yes, we live by faith and not by sight, but we must not live by foolish faith. Charles Manson honestly and passionately believed that God told him to kill those people in the 70s, but we think he is mentally unstable. We can see how he should have done some examination of his assumptions. We need to do the same, mostly because of the second reason.

The second reason this study is relevant is because of the world of apologetics. Apologetics is "a branch of theology devoted to the defense of the divine origin and authority of Christianity" (*Merriam-Webster*). In short, apologetics is the process of defending the faith, and we never really know when we will be called upon to defend our faith.

If for no other reason, I need to know the answer to this question because I am a parent. While a six year old might accept the Bible as the inspired word of God without question, one day the child will become a thirteen year old who will challenge everything. When that child asks me, "How do we know the Bible is the Word of God?," I need to be ready to answer that question.

But even if you are not a parent, you have co-workers, friends, and neighbors who will question you about your faith. And their questions may not be accusatory or belittling. They may be the barriers that are keeping them from faith. I want you to be equipped for the good work of sharing your faith with those who have yet to put their faith in Christ.

Before we get into the one story of God's relationship with His people as told in the Bible, let's examine this question about the origins of the Bible by focusing on four key terms. Each term will describe a step in the process of God's Word moving from His heart to our hands.

Inspiration

The fist concept to consider is the inspiration of the Bible. By inspiration, we are speaking about

> *The supernatural influence of the Holy Spirit upon the Scripture writers which rendered their writings an accurate record of the revelation or which resulted in what they wrote actually being the Word of God. (Erickson, 199)*

As we try to pick apart this process, we should remember the words of the apostle Peter,

*For no prophecy was ever produced by the will of man, but men spoke
from God as they were carried along by the Holy Spirit. (2 Peter 1.21)*

Inspiration is an attempt to understand the "how" of 2 Peter 1.21. How did the
Spirit move a person to speak and write on God's behalf?

What we are talking about is the work of the Holy Spirit. The apostle Peter
spoke about this work when he quoted from Psalm 69 in one of his first
sermons.

*Brothers, the Scripture had to be fulfilled, which the Holy Spirit spoke
beforehand by the mouth of David concerning Judas. (Acts 1.16)*

Peter understood the Scriptures to be nothing less than the Spirit speaking
through the writers.

Whatever we say about inspiration, it is an attempt to understand the work of
the Spirit of God speaking through the writers of the Scriptures to us.

Theories of Inspiration

Because this is a difficult process to understand, several different theories
about how the Spirit of God carried out this work have developed. Depending
upon which theory we embrace, it will determine how we treat the Scriptures.

We all have a "theory of inspiration" even if we are not able to articulate it or
even define it. We each hold core beliefs about what to do with this book, and
how it relates to God, and what kind of authority it has over our lives.

The Intuition Theory

The intuition theory says that the Scripture writers had a high degree of insight.
They were a type of religious genius. The work of the Spirit was to give them a
brilliant religious mind at birth, but there was no particular revelatory work of
the Spirit at the moment of writing down the sacred text.

If we adopt this view of inspiration, then we are relatively free to abandon the
text when we feel like we have reached a higher level of religious insight than

the biblical writers. In fact, the Word of God is nothing more than the wisdom of people, which is ever changing.

The Illumination Theory

The illumination theory moves beyond the intuition theory by seeing the Spirit at work in heightening the normal powers of the Scripture writers at the moment of writing the sacred text. Though the writers were given an increased perception about spiritual matters, there was still no direct revelation from the Spirit to the writer, just an increased ability to discover truth.

Once again, if we adopt this view, we are free to abandon the truth claims of the Scriptures whenever we feel that the Spirit gives us an increased ability to discover truth that might trump that of the Scripture writers.

The Dynamic Theory

The dynamic theory begins to see the Spirit and writer at work together in the producing of the sacred text. In this theory, the Spirit directed the thoughts and concepts of the writer to the thoughts and concepts he or she should have while allowing the writer's own distinctive personality to come into play in the choice of words or expressions.

For example, the Spirit led Paul to the truth that we are struggling with spiritual forces in this world, but Paul's personality described that struggle using an analogy of armor and weaponry (see Ephesians 6.10-12).

So, the question is, "What is inspired"? Did the Spirit inspire merely the thought or did the Spirit inspire the exact expression of that thought? In this view, the Word of God is really found behind the text, behind the expression of that Word.

Some who understand inspiration in this way have tried to discover the thought behind the expression, even liberating the thought from the expression. Often, the end result is that the identified thought bears little resemblance to the original expression.

With this theory of inspiration, like the ones before it, the text itself is not inspired.

The Verbal Theory

The verbal theory sees the work of the Spirit as so intense that the exact word which God wanted the writer to use at that point was used. This goes beyond just the influence of thought, but to the selection of the words used by the author. At this point, inspiration involves revelation which led to an inspired text, a sacred text. The actual words on the page are inspired.

Here, the text itself takes on the power of sacred text. The actual word chosen is the inspiration of God, not just the ideas behind them.

The Dictation Theory

The dictation theory sees the writers as little more than just secretaries to whom the Spirit dictated the divine text. We see this in Moses on Mount Sinai and with John in the Book of Revelation where the angel said to John, "Write what you have seen" (Revelation 1.19).

Choosing a Theory of Inspiration

Which one of these theories is correct? The best way to handle that question is to look at how the New Testament writers and Jesus treated the sacred text of their times, what we call the Old Testament.

First, Jesus and the New Testament writers viewed Scripture as revelation from the Spirit. We have already noted that Peter understood Scripture as the Spirit speaking through the Scripture writer.

Second, Jesus viewed the words of Scripture as inspired by God. Consider the following exchange between Jesus and the religious leaders from John 10. Jesus was debating with the Jews about whether or not He was the Messiah. Jesus claimed to be one with the Father, and the Jews accused Him of blasphemy. In response, Jesus said,

Is it not written in your Law, 'I have said you are gods'? If he called them gods, to whom the word of God came, and the Scripture cannot be broken, what about the one whom the Father set apart as His very own and sent into the world? (John 10.34-35).

Exposition of this text is difficult and not the focus here. I quote this verse for two reasons.

Notice that Jesus said that the word of God came to the Scripture writer. Scripture, according to Jesus, was the result of a revelation from God by the Spirit. Moreover, notice how much emphasis Jesus put on the plurality of the word "gods." In other words, Jesus was implying that the specific word chosen by the Scripture writer was the result of the Word of God coming to the writer through the Spirit.

So, either the verbal or the dictation model seems to best represent the biblical view of inspiration of the Old Testament. The word of the Lord came to the Scripture writer in such a powerful way that the end result was that the writer used the exact words desired by the Spirit. The Spirit worked through the distinctive personalities of each writer, but the end result was an inspired text, down to the word choice.

The primary reason for choosing a theory of inspiration wisely is because it will determine how much authority we apply to the words of the sacred text themselves. How authoritative is the text? According to Jesus, the words on the page are the Word of God as revealed through the Spirit to the Scripture writers, and God continues to speak through the Scriptures to us today.

Canonization

When Jesus walked this earth, He knew of a sacred text. It was called "Scripture," and it was what we call the Old Testament.

The fact that the Jews had a collection of sacred writings is quite amazing. When Jesus lived, books were not printed on pages collected together. They were written on scrolls. These were large and did not contain much text. For instance, one scroll might be able to contain the book of Genesis, but not much more. To read the Old Testament would require you to go to a place where over 25 scrolls were stored.

So, it was not a matter of one book being agreed upon by the community of faith as being "sacred." It was the matter of a collection of scrolls being agreed upon by the community of faith as being "sacred."

From the beginning, we know the Lord commanded a few men to write down certain things for future generations to know. The Lord told Moses to write down the law and store it beside the Ark of the Covenant (see Deuteronomy 31.24-26). The Lord told Jeremiah to write down His words. His scribe, Baruch, actually wrote down the prophet's words twice (see Jeremiah 36.4). Though not told to, Joshua wrote down his testimony and placed it in the sanctuary (Joshua 24.26).

Of course, writing something down and having it viewed as sacred text are two different things. I write newsletter articles for our church all the time, but no one in their right mind would confuse them with sacred text. However, the Old Testament gives testimony that these writings were seen as Scripture. For instance, Josiah and Ezra both read the Book of the Law before the people as sacred text (see 2 Kings 22.8 and Nehemiah 8.1). In addition, Daniel referred to Jeremiah's writings as "Scripture" (see Daniel 9.2).

By the time of the New Testament, we know the Jews of the first century regarded this collection as sacred text. For instance, John 7.42 calls the book of Micah "Scripture" (see John 7.42). Peter quoted from Psalm 69 in Acts 1 and called it "Scripture." Paul quoted Genesis 15.6 in Romans 4, calling it "Scripture." James called Leviticus 19.18 "Scripture" in James 2.8.

So, the early church was convinced that the writings of the Old Testament were indeed Scripture. How did they get from the writing stage to the sacred text stage?

The Concept of Canon

This question is really about the "canonization of Scripture." Of course, this is just the language that stuffy theologians use to describe the process by which the community of faith came to view the collection of writings as sacred text.

The word "canon" means rule or standard. Throughout history, "canon" has meant different things for the church. It first designated certain rules that church members were to follow. The Catholic Church still issues "Canon Law" and even has its own set of Canon lawyers. Also, each local church would have a list of approved clergy called "the canon of clergy." Sometime around the 4th century AD, "canon" came to mean the rule and norm of the Christian life and faith. Part of this determination was the list of books sacred to Christians.

To understand how the Bible was canonized, let's look at each of the two Testaments separately.

The Canonization of the Old Testament

The canonization of the Old Testament took place in three stages which are parallel with different sections of the Old Testament.

The Pentateuch (the first five books of the Old Testament) had almost universal recognition by God's people as sacred text because the Lord told Moses to write down the words He spoke to him and to keep them with the Ark. From the beginning, these were the Scriptures of God's people. For that reason, the Book of the Law is referenced over and over again in the Old Testament story. The Pentateuch was probably stabilized in its present form before 1000 BC. By this time, David was eloquently speaking of his love and devotion to the law (see Psalm 119). So, this first section was very early adopted by the community of faith as Scripture.

The second part of the Old Testament, the Prophets, was divided into two groups. The Former Prophets (Joshua, Judges, I and II Samuel, and I and II Kings) were completed as one collection of writings sometime during the exile (608 to 538 BC). Notice, this section includes historical events up until the exile. The second group is called the Latter Prophets (Isaiah, Jeremiah, Ezekiel, and the 12 Minor Prophets) and must have been collected sometime after the writing of Micah (450 BC). Daniel spoke of the prophecies of Jeremiah as recorded in Scripture, so parts of it must have already been accepted as such as early as Daniel's captivity in Babylon (see Daniel 9.2). Both groups appear to be canonized by 180 BC since *Jesus Ben Sira*, an apocryphal book on wisdom, lists these books and refers to them as Scripture.

The last section, the Writings (the wisdom books, Ezra, Nehemiah, and I and II Chronicles) were the last collection to be seen as sacred text. When they were collected as one group is hard to determine. Five of the books, each written on a separate scroll, were read at different annual feasts. (Song of Solomon at Passover, Ruth at Pentecost, Lamentations on the ninth of Ab which was the day Jerusalem was destroyed in 586, Ecclesiastes at the Feast of Tabernacles, and Ester at Purim.) Though we don't know when the whole collection was put together, it was at least finalized by 150 BC.

When did the three collections come together as one? Tradition says that the Council of Jamnia (around middle of second century AD) "fixed" the canon of the Old Testament. The truth is that the canon was already established as early as the second century BC. The meeting at Jamnia was more an organization of one rabbi who met with other scholars to debate whether some of the books already included in the canon should remain.

However, the most powerful evidence of the earlier canonization of the Old Testament is the Septuagint (LXX), the Greek translation of the Hebrew Old Testament. I will explain the Septuagint in detail later on, but this important translation was finished around 150 BC. The LXX is the most powerful witness for a canonized collection of sacred text early in the second century BC.

The Apocrypha

What about those other books that we often call the Apocrypha?

This term is extremely confusing to most Protestants. Though the term actually means "hidden," we use it the way Jerome did. Jerome was one of many whom we refer to as "early church fathers." These were early church leaders, both theologians and pastors, who lived in the first couple of centuries after the birth of the church. Their extensive writings solidified many doctrinal questions and give great insight into the status of the Scriptures within the church.

To Jerome, the books written during the last two centuries before Christ and the first century of the Christian era were all considered the Apocrypha and not part of canonical Scripture (Metzger, 161). However, in the Greek and Latin copies of the Old Testament, these books were included and interspersed in the Old Testament where they would likely fit into the story.

The 39 books found in the Hebrew Old Testament (the same ones that are in the Protestant Bible) are often called "protocanonical" while the seven additional books found in the Greek Old Testament (the Septuagint) are called "deuterocanonical." Roman Catholics, in their English translation of the Old Testament, include these seven deuterocanonical books interspersed among the 39 protocanoncial books. The Council of Trent (1546) accepted these as canonical Scripture.

On the other hand, Protestant Bibles list the deuterocanoncial books among the Apocrypha section between the Testaments and do not consider them as canonical.

To make matters more confusing, the Eastern Orthodox Church accepts as canonical the 39 protocanoncial books, the Catholic's seven deuterocanoncial books, and an additional seven to eight books (above and beyond the deuterocanonical books). The Roman Catholics refer to these as the Apocryphal and do not consider them canonical.

As you can see, many groups use the same term to refer to different sets of writings.

Why are none of these books not considered to be canonical by Protestants if the LXX included them? The primary reason is that Jerome excluded them in his Latin version of the Bible, the *Vulgate*, which was finished in the 5th Century AD. A fuller discussion of translations will come later, but this Latin translation was the exclusive translation used by the church for over a thousand years. Not until the Council of Trent (1546) did the Catholic Church accept the apocryphal books as canonical and put them back into the canon. Protestants rejected that decision keeping with the 1000 year tradition of rejecting the apocrypha.

By the time of Christ, there was a set of Scriptures for God's people. Of course, another Testament was coming. How did that become part of the canon?

The Canonization of the New Testament

Most of the biblical writers probably did not know they were writing Scripture. As far as we know, only the Book of Revelation was written by a direct order of the Lord. The New Testament began as the early church sought to share and remember the Christ that had changed the world.

The first stories of the life of Christ, the gospels of Mark and Luke, were both written in the 60s with Matthew following around 80 AD, and John perhaps as late as 90 AD. However, the first document written that would eventually become part of the New Testament was one of Paul's letter's (either I Thessalonians or Galatians) written around 50 AD.

Most agree that the documents contained in our New Testament were all written and even circulating among churches by the middle part of the 2nd century AD, but we have little evidence that they were recognized as a group of Scriptures until Athanasius, the bishop of Alexandria, listed the 27 books of the New Testament as canon in 367 AD.

Surprisingly, the early church did not have a pressing need to develop a new canon of Scriptures to add to the existing collection (of what we call the Old Testament). They were content to use the Old Testament to preach Christ. You will notice that all of the sermons in the book of Acts were based upon Old Testament Scriptures.

It was outside forces that forced the church to formulate a canon, and even then, the church struggled for centuries over the closing of this canon.

The first outside (though he may have considered himself "inside") force was a teacher of the 2nd century (around 140 AD) named Marcion. Marcion taught that the God of Jesus, full of love and grace, was incompatible with the God of the Old Testament, full of judgment and wrath. Therefore, he dropped the Old Testament and any New Testament writing that referred to it or valued it. He developed a list of canonical Scriptures that included Galatians, I and II Corinthians, Romans, I and II Thessalonians, Laodiceans (what he called Ephesians), Colossians, Philemon, Philippians, and the gospel of Luke but purged of all Old Testament quotes and allusions.

Many question which came first, the chicken (Marcion) or the egg (canon)? In other words, did Marcion develop his canon to refute one developed by the early church or did the early church develop a canon to refute Marcion's? The position taken here is that our canon was a reaction to Marcion's.

Marcion presented one challenge to the church: he narrowed the canon too much. The Montanists presented the exact opposite challenge: they opened the door too wide. The Montanist movement of the 2nd century AD sought to elevate the voice of modern prophecy to the level of Scripture. So, this group added new Scriptures, novels, and spurious gospels to their canon as they received revelation from God. The canon of the early church was developed to narrow down the list and to exclude these spurious works.

The Standard of the Canon

So, how did it all come together? The need for a Christian canon was great for the early church, though they would not have used the term. They needed some rule and guide to distinguish between the variety of Christian writings being passed around. Which ones were to be read in the churches? Which ones were authoritative for doctrine and ethics? Three major criteria seem to dominate the decision process: orthodoxy, apostolicity, and acceptance.

Orthodoxy

The standard of orthodoxy means that a book had to be consistent with the basic doctrines already recognized as normative by the church. What this means is that doctrine existed before the formal New Testament. This demonstrates what many call the Canon of the Apostles, the idea that the apostles teachings were circulated in some form (possible orally) and these were the foundation of the early church (see Acts 2.42). When it came time to fix the canon, only those books that agreed with what the church had already been taught by the apostle's teachings were considered canonical.

Consider the opening argument of Galatians. Paul was amazed that some in the church of Galatia had abandoned the gospel of Jesus for another gospel, one that really was no gospel at all (see Galatians 1.9). Paul was not writing about the written gospels but the gospel message itself. Paul was writing this letter about ten years before the first gospel was written. In other words, before a gospel was written down there existed a "gospel" to which Paul referred to in

Galatians 1. Orthodoxy came from adhering to that gospel, not the written gospels.

Apostolicity

The standard of apostolicity makes sense once we understand the standard of orthodoxy. Canonical books were those who were either authored by an apostle (one who met Jesus or followed Jesus while He walked on this earth) or by a close follower of an apostle. The gospels tells us that Jesus Himself designated the apostles.

> *And he appointed twelve (whom he also named apostles) so that they might be with him and he might send them out to preach (Mark 3.14-15).*

These apostles, and their close associates, authored the Scriptures. For instance, the gospel of Matthew was written by the disciple bearing his name. Paul knew Jesus through his experience on the road to Damascus. Luke was a traveling companion of Paul and is considered to be of apostolic origins.

A key factor in determining whether a work should be accepted into the Christian canon was its connection to an apostle.

Life of the Church

The last standard, acceptance by the churches, means that writings were accepted into the canon because they had become a part of the life of the church. Books were only considered for the canon if they were already being used by the church to teach doctrine and the normative Christian life. In addition, it helped if these books were quoted by early church fathers or bishops.

Closing the Canon

Even though the canon appears to be constant by 367 AD when Athanasius the bishop of Alexandria listed the canonical books of the New Testament, the debate still smoldered for years. Many bishops and theologians continued to refer to and quote from non-canonical books, like *The Shepherd of Hermes*, in their writings. Shocking as it may sound, the church did not officially "fix" the modern 27 book New Testament canon until 1546 at the Council of Trent.

But, the truth of the matter is by the 4th century AD, the church had its canon in its hands, and it looked like what we have in our hands, but of course, in a different language. How did it get from canonization to our hands?

Transmission of Scripture

Having talked about the inspiration of the Scriptures and the canonization of the same, we now must examine the issue of transmission, or the passing down of that text from the original authors to us. Why is this relevant to us today? Why should we care about this? How does knowing this impact our walk with Christ?

On one level, it impacts us because it gives us greater confidence in the leather bound book we hold in our hands to know that it faithfully represents the revelation of the Spirit to Moses, Paul, and others. We need assurance that it accurately records the inspired sacred text. It is important that we know it is the Word of God when we read it for personal devotions and when we teach it to our children. We need some assurance that some editorial board has not altered the original text of the book of Romans to make it more "marketable."

On another level, it helps us to better understand why there are so many different translations and which one might be best for us. We will examine this in greater detail in a few moments, but we do have to make a choice about which translation to read, to study, and to memorize. This information will inform our discussion.

But there is another element that is of interest in this discussion. We have talked about how the Holy Spirit revealed the Word of God to the authors. We have talked about the work of the Spirit in leading the church to recognize which texts are sacred. Here, we see another example of the work of the Spirit: preserving His sacred text through the restraints of history and fallen humans.

The historical challenges of passing down a text from Moses to us were daunting: the physical distance from Canaan to North America, the deceit of people who would destroy the revelation of God, the simple ignorance of good intentioned people, wars and infighting where precious things were destroyed, the lack of writing utensils in antiquity, and even the innocent ability to misplace things. Through all of this, the Lord preserved His revelation to us.

Writing Tools

When the Spirit spoke to the author, the author wrote those words down on various writing tools. Understanding the various writing tools and developmental stages of writing helps us gain a better understanding of the process by which God's breath became a sacred text.

Stone

The earliest writing tool was a stone tablet or stone wall. The primary biblical example is the stone tablets of Moses.

> *Come up to me on the mountain and wait there, that I may give you the tablets of stone, with the law and the commandment, which I have written for their instruction. (Exodus 24.12)*

Another historical example is the Rosetta stone, a granite stone slab bearing in inscription an hieroglyphics, demotic, and Greek inscribed in 196 BC. The Rosetta Stone was discovered in 1799 in Egypt. Because the stone was inscribed in these three scripts, scholars were able to decipher the hieroglyphics used by the Egyptians. It is now in the British Museum in London.

Clay and Wooden Tablets

Later, people developed clay tablets to write upon. The prophet Isaiah was told to "Write it before them on a tablet and inscribe it in a book, that it may be for the time to come" (Isaiah 30.8).

Papyrus

The Egyptians developed the first major improvement in writing tools. They took a reed plant, cut it into strips, and glued the strips in a perpendicular patchwork like pattern to make paper. These were formed into long scrolls. The longest of these scrolls was 120 feet, but scrolls over 30 feet were hard to handle. These papyri not only preserved better than normal paper, but the conditions in Egypt (dry, arid soil) preserved many old papyruses that have been found in the last 100 years. The papyrus was in use in Egypt long before Moses ever wrote the Torah.

The scroll became the primary writing tool of antiquity. God told Jeremiah,

> *Take a scroll and write on it all the words that I have spoken to you against Israel and Judah and all the nations, from the day I spoke to you, from the days of Josiah until today. (Jeremiah 36.2)*

Parchment

The next innovation in writing was the parchment. A parchment was a dried animal skin with the hair and other elements scraped off. These had the added value of being erasable and reusable. They were often in scrolls, but would later be combined into book form (also known as codices). The Dead Sea scrolls were written on parchment.

Paul spoke of the parchments when he wrote to Timothy,

> *When you come, bring the cloak that I left with Carpus at Troas, also the books, and above all the parchments. (2 Timothy 4.13)*

Paper

The common writing tool of today is paper; however, paper was not invented until around 900 AD. Not only were the original documents not written on paper, but the copies of the copies that we depend upon today for our translations were not written on paper.

Textual Criticism

An important science that deals with the area of the transmission of the text is "textual criticism." The goal of textual criticism is to reconstruct the original text as it was first written down. You may ask, "Why do we need an entire science to reconstruct the original text?

No Autographs (Original Writings) Survive To This Day

The first reason we need textual criticism is that we simply do not have the original writings of Moses, Paul's letters, or Luke's account of the spread of the early church. No autographs, as original writings are called, survive to this day. This may be a huge blessing because we can only imagine the idolatry that would be given to an original copy of John's gospel. Nevertheless, since we don't have a copy of the original, we have to try to reconstruct it from copies of the original.

All We Have Left Is Copies Of Copies

We must remember that the printing press was not invented until 1450 AD. Prior to that, all copies were made by hand. To compound the problem, all we have left are copies of copies. For example, we only have a copy that was written almost 1500 years after Moses lived. As discouraging as this might seem, we have to realize that all books of antiquity rely upon copies of copies for their text. The goal is to try to find the best copy of the original. To do this, we must consider three issues.

Three Issues: Quantity, Accuracy, And Time

The first issue is how many ancient texts do we have in our possession today that are early copies? The more copies we have, the more confident we can be that these copies reflect the original.

Accuracy speaks to the quality of the manuscripts. In other words, do the copies of the text accurately reflect the original from which the copy was made?

The final issue deals with distance between the time the author wrote the original and when the copy was made. In other words, how much space is between the original and the document? The less time between the two, the more reliable the copies are considered to be.

Comparing Textual Evidence

How does the textual evidence for the Bible compare with the textual evidence for other writings? Let's compares the Bible with four other major bodies of literature.

- Caesar's *Gallic Wars* was written around 54 BC. We only have 9 or 10 good manuscripts upon which to base our understanding of the original. The oldest of these is 900 years older than the original.

- Of all the 142 books of *Roman History* by Livey which were written between 49 BC and 17 AD, only 35 have survived. None of the copies are older than the 4th century AD.

- Of the 16 books of the *Annals* of Tacitus, who lived 55 to 117 AD, only 10 remain in full and two in part. None of the copies are older than the 9th century AD.

- Of the writings of Plato, the earliest is 1300 years later than the original writings.

- But, for the New Testament, we have over 5000 complete or partial manuscripts. The oldest is from the second or third century, not more than 100 years after the original was written.

When compared with the gap between the autographs and copies of the other historical examples, the manuscript evidence for the New Testament is staggering (Boa, 93).

Handmade Copies

With all of the copies of copies, mistakes were inevitable. In fact, considering the challenge of copying even a short letter from Paul, it is amazing that there are as few mistakes as there are. For example, consider what it would take to copy the third chapter of John by hand today.

If you were to be copying the Greek manuscript of John, you would be staring at a document with no spaces between words, no periods at the end of sentences, no capital letters to identify proper nouns, and no commas or other punctuation marks. What kind of mistakes might you make in copying that chapter? If it were me, I would misspell words, leave out a word or maybe even a line, and I might repeat a word, letter, or lines. These are the exact mistakes that are most common among the manuscripts of the New Testament.

Scribes Tried To Correct Perceived Mistakes

These mistakes were passed down as new copies were created. This created a ripple effect because the next scribe was faced with the issue of dealing with the known error. For example, if you were making a copy of John 3 and you came to verse 16 and the text in front of you was "God so loved the universe" but you knew the original read "God so loved the world," what would you do?

You might copy the text in front of you without making any changes. Or, you might copy the original but put a note in the margin that you think it is wrong. Or, you might correct the original but make a marginal note indicating such. Or, you might just correct the original without any notation.

Now, you have created a problem for the person who will make a copy of your corrected copy. Does the next scribe copy the corrected copy along with marginal notes? Does he change the text to reflect what the marginal notes say was the right reading? Does he remove the marginal reading because he agreed with the incorrect reading? Or, does he change it back to the original because he knew of another copy that contains that reading? How the scribe handles this change will affect the next scribe, and so the ripple goes.

Many of us are aghast at how a scribe might "edit" sacred text, but at the time, copying a letter of Paul or a story of the life of Jesus was not seen as copying "sacred text." Of course, years later, after the canon was set, copying the sacred text was a different matter, but the early copies were easily modified. After all, what difference does it make if we make a few changes of a paragraph of Max Lucado's book when we email it to a friend?

What changes might they have made? Perhaps they would add a better ending to the book or correct word choice or grammar. All of this adds up to over 200,000 variant readings among the 5000 Greek New Testament manuscripts.

Only a fraction of the New Testament is in question, but how can we trust any of it to be accurate? Trust is developed through extensive study. According to Westcott and Hort's *Introduction to the NT in Original Greek (Volume 2)*, about 87% of the New Testament is accepted without question as true to the original. Of the remaining 13%, the majority of these differences are scribal errors (misspelled words, repeated words, left out lines, etc.). Less than 2% of the New Testament is in any real question. Of these, the majority are truly trivial matters that have almost no impact on meaning. That leaves about .1% of the text that is truly a question of textual criticism.

So, we do have a Bible that is 99.9% faithful to the original author's manuscript.

How Does Textual Criticism Establish the Best Text?

We claim to have a Bible that is 99.9% faithful to the original. What is the process by which textual critics have gone through to get back to the original writings?

First, they try to discover the earliest manuscripts. The earlier the manuscript, the more likely it is to be free from errors, though this is not always the case.

Second, they look at early translations into other languages. If a Greek translation of the Hebrew Old Testament is found that dates back to 100 BC, that would tell us a lot about the Hebrew text the authors used to translate. That would help us to reconstruct the original Hebrew text.

Third, they look at quotations of early church fathers. By studying their quotes of the Old and New Testament, we can get a clue as to the text they were familiar with. By doing so, we can better reconstruct the original text.

Old Testament Transmission

Masoretic Text

Until a shepherd boy stumbled across a cave by the Dead Sea while looking for some lost sheep, the oldest copy of the Old Testament was from the 9th century

AD. So, if the Old Testament was fixed around the second century BC, the oldest copy was at least a thousand years older than the close of the Old Testament canon. When that little shepherd boy threw a rock into a cave, his rock changed the world.

In 1947, his rock hit several clay jars filled with various scrolls. This collection of scrolls is called the Dead Sea Scrolls (DSS). These date back to 100 BC, around 100 years after the Old Testament text was probably fixed. The DSS contains most of the Old Testament (except Esther) along with some other books that we do not consider to be sacred text. This finding helps us realize that the Old Testament text we have today is almost exactly like the Old Testament before 100 BC. Unfortunately, we know very little about copies of the Old Testament before 100 BC.

By 100 AD, the Old Testament text was standardized due to the destruction of the Temple (70 AD) and a great fear among the Jews of losing something very precious. In addition, Rabbi Akiba (who died in 135 AD), a vigorous opponent of Christianity and a scholar of Old Testament Hebrew, worked hard to standardize the Hebrew Old Testament text out of a dislike for the Septuagint (LXX) used so predominately by the Christian community.

With a standardized text in place by 100 AD, the transmission of the text was made simpler, even more so when the Masoretes, a group of scribes who worked from 500 AD to 1500 AD, took over the job of copying the text. This is why the standardized Old Testament text is often called the "Masoretic Text." They were meticulous about making copies. Here are only a few of their rules when it came to making copies of the text.

1. Only parchment from clean animals could be used.

2. Each column would have between 48 and 60 lines.

3. Letters should suspend from the lines.

4. No word could be written from memory and each word had to be sounded out before being written.

5. The scribe must wipe the pen clean before writing the name of God, YHWH.

6. If more than 3 errors were found on one sheet, the entire scroll would be condemned.

Masorete scribes counted the number of lines on a page, the number of letters on a line, and the number of pages in a book. Each of these counts was compared to the standardized text. If they differed, they knew there was a problem. For this reason, there is little struggle with the Old Testament text. What we have is faithful to the original Old Testament.

Septuagint (LXX)

One of the most significant translations of the Hebrew Old Testament is the Septuagint.

When Alexander the Great conquered the world in 333 BC, Greek became the common language throughout much of the world. Jews, particularly those who were scattered throughout the world through the exile (also known as the Diaspora), could no longer read Hebrew. So, a Greek translation of the Hebrew was developed. Probably finished around 250 BC, the manuscript is called the Septuagint (meaning 70) because tradition says that 70 scholars worked on the translation. It is usually abbreviated LXX. The oldest copy of the LXX is from 150 BC, only 100 years after it was written. As we have already said, the Jews rejected the LXX after the Christian church began to use it so heavily. So, all the copies we have of the LXX have been preserved by Christians. Some Jewish leaders would even begin to refer to it as the work of the devil.

Its value lies in that most of it is a word for word translation of the Hebrew text. So, it is a faithful witness to the original Hebrew text that even predates the Masoretic text. Also, this was the Bible of the Greek speaking Christians of the early church. This is the Bible from which Jesus and New Testament writers quoted.

Latin Vulgate

Around 400 AD, Jerome, one of the early church fathers, translated the Bible (Old Testament from Hebrew, not the LXX) into Latin, the common language of the educated masses. This translation is called the *Latin Vulgate* because "vulgate" means common. This would be the basis for all other translations into all other Western European languages until the 16th century. What this means is that no one else tried to reconstruct the Hebrew Old Testament for the next 1200 years after Jerome published the *Vulgate*. One of the impacts of the *Vulgate* was the removal of the apocrypha books from the accepted canon.

New Testament Transmission

Two Most Important Texts

Of the over 5000 Greek manuscripts, there are two major Greek manuscripts of the New Testament. Textual critics like to give names and symbols to the manuscripts they study. The first major manuscript is called Sinaiticus (assigned the symbol ℵ), and it dates back to the 4th century AD. This manuscript contains most of the Greek Old Testament and all of the New Testament. It was first published in 1862. The second major manuscript is called Vaticanus (assigned the symbol B), and it also dates back to the 4th century AD. It was published in 1867. These are the two most reliable manuscripts.

Translations

Not only was the Spirit of God at work inspiring the Scripture writers and in preserving the text for future generations, the Spirit was also at work translating that text into the language of the people.

The Hebrew Old Testament, the Greek Old Testament, and the Greek New Testament became locked behind the door of the Latin Vulgate for almost a thousand years. During the "Dark Ages," the average person could neither read a Latin text nor had enough personal wealth to purchase a hand written copy of the Scriptures. While there were some local attempts to translate the Scriptures into the language of the people, this process did not start in earnest until John Wycliffe.

John Wycliffe

John Wycliffe was convinced that the Bible and the codification of God's law should be widely available in the vernacular since every man was God's tenant-in-chief directly responsible to God. Although he probably did not finish his work before his death, his co-workers did. The first edition was completed around 1384. This English translation was based upon the Latin text.

Guttenburg Bible (1456)

With the invention of the printing press, the work of creating copies of the Bible became much easier. The first major work to come off the printing press was a copy of the Latin Bible named after the publishing house (Guttenburg). Even after the advent of the printing press, the Bible still remained un-printed in English.

Erasmus (1516)

In 1516, Erasmus took a giant leap forward for mankind: he created the first printed edition of the Greek New Testament. Until then, the only printed Bible was in Latin, and other translations were all based upon the Latin version instead of the Greek and Hebrew.

Unfortunately, Erasmus was only able to use the Greek mansucripts which he had access to at the time. At the time of Erasmus, the best manuscripts had still yet to be found. In some places, he supplied the Greek from the Latin in order to make the Greek edition complete. Most of these errors were corrected in later editions, but a few were not. For example, there are two words in Revelation 22 in Erasmus' text that were not in any Greek manuscript, and there is a spurious text about three witnesses in 1 John 5.7.

Textus Receptus (1633)

In 1633, a printing house published another copy of the Greek New Testament. There is nothing significantly different about the text since it was actually the same text as Erasmus. The major addition of this publication was the claim by the printing house to the reader: "You have received the text received by all in which we give nothing changed or corrupted." This was later to be understood as the "textus receptus." Though this sounds like something the Road Runner bought from an ACME catalog, it became a common phrase. Often referred to as the "received text," it was the basis of almost all translations up until the 19th century, including the King James Version.

Tyndale (1534)

William Tyndale was convinced "that religious confusion stemmed from a widespread ignorance of the Scriptures, even among the clergy" and he hoped that "every plowboy could read the Scripture for himself" (Thomas, 14). So, he produced a translation of the Bible in everyday English in 1534. Tyndale's translation was the first printed English translation based upon the original languages (Greek and Hebrew). For all his trouble, he was executed on October 6, 1536 for such a heretical act. Of course, this translation was still based upon the Greek text of Erasmus. 90% of the King James Version is Tyndale's text.

Coverdale (1537) and the Great Bible (1539)

Miles Coverdale, a friend of Tyndale, used Tyndale's translation to produce the Coverdale Bible in 1537. This was the first English Bible to separate the apocryphal books from the rest of the OT books and was also the first English edition to be printed on the printing press.

He was recruited by Oliver Cromwell to be a part of the team that produced the Great Bible of 1539. This was the official edition placed in all English parish churches. It was called "great" because of its size. Even today, the Psalter of the English Book of Common Prayer is from the Great Bible and not the King James Version.

Geneva Bible (1560)

The Geneva Bible was published in 1560 and was considered by many to be the best English translation that ever appeared until the King James Version was produced 50 years later. It was the Bible of Shakespeare and the Pilgrims. In fact, it was used long after the "new and fond thing vainly invented" King James Version was introduced. Cromwell's army traveled with the *Soldier's*

Bible which was the text of the Geneva Bible. The last edition was printed in 1644.

It was obviously better than any other English version but the developers were out of the Queen's favor, so its popularity demanded a revision of the Great Bible. This revision was called the Bishop's Bible.

King James Version (1611)

When James became King, there were two competing Bibles in the English church. The Bishop's Bible was used in the churches, but the Geneva Bible was used in private readings by the laypeople. So, the church leaders asked the King to authorize the production of a new translation that would be the official Bible of the English Church. About 50 translators were involved, and they followed the following rules: the Bishop's Bible was to be the standard, the Hebrew and Greek texts were to be examined, and all other English versions were to be consulted.

To prevent the reading from being too stilted, a variety of words were used in rendering the Greek and Hebrew. For example, the Greek word *katargeo* is used four times in 1 Corinthians 13.8-13, but the KJV translated it variously as fail, vanish away, done away, and put away. The translators purposefully retained ecclesiastical words like charity and church and used italics to indicate words not in the original Hebrew or Greek. The original KJV still included the Apocrypha. This Bible was first published in 1611.

A few of the early editions produced several comical errors (Ewer, 202). For instance, Matthew 23.24 reads "strain at a gnat" instead of "strain out a gnat," and it remains so today. In the 1631 edition, the "not" was left out of the seventh commandment. This edition was so named the "wicked Bible" because it encouraged people to commit adultery. The 1717 edition published the heading of Luke 20 as the "Parable of Vinegar" instead of the Parable of the Vineyard and was so named the Vinegar Bible. The 1795 edition was called the Murderer's Bible because Mark 7.27 read, "Let the children first be killed" (instead of filled).

The KJV quickly became known as the Authorized Version because it was the version authorized by the king to replace the Bishop and Geneva Bible. The modern version is the result of a revision in 1769 in which the Apocrypha was removed.

Though it did eventually win out, it received great criticism at first. One critic said,

> *The cockles of the sea shores, and the leaves of the forest, and the grains of the poppy may as well be numbered as the gross errors of this Bible, disgracing the ground of our own hope. (Ewert, 203)*

It is important to remember that the KJV was based upon the Greek text printed by Erasmus at a time when the best manuscripts of the fourth and fifth century had not yet been discovered. There were only 25 manuscripts to study, while there are over 5000 Greek manuscripts known to scholars today (Lewis, 42). While some consider it to be the first English translation of the Bible, it was actually published almost 230 years after Wycliffe's English translation.

It continues to be treasured as an excellent piece of literature, but many verses are hard to understand today. For example: "Thou shalt destroy them that speak leasing" (Psalm 5.6), "Solomon loved many strange women" (I Kings 11.1), "I trow not" (Luke 17.9), and "We do you to wit of the grace of God" (II Corinthians 8.1). While it did give the church one version to memorize and the poetic language is great for public reading, the English language in America has changed much since 1611.

The Need for a New Translation

The KJV was the dominate translation for over 200 years, but two issues pushed the need for a new translation.

First, through the extensive work of biblical archeologists, many new manuscripts were discovered. In addition, many Greek papyri were found in Egypt that illuminate scholar's understanding of the Greek language. A rash of new lexicons were written to replace the old. Biblical scholarship had simply marched so far forward that it demanded a new translation.

Second, the English language had changed much from the time of King James.

With the discovery of new manuscripts, with a better understanding of the Greek language, and with the changing usage of the English language, new English translations were needed and sought.

English Revised Version (1881)

After Vaticanus and Sinaiticus, the best and latest manuscripts, were discovered in the middle of the 19th century, Westcott and Hort produced a new Greek translation of the New Testament in 1881. At the same time, 54 English translators and 30 American translators published the English Revised Version in 1881. While they tried to bring the Authorized Version in line with Greek and Hebrew, they did not try to modernize the old English. While the Greek text was better, the English was almost worse. Spurgeon called it, "Strong in Greek; weak in English" (Ewert, 209).

American Revised Version (American Standard Version) (1901)

The American translation team of the ERV was disappointed that the old English language was not modernized. Since their suggestions were largely ignored by the ERV or placed in the appendix, they worked with Thomas Nelson and Sons to publish the American Revised Version in 1901.

They excluded 16 whole verses and 122 parts of sentences from the KJV based upon manuscript evidence (Lewis, 80). For example, the doxology at the end of the model prayer (Matthew 6.13), the troubling of the water at the pool of Bethesda (John 5.3-4), the prayer phrases of Luke 11.2-4, the Johannen Comma (1 John 5.7), and Acts 8.37.

New King James (1982)

The New King James Version (NKJV) was published in 1982. While it claims to be the first revision of the KJV, this is not completely accurate. Jay Green published the King James II Version in 1971, but it was the work of one man and not highly regarded. The NKJV was the work of 119 scholars, but largely ignored modern textual scholarship since 1611.

Proliferation of Translations and Paraphrases

It would be nigh unto impossible to list and describe all of the English translations since the ARV. Several groups and individuals tried to combine modern textual scholarship and updated English. The Moffatt Version (1928), JP Phillips (1958), New English Bible (1970), Good News Bible (1976), the Amplified Bible (1965), and the Message (1993) are just a few of the more popular ones.

Revised Standard Version (1952)

One of the most respected attempts to modernize the language and adhere to modern scholarship was the Revised Standard Version (RSV) of 1952. It is regarded by many in academic circles as the best English translation. The New Revised Standard Version (NRSV) was published in 1989 with gender inclusive language.

Jerusalem Bible (1956)

The Jerusalem Bible (JB) was the first complete Catholic Bible translated into English from the original languages. The Apocrypha books were placed where they stood in the LXX. It contains more poetry that any other English translation. American scholars would later produce the New American Bible in 1970.

New American Standard Version (or Bible) (1971)

After almost 70 years, the American Standard Version was beginning to disappear from use. So, the New American Standard Version (NASB) was published in 1971. It remains a good study Bible for it adheres more literally to the original languages. It was the first to capitalize the pronouns when referring to deity.

The Living Bible (1971)

Kenneth Taylor, President of Tyndale House Publishers, produced his own paraphrase of Scripture in 1971. It began as a translation of the New Testament epistles, but not a single publisher was interested in it. However, Billy Graham ordered 50,000 for his TV viewers. The response was so great that Taylor started his own publishing house (Tyndale) to print them. His basic text was the ASV (he did not know Greek or Hebrew), and his rigid evangelical position was his guiding light.

The New Living Translation (NLT) of 1996 is based upon the same language standards as the Living Bible but used more modern scholarship. A team of 100 scholars worked to produce this dynamic equivalent text.

New International Version (1978)

The next major translation work, and the one that remains as the predominate translation in the American church, is the New International Version (NIV) of 1978. It was written on an eighth grade reading level (the average reading level of American adults) and is considered by many to be the best all purpose Bible to English speaking Christians for public worship, private study, and memorization.

In 2011, the NIV was updated to include gender neutral language, but this did not affect the pronouns referring to God.

English Standard Version (2001)

The most recent update of the Revised Standard Version, the English Standard Version (ESV), was published in 2001. It is an essential literal translation, a translation philosophy that is much closer to "word for word" than "thought for thought." Many of the words and phrases flow from the Tyndale tradition, though the archaic language has been brought into current usage. The ESV is increasing in popularity, both among scholars and lay persons.

All of the Scripture quotations in this book are from the ESV.

Choosing a Bible Translation

Literal, Dynamic, or Free?

When choosing an English translation of the Scriptures, we need to keep in mind the theory of translation. This has to do with the degree to which one is willing to go in order to bridge the gap between the original language of the author and the English translation.

For example, how should "lamp" be translated? Should it be flashlight, torch, or just lamp? What should be done with "greet one another with a holy kiss"? Does this become a "handshake of Christian love" in non-kissing cultures? Each translation has a theory that guides which English word or phrase is used to translate the original languages.

Literal

The literal theory of translation attempts to keep as close as possible to the exact words and phrasing of the original languages while still making sense in the English language. A literal translation will keep the historical distance intact at all points. The New American Standard and the King James Version are literal translations.

Free

The free translation theory attempts to translate the ideas from one language to another with less concern about using the exact phrasing or words from the original. Sometimes called a paraphrase, it tries to eliminate as much of the historical distance as possible. The Living Bible and the Message are free translations.

Dynamic Equivalent

The dynamic equivalent translation seeks to translate words, idioms, and grammatical constructions of the original language into precise equivalents in the English language. Such translations keep historical distances on all historical and factual matters (measurements, currency, etc.) but updates matters of language, grammar, and style. These are often called "thought for thought" translations. The New International Version is a dynamic equivalent translation.

Questions to Consider

Here is a short list of questions to ask when comparing and choosing a Bible translation.

- Is the translation the work of an individual or a team?
- What original manuscripts are they using?
- Is the translation literal, dynamic, or free?
- What style of the English language is being used?
- How widely accepted is the translation?
- How readable is it?
- Am I wanting a Bible for in-depth study or devotional reading?

How you answer each of these questions will impact which Bible translation you will choose.

Let The Story Begin

Now that we have a Bible in our hands, and we know where it came from and how it came from God's heart to our hands, and we have chosen an English translation from which to study, let us now turn to the text itself.

Let the story begin.

Introduction

The story of the Bible will span over 2000 years and cross three continents. It will weave a myriad of nations, people groups, and religions into one, long story. Like all good stories, this great story needs a good introduction. It should peak interest, foreshadow some of the impending conflict, and lay the background information for the story that follows.

This is the best way to think about the first eleven chapters of the book of Genesis: as background for one large story of God's relationship with His people. What follows the introduction is not a collection of unconnected stories like the *Arabian Nights* or *Mother Goose Fairy Tales*. It is one story with one plot line. One of the primary reasons that we have such a problem understanding the relevance of particular portions of the Bible, mainly the prophets of the Old Testament, is that we have a poor grasp on the one story of the Bible.

The story of God's relationship with His people begins in the garden and ends in glory. It is a story of love and rebellion, of a wayward son and a loving father, and of the rise and fall of a people group. The story will not only span 2000 years, but it will weave its characters through a progressive and growing understanding of what it means to live in relationship to the Creator. The characters vary. Some are noble and faithful, others are wicked and rebellious, but they all fit into one long storyline that brings light into the darkness. And, at the appropriate moment in the story, the Light will burst into the story once and for all. God will reveal Himself to His creation through His Son, and in one moment, all the other plot lines and characters suddenly make sense.

This is our aim as we read the story. We want to find this one storyline of God's relationship with His people. We want to understand how the individual stories fit into the larger plot. As we do this, we will find that God still speaks even through the parts of the Old Testament that we had long given up on. You know those parts of the Old Testament where the pages of your Bible are still stuck together because you have never read them? Even those sections are still profitable for teaching, correction, training, and equipping if we can understand them in light of the larger story.

So, we turn our attention to the introduction to this wonderful story.

Creation

There are three parts to this introduction material.

The first section presents the story of creation, how God created the heavens and the earth. While our western minds want to focus on the "how" of creation, the primary goal of this section is to focus on the "Who" of creation. The creation account tells us about the grand architect behind this thing we call life. "For from Him and through Him and to Him are all things" (Romans 11.36).

"In The Beginning, God…"

The story of creation begins with such a simple phrase, but it contains so much spiritual depth. From these auspicious beginnings, three critical concepts begin the biblical story.

First, the story has a beginning. Contrary to the theory of Darwinian evolution, the story of creation means that life had a beginning, and therefore, has direction. The endless cycle of birth and rebirth, or evolution after evolution, leaves us with a hopeless existence void of direction or purpose. However, the biblical story of creation is very different. This creation has a direction, a purpose, and meaning.

Second, before there was anything, there was God. The Lord did not create the heavens and the earth out of available materials. No, He created all that is *ex nihilo*, a Latin phrase meaning "out of nothing."

While no argument for the existence of God can totally convince a skeptical mind, an honest and logical search will lead to the conclusion that it is more logical to conceive of a designer creating an ordered universe than it is to think of our ordered universe resulting from a chaotic big bang.

> *For what can be known about God is plain to them, because God has shown it to them. For his invisible attributes, namely, his eternal power and divine nature, have been clearly perceived, ever since the creation of the world, in the things that have been made. So they are without excuse. (Romans 1.19-20)*

The third critical issue occupies most of our questions surrounding the act of creation: how did it happen? Inquiring minds want to know. Did the act of creation take place in six twenty-four hour periods or does the idea of a "day" mean something different?

The Hebrew word *yom* can mean anything from a twenty-four hour period to a general division of time. Further, the fact that the sun and the moon were not created until day four, and these are signs for the days and seasons (see Genesis 1.15), has led many to understand the "days" of the creation account to mark periods or stages of creation. However, many hold firmly to the idea of a six literal day creation period and would mark anything less as a "liberal" theological position. This is a heated question. However, it is "always dangerous to shout where God has whispered" (Sproul, 5). The point of the creation story is that all things came into being through God; in faith, we must leave the how in His hands.

These complicated questions can sometimes obscure the most basic truth found in the creation narrative: God pre-existed creation, God was the author of creation, and creation is accountable to God, its Creator. While the how of creation might forever elude our earthly mind and we might come to different conclusions regarding things like micro-evolution and the time period of creation, we can agree upon the core truths revealed in the creation account.

"In His image…"

Another key truth in the creation story is that God created men and women in His image.

There is something radically different about mankind. Unlike the animal kingdom, men and women have the ability to think and reason, have a moral conscience, and have the ability to relate to each other and to God. Within mankind lies the breath of God, the soul that transcends our physical bodies (see Genesis 2.7). It is in this soul that we find life, even this side of eternity. Jesus Himself said, "I came that they may have life and have it abundantly" (John 10.10). Billy Graham is famous for saying that we have all been created with a "God sized whole in our heart." It is in our soul that we find life, and it is in our soul that we experience the absence of life: death.

Sin

The second part of the background material is the presence and principle of sin.

Every good story has conflict, and the conflict in the story of God's relationship with His people rears its ugly head in chapter 3. There is no way to understand the life of Jesus, heaven or hell, or any view of salvation without a biblical and correct concept of sin. It is the problem to be solved, the source of conflict both among mankind and between mankind and God.

A simple definition of sin might be "doing something wrong." While this is a basic definition, a student of the Bible will need a deeper understanding of this basic biblical doctrine. The Bible uses several key terms to paint a vivid picture of this thing called sin. Let's focus on four key words used for sin.

The first word is transgression which means "to cross over a line established by God." Sin is transgressing over a limit or boundary established by the Creator. We cannot step over a limit that has not been established. With the law, the boundary lines were set. And all of us have stepped over them.

The second word is rebellion which means "to rebel against His authority." In rebellion, we deny the Lord's position as our Creator and Sovereign who has the right to direct and command our lives. The sinner is one who has mounted a mutiny against the King of Kings.

The third word is perversion which means "to twist God's original intention for creation." Through our sinful choices, we have perverted God's creation, twisting it from a community of holiness and love into a culture of impurity and selfishness. This word is often used in reference to sexual purity. For instance, "And you shall not lie with any animal and so make yourself unclean with it, neither shall any woman give herself to an animal to lie with it: it is perversion" (Leviticus 18.23).

One final word is disobedience which means "to break a rule set up by God." This is not only prohibitive rules ("Thou shall not...") but also the affirmative commands ("Love your neighbor..."). We sin when we break both forms of God's commands.

In the garden, Adam crossed over a line established by God and broke a simple command. He perverted God's design for creation in his disobedience. The story of Adam and Eve demonstrates what has happened in all of our lives: "All have sinned" (Romans 3.23).

Consequences

The third and final part of the background material is the consequences of mankind's sin. The story moves from a beautiful garden to isolation, anger, disorder, and every evil thing. First, Adam and Eve were cast out of the garden and out of basic fellowship with their Creator (Genesis 3). Then, sin infected the individual's ability to live in harmony with each other. This is vividly illustrated in Cain's murder of his brother, Abel (Genesis 4).

God recognized that the intent of mankind's heart was only on evil (Genesis 6.5), and He decided to destroy it all and start over with one righteous man, Noah and his family. But even after a fresh start, the descendants of Noah were once again impacted by sin. Destroying all the bad people was not able to destroy the problem of sin.

People groups were formed with enmity towards each other (Genesis 9-10), and the nations tried to organize to make a name for themselves (Genesis 11). However, God frustrated those plans, confused their languages, and scattered them over the entire earth.

In simple language, the consequence of sin was, and still remains, destruction. Sin destroys our relationship with God, it destroys our relationship with others, and it destroys our relationship with ourselves.

So, the background material of Genesis 1-11 sets us up with some basic information: God made all that there is, we have all chosen to sin, and the consequence of that sin is destruction.

Patriarchs

The rest of the book of Genesis is the story about the Patriarchs. According to the dictionary, a patriarch is

> *One who is head of a social organization marked by the supremacy of the father in the clan or family, the legal dependence of wives and children, and the reckoning of descent and inheritance in the male line. (Merriam-Webster)*

The story of God's people begins in a culture dominated by the father of the clan. The story and history of God's people are traced through these patriarchs.

As we study their lives, we need to remember that the Scriptures will describe their lives, both good and bad. Much of what they did was not holy or righteous, and were not acts of faith. They lived in a period of salvation history not only before Christ, but also before the law. God had yet to reveal to them, in detail, His expectations of the covenant relationship. They were living in Romans 1.20.

> *For his invisible attributes, namely, his eternal power and divine nature, have been clearly perceived, ever since the creation of the world, in the things that have been made. So they are without excuse. (Romans 1.20)*

However, they did not have the fullness of revelation available to Paul or even Moses. So, while much of their transgressions were due to their sin nature, some was due to the salvation age in which they lived.

Abraham

The first patriarch was Abraham. More than just the first in the long line of clan leaders, Abraham was truly the beginning of the story of faith.

In Genesis 12, God began the plan of buying back a lost and dying creation, a humanity totally wrecked by the devastation of sin. The story of Abram, whose name was changed to Abraham in Genesis 17.5, began with his call experience.

> *Now the Lord said to Abram, "Go from your country and your kindred and your father's house to the land that I will show you. And I will make of you a great nation, and I will bless you and make your name great, so that you will be a blessing. I will bless those who bless you, and him who dishonors you I will curse, and in you all the families of the earth shall be blessed. (Genesis 12.1-3)*

All the people of the earth will be blessed through Abraham, through the faith relationship between God and His people that began to build through Abraham. For this reason, Abraham is considered the father of faith, and the father of all those who are of faith.

> *And the Scripture, foreseeing that God would justify the Gentiles by faith, preached the gospel beforehand to Abraham, saying, "In you shall all the nations be blessed." So then, those who are of faith are blessed along with Abraham, the man of faith. (Galatians 3.8-9)*

All nations will be blessed when they put their faith in God, and ultimately, in His Son, our Savior, Jesus Christ. The gospel does not really begin in the New Testament. It was preached in advance to Abraham.

Abraham is regarded by the Jewish people as "Father Abraham." He is the most significant figure in the life of the Jews, even more so than our favorites of Moses and David. "We are children of Abraham," the Pharisees proudly proclaimed to Jesus (see John 8.39).

The life of Abraham is the story of faith. In fact, his life is described as such in the "Faith Hall of Fame" of Hebrews 11. The writer of Hebrews gave several illustrations of Abraham's faith. First, when called to go to a place he would later receive as his inheritance, Abraham obeyed and went, even though he did not know where he was going (Genesis 12 and Hebrews 11.8). Next, he became the father of many nations even though his wife of many years was barren (Genesis 21 and Hebrews 11.11). Finally, the writer of Hebrews tells us of how Abraham was willing to offer Isaac as a sacrifice in obedience to the Lord's instructions (Genesis 22 and Hebrews 11.17).

Other well known stories can be found in the material on Abraham's life in Genesis. His relationship with his nephew, Lot, is described in Genesis 12-14 along with the horror of Sodom and Gomorrah (Genesis 19). In Genesis 17, God instituted the covenant of circumcision with Abraham, a sign of the covenant between God and Abraham.

Isaac

The story continues through the life of the second patriarch, Isaac, the son of Abraham.

Isaac's life is described primarily in Genesis 25-27. His influence and mark on the pages of Scripture are not as significant as was his father's. Isaac is mostly remembered for his near death experience as a child and by the struggle between his two sons, Jacob and Esau.

Jacob

The story continues through the third patriarch, Jacob. However, the story gets much more complicated.

While in Abraham, we find a faithful figure with a few flaws and weak moments, it seems in Jacob we find a weak figure with a few good moments. From the beginning, Jacob was at odds with his twin brother, Esau. Born first, Esau was the rightful heir of the birthright and should have become the third patriarch. However, with the help of his mother, Jacob deceived his aging father into blessing him on his deathbed (Genesis 27).

Another significant event in Jacob's life is described in Genesis 32. Here, he wrestled with God by the banks of the Jabbok River. In a truly marvelous, life changing moment, Jacob physically wrestled with God. God appeared to him in the form of a man, and Jacob wrestled with Him all night. At the end, the Lord changed his name to Israel, which means "He struggles with God."

Was this a positive or negative term? Is struggling with God a good characteristic (as in one who walks with the Lord and seeks His face and strives to be obedient) or a negative quality (as in one who is contentious and rebellious)? Or, is the name intentionally fluid so that it would describe the people of God for generations? However we understand it, this name identified the people of God for almost 2000 years. Jacob's descendents will forever be known as the people of Israel or as the children of Israel.

Jacob, along with his two wives and two servants, had twelve sons (Genesis 35). The twelve tribes of Israel are traced back to the twelve sons of Israel.

Joseph

The final patriarch was Joseph, one of the twelve sons of Israel. Joseph's story is told in Genesis 37-50, by far the largest narrative portion of the first book of the Bible. It contains some of the most well known stories of the Old Testament, and is a fascinating story.

Joseph was the favorite child of Israel, and he was despised by his brothers accordingly. Joseph didn't help his case by sharing his dreams of greatness with them (Genesis 37). In anger, they sold him as a slave, and Joseph found himself in Egypt as a servant to one of the Pharaoh's officials, Potiphar.

However, the Lord blessed him, and he was treated with honor until he was falsely accused of sexual immorality by Potiphar's wife (Genesis 39). He was thrown into prison where he met the Cupbearer and Baker, both servants to Pharaoh and plagued by strange dreams. Given the gift of interpreting dreams by the Lord, Joseph interpreted their dreams, and one of them was restored to his position.

When the Pharaoh later had bad dreams himself, the Cupbearer told the Pharaoh about Joseph. After bringing peace of mind to the Pharaoh by interpreting his dreams, Joseph was promoted to second in command in Egypt and in charge of preparing the nation for the upcoming famine (Genesis 41). When the ensuing famine overtook the whole land, the other sons of Israel came to Egypt to buy some bread. Joseph revealed himself to his brothers through a fascinating series of events. Afterwards, they were restored in their relationship with Joseph. Also, they moved with their families into the most fertile region of Egypt, the Nile Delta.

Joseph's life ends with one of the most powerful quotes of the entire Old Testament. After years of turmoil and misery as the result of being sold into slavery by his own brothers, Joseph did not hold a bitter memory of his past. Instead, he said, "As for you, you meant evil against me, but God meant it for good, to bring it about that many people should be kept alive, as they are today" (Genesis 50.20).

The book of Genesis ends with the children of Israel living in splendor in the land of Egypt. Of course, this will quickly give way to a people enslaved in the very land where they lived in splendor, but that is the subject of the next chapter.

Conclusion

The book of Genesis is the book about beginnings: the beginning of the world, the beginning of sin, and the beginning of God's plan to buy back a lost and dying creation. It is a story that is told through the lives of the four patriarchs: Abraham, Isaac, Jacob/Israel, and Joseph.

We read these stories as stories of faith. They wrestled in their immaturity to gain a better understanding of what it meant to trust God and to follow Him. They weren't always right, and they were not worthy of God's blessings and selection, but that is what faith is about. They struggled in their faith because following God in the real world is not easy. Sometimes, we don't make good choices, but God forgives us and calls us back into following Him.

Faith on this side of the cross differs because of the Spirit. While Abraham had faith, he did not have the law, nor did he have the indwelling Spirit. New covenant believers are filled with the Spirit of God who bears righteous fruit in our lives. Abraham was still living under an old covenant, a covenant of works righteousness. No one is made right with God by observing the law, and that included Abraham. Abraham's life is a prime example of the reason why Christ came to set us free from the law. Even the most faithful person of all time could not fulfill the law.

The New Testament teaches us that the effects of Adam's sin impacts us all. The consequences of Adam's sin was more than just a bad example. Sin came into the world through that one man (see Romans 5.12), and death continues to reign in creation because of the sin of that one man (see Romans 5.17). The work of Christ conquered the work of Adam's sin.

> *Therefore, as one trespass led to condemnation for all men, so one act of righteousness leads to justification and life for all men. For as by the one man's disobedience the many were made sinners, so by the one man's obedience the many will be made righteous. (Romans 5.18-19)*

As we read the story of Adam and his removal from the presence of God, his story impacts us all.

Making It Profitable

At this moment, you have a crucial choice to make.

You have already made the choice to deepen your understanding of the Bible by purchasing this book. And you have taken a deeper step by actually reading this book instead of just letting it rest on your nightstand. And now you have almost made it through one third of the book.

You will be tempted to turn the page and start reading the next act in this wonderful story. But I want you to value your spiritual development enough to resist that urge. Please don't be content to merely learn about the Scriptures. Don't be content with knowledge about the Bible. Pursue the Living Word.

I want to challenge you to strive to experience the Scriptures through the spiritual disciplines of daily Bible reading, meditation, Scripture memory, and prayer. If you just learn about the Bible, but never experience Christ through the Bible, then it won't matter how much you learn because the Bible will never become profitable to you.

Take the time to make it profitable.

Daily Bible Readings

There are a variety of ways to plan your daily Bible reading. At the end of the book, I list various online resources to help you develop your own Bible reading plan after you finish with this book. One way is to follow a Scripture reading program much like I hope you will be doing as you read this book. You will notice that I have included only six days of daily readings instead of seven. It is my hope that on the seventh day you will be reading the Scriptures as part of your church worship experience.

This week's daily readings will encourage you to pair an Old Testament reading with a New Testament reading. You will notice that the two readings are connected, and I would challenge you to pay attention to how they are connected, and to see how God might be speaking to you through that connection.

Meditation

To meditate upon something is to think deeply about something and about how that truth might impact your life. Please don't just read the daily readings, but take the time and put forth the effort to meditate upon them.

I encourage you to use the SOAP method of journaling to meditate upon the daily readings. Allow the Spirit to highlight one or more verses of Scripture from the daily reading and write those verses down in your journal. Write down a few observations about that verse. Was there a spiritual truth you encountered today? Then, take some time to think about how this verse might apply to your life. And don't forget to spend some time talking to God about what you hear Him saying to you.

Suggested Memory Verses

So God created man in his own image, in the image of God he created him; male and female he created them. (Genesis 1.27)

And I will make of you a great nation, and I will bless you and make your name great, so that you will be a blessing. I will bless those who bless you, and him who dishonors you I will curse, and in you all the families of the earth shall be blessed. (Genesis 12.2-3)

But Joseph said to them, "Do not fear, for am I in the place of God? As for you, you meant evil against me, but God meant it for good, to bring it about that many people should be kept alive, as they are today. (Genesis 50.19-20)

For what can be known about God is plain to them, because God has shown it to them. For his invisible attributes, namely, his eternal power and divine nature, have been clearly perceived, ever since the creation of the world, in the things that have been made. So they are without excuse. (Romans 1.19-20)

For by him all things were created, in heaven and on earth, visible and invisible, whether thrones or dominions or rulers or authorities—all things were created through him and for him. And he is before all things, and in him all things hold together. (Colossians 1.16-17)

By faith Abraham obeyed when he was called to go out to a place that he was to receive as an inheritance. And he went out, not knowing where he was going. (Hebrews 11.8)

Day One: Genesis 1.1-31 and Colossians 1.15-20

S: _____

_____

_____

_____

_____

_____

_____

O: _____

_____

_____

_____

_____

_____

_____

A: _____

_____

_____

_____

_____

_____

_____

P: _____

_____

_____

_____

_____

_____

_____

Day Two: Genesis 3.1-24 and Romans 5.12-21

S: _____

_____

_____

_____

_____

_____

_____

O: _____

_____

_____

_____

_____

_____

_____

A: _____

_____

_____

_____

_____

_____

_____

P: _____

_____

_____

_____

_____

_____

_____

Day Three: Genesis 12.1-9 and Romans 4.1-12

S:

_____
_____
_____
_____
_____
_____
_____

O:

_____
_____
_____
_____
_____
_____
_____

A:

_____
_____
_____
_____
_____
_____
_____

P:

_____
_____
_____
_____
_____
_____
_____

Day Four: Genesis 22.1-19 and Romans 4.13-25

_S:_ _____

_____
_____
_____
_____
_____
_____
_____

_O:_ _____

_____
_____
_____
_____
_____
_____
_____

_A:_ _____

_____
_____
_____
_____
_____
_____
_____

_P:_ _____

_____
_____
_____
_____
_____
_____
_____

Day Five: Genesis 37.1-36 and Romans 12.14-21

S:
_____
_____
_____
_____
_____
_____
_____

O:
_____
_____
_____
_____
_____
_____
_____

A:
_____
_____
_____
_____
_____
_____
_____

P:
_____
_____
_____
_____
_____
_____
_____

Day Six: Genesis 50.1-21 and Romans 8.26-30

S: _____

_____

_____

_____

_____

_____

_____

_____

O: _____

_____

_____

_____

_____

_____

_____

_____

A: _____

_____

_____

_____

_____

_____

_____

P: _____

_____

_____

_____

_____

_____

_____

5 | ACT 2 | MOSES AND THE EXODUS

At this point, the people of God were living in Egypt, living under the protection and provision of the second in command to the Pharaoh, Joseph. They settled in the most fertile region of Egypt, the Nile Delta, and things could not be looking better. But, as the next section of the story unfolds, things couldn't be worse.

Decades passed since Joseph was alive, and a new Pharaoh was in charge who did not know about Joseph. He enslaved the Hebrews to prevent them from rebelling against the Egyptians and perhaps taking over the land (Exodus 1.8-10). The Pharaoh used the Hebrews as forced labor to build two cities, Pithom and Raamses.

To an oppressed people, God sent a man like no other.

The Dating of the Exodus

The entire Old Testament revolves around two key events: the exodus and the exile. While the exile will be the subject of later chapters, the first key event is associated with the life and ministry of Moses: the exodus. The title for the second book of the Old Testament is given to us by the Greek translation of the Hebrew Old Testament. The LXX entitles this book, "Exodus," or Greek for "exit." Therefore, the exodus is the event in the Old Testament where the people of God "exited" Egypt and journeyed towards the Promised Land.

When did the exodus take place? We know that Solomon completed the Temple in 960 BC. Furthermore, the writer of the book of Kings tells us that the exodus took place 480 years before the Temple was finished (1 Kings 6.1). So, the exodus must have taken place around 1440 BC.

Since most of the Old Testament material wanders around loosely in our minds, like spare change in the kitchen drawer, it helps to drive a few historical posts into the narrative landscape so that the other stories can be put in proper perspective.

There are certain benchmark dates that will be emphasized in this book: the exodus (1440 BC), construction of Solomon's temple (960 BC), the split of Israel and Judah (921 BC), the fall of Israel to Assyria (721 BC), the fall of Judah to Babylon (586 BC), the rebuilding of the Temple (515 BC), the birth of Christ (4 BC), and the fall of Jerusalem (70 AD). Keeping these dates firmly in mind will help the reader of the Bible to place other events in their chronological order.

The Call of Moses

After a brief introduction to the crisis in Egypt and the birth and young adult life of Moses, we find ourselves at the burning bush, the place where the Lord called Moses into service. Moses was reluctant to believe that the Lord would choose or use him for such a mighty task. He gave four excuses that sound hauntingly familiar as we continue to use them today to avoid God's call.

Moses first reaction was to say, "Who am I that I should go to Pharaoh?" (Exodus 3.11). He made a good point. There was little to commend Moses to such a post. His only real claim to fame was that he murdered an Egyptian and had to flee the country because the Pharaoh put a price on his head.

Like us, Moses could not see his unique qualifications for the job. He was raised as the son of Pharaoh (see Exodus 2). This meant he received the best military and political training possible. After his banishment from Egypt, he spent the next forty years in the desert working the flocks and learning how to survive in the wilderness. He was perfectly trained and qualified for his mission of leading a large group of people on a wilderness journey.

The Lord's answer to Moses' first question was basically, "It doesn't matter who you are because I will be with you." This led naturally into Moses' second question, "Who are You?" His fellow Israelites would surely want to know, so God revealed the most sacred of all names to the Jewish people: Yahweh or "I AM" (Exodus 3.14).

The name is the Hebrew "to be" verb, and its translation has spawned a volume of work trying to encompass the depth of the name. The God of Abraham is the "I am," the "I am who I will be," or the "I will be who I have been." The great I AM. The Lord is the All-sufficient One.

"But they will not believe me" (Exodus 4.1) was Moses' third objection, and a good point at that. After all, why would they? Why would anyone believe that a man had met the sovereign Creator of the universe at a burning bush in the desert? So, the Lord gave Moses three signs: his rod would turn into a snake, his hand would turn leprous when placed in his cloak, and the water from the Nile would turn to blood. The people would be convinced by such wondrous signs.

But, Moses was a stubborn lot. He refused to budge. His fourth and final excuse was his speaking inability. He had never been eloquent. So, the Lord gave Aaron, his brother, as an assistant to help him with the duties of public speaking.

Convinced of his call and confident in the power and presence of the Lord, Moses set off for the Pharaoh's palace.

The Plagues

The Lord told Moses that the Pharaoh would not easily allow the Hebrews to leave Egypt. After all, why would he allow a labor force of over two million people to simply walk away? He would have to be forced into allowing the people to go. So, the Lord sent a series of plagues on the land.

The False Gods of Egypt

Each of the ten plagues attacked one of the gods of Egypt. For instance, cows were viewed in Egypt as sacred. Later, the people would rebel against Moses and the Lord by building a golden idol (see Exodus 32). Why did the people build a golden calf instead of a donkey or snake? Because it was one of the many gods that were worshipped in Egypt. So, the fifth plague was a terrible plague on the livestock to demonstrate that the Lord was sovereign over every created thing.

The final plague, the death of the first born, was the most serious challenge to the false gods of Egypt. The Pharaoh was believed to be the incarnation of the Sun God, and his first born son would be the next in line to receive this divine incarnation. The final plague killed all the first born in Egypt and demonstrated the Lord's sovereignty over even the Pharaoh and the sun god.

Good Riddance!

The plagues were unpleasant events orchestrated by God for two basic reasons. The first was to force the Pharaoh to allow the Hebrews to leave. Otherwise, he would not be inclined to allow his slave labor force to just leave.

But, not only did God need to force the Egyptians to allow the Hebrews to leave, He also had to convince the Hebrews to leave, too. Remember, the Hebrews were living in the most fertile area of the Nile valley, and even though they were in harsh, slavery conditions, life was still better there than in the desert. They would often complain to Moses about how they should have stayed in Egypt because they at least had enough food and water for survival (for example, see Exodus 16.3).

Sometimes the greatest struggle is moving the people of God from good to better or from better to best. We easily find contentment in small blessings, and this contentment prevents us from stepping out on faith towards the Promised Land of the future. However, the land of promise lies on the other side of the deserts of barren journeys. Most of God's people have needed some degree of nudging to get them to leave the good for the best.

For example, the apostles were quite content to remain in Jerusalem after Jesus returned to the Father even though the Lord commanded them to be witnesses in Jerusalem, Judea, Samaria, and unto the ends of the earth. Since they wouldn't leave, the Lord brought a great persecution against the church, and the disciples fled Jerusalem for the ends of the earth, taking the gospel with them (see Acts 8.1).

We often need the plagues to make us want to leave the land of the good for the land of the best.

Warnings about Hardened Hearts

The first nine plagues showed a clear pattern. The first of each triplet of plagues was accompanied by a lengthy warning to the Pharaoh. The second was accompanied by a short warning, but no warning was given in the case of the final plague of each triplet. It was as if the Lord was saying to Pharaoh, "I gave you one chance, I gave you another chance, and I gave you a third chance, but you still refused to listen to me."

With each warning, and even with each horrible plague, Pharaoh refused to listen to Moses. He continued to harden his heart. There is a simple lesson in the hardening of Pharaoh's heart. Each time we refuse to listen to the Word of the Lord, our hearts grow more callous. If we continue on this pattern, there will grow a time when we are no longer able to hear. Our hearts will be hardened, and even though the miraculous signs abound, we will be unable to see or respond to the word of the Lord. The simple truth: when the Lord speaks, listen and obey lest your heart be hardened.

The Tenth Plague and Salvation

The tenth plague was entirely different. The opportunities for Pharaoh to let the people go were over. Judgment was coming.

The people were instructed in Exodus 12 to prepare for the tenth plague with very specific details. Each family was to take a male lamb, without defect. They were to slaughter it, place some of the blood on the doorpost of their house, and then eat it with their families as a ceremonial meal. In addition, they were to eat bread without yeast and bitter herbs. That night, the death angel would pass through the land and kill the first born of mankind and animals.

This meal became the most important feast in all of Jewish life: the Passover. As described in Exodus 12, this meal was to be celebrated by the Jews each year for generations eternal as a memorial of this deliverance. After the exodus, the observance of the Passover was dependent upon the presence of the Tabernacle or the Temple since the lamb had to be offered as a sacrifice. So, the Passover was not observed during the exile but was re-established during the time of Ezra (see Ezra 6.19-22).

The Passover endured many changes after the destruction of the Temple in 70 AD by the Romans. The sacrificial lamb was removed from the observance and the focus shifted to the unleavened bread.

The Passover Meal, instituted with the tenth plague, provides much insight into the salvation story. In Scripture, we often find "types," one event or person that will become a model for future events or people. These types foreshadow or inform future events. There are many Old Testament types, or foreshadowings, of Christ.

In the tenth plague, we find a foreshadowing or type of the salvation event of Christ's death on the cross. In other words, the Lord was preparing His people to receive Jesus' death on the cross for our salvation through the annual observance of Passover.

The Lamb of God

In the Passover meal, the lamb was the central element of the meal. This lamb had to be perfect, without defect. Early in the life of Christ, John the Baptist would declare that Jesus was the Lamb of God, provided by the Father to take away the sins of the world (see John 1.19). Unlike the Passover lamb, the Lamb of God was able to fully take away our sins (see Hebrews 10.11-12).

Substitutionary Death

Remember, the tenth plague and its corresponding Passover meal was instituted long before the sacrificial system had been revealed to Moses. In other words, before the Hebrews had ever sacrificed a lamb at the altar of the Tabernacle or the Temple, before they were presented with a system where a sacrificed animal could bring the forgiveness of sins, they were to believe that the blood of a lamb would protect them from the death angel on that fateful night in Egypt.

God was laying the groundwork of the substitutionary nature of the atonement. The substitutionary atonement is a fancy theology term which means that

Christ's death substituted for our own. He died in our place. The Passover lamb pointed the people of God to this expectation of salvation.

The Shedding of Blood

Modern Jews do not like to talk about the bloody sacrifices of the Old Testament. In fact, many scholars today would shudder at the gross and barbaric nature of the blood sacrifices of both the Old Testament and the Passover. Jewish rabbis teach today that we have moved beyond this barbaric practice, but there was a very important principle established on the night of Passover that teaches us so much about the death of our Lord and Savior.

The writer of Hebrews wrote, "Indeed, under the law almost everything is purified with blood, and without the shedding of blood there is no forgiveness of sins" (Hebrews 9.22). Why is the shedding of blood necessary for forgiveness? Why can't the Lord be pleased with a financial gift or a grain offering? What is so important about blood?

The book of Leviticus gives us the answer. "For the life of the flesh is in the blood, and I have given it for you on the altar to make atonement for your souls, for it is the blood that makes atonement by the life" (Leviticus 17.11). So, atonement is only possible through the blood of one life poured out in substitution for another. The wages of sin is death (see Romans 3.23), either ours or another's. In the Passover meal, the people of God were beginning to see that the only way to salvation is through the shedding of blood of one life on behalf of another.

The Lord's Supper

It was this annual Passover meal that Jesus celebrated with His disciples on the last free night of His life. However, Jesus radically transformed this meal by describing the wine as the new covenant in His blood, and the bread as His body given for them (see Luke 22.19-20). Jesus became the Passover Lamb as prophesied by John the Baptist (see John 1.29), and it was the spilling of His blood that saved His people from their sins.

The Wrath of God

Before we leave the tenth plague and the Passover meal, there is one more important observation that is often missed when discussing that fateful night in Egypt.

From what were the people of God spared when they put their faith in the Passover lamb? Were they spared from the wrath of the Egyptians? Were they spared from the power of the Pharaoh? No, they were spared from the wrath of God.

Another key component in the New Testament picture of salvation is that our sins have brought upon ourselves the wrath of God. The apostle Paul wrote extensively about this wrath.

> *Among whom we all once lived in the passions of our flesh, carrying out the desires of the body and the mind, and were by nature children of wrath, like the rest of mankind. (Ephesians 2.3)*

> *For the wrath of God is revealed from heaven against all ungodliness and unrighteousness of men, who by their unrighteousness suppress the truth. (Romans 1.18)*

> *Since, therefore, we have now been justified by his blood, much more shall we be saved by him from the wrath of God. (Romans 5.9)*

The biblical picture is quite clear. Sin brings on the wrath of God. One of our needs for salvation is to be saved from this coming wrath of God that is being stored up against all unrighteousness. God provided a Lamb so that we might escape this coming wrath just like the Passover lamb provided an escape for God's people from the wrath of God revealed through the death angel.

The Exodus Miracles

The exodus officially began with the Pharaoh yielding to Moses' demands after the tenth plague. The people, probably over 2.5 million of them, left Egypt in haste as prophesied by the eating of unleavened bread during the Passover meal (see Exodus 12.12). The figure of 2.5 million Hebrews leaving Egypt is an estimate based upon the period of years the Hebrews were in Egypt in conjunction with the total number of all the men who were of military age according to later census figures. Since the census in Numbers 1.46 yielded 603,550 fighting men, the total number, including estimates for women and children, would be about 2.5 million.

Before the free labor force had left Egyptian soil, the Egyptian neighbors gave the Hebrews gold and articles of clothing for their journey (see Exodus 12.35-36). This marked the beginning of the single most important event in the history of the Jewish people: the exodus.

The journey from Egypt to the Promised Land was not a simple matter. Not only was the journey long and difficult with such a large group of unprepared people, but the Lord had so much work to do to turn these people into a covenant nation. The next 40 years would be the single greatest display of the power and presence of God in the history of mankind.

Every day, the people saw the presence of God in a cloud that led them by day and a pillar of fire that led them by night. The most basic needs of food and shelter were miraculously provided by the Lord Himself. The clothes on their back and the shoes on their feet never wore out (see Deuteronomy 29.5). They gathered miraculously provided manna every morning for their daily meals. Fresh water poured forth from rocks in the wilderness. They watched as the Red Sea parted in two, and they stepped on dry ground instead of a mushy riverbed. They watched their leader meet with the divine regularly as the cloud descended over the tent of meeting.

One would think that as the people of God lived in the presence of such miraculous displays of God's power, presence, and care, that they lived in faithful harmony with what they witnessed. However, the greatest period of God's miracles only produced the greatest period of the rebellion of God's people. The Psalmist reflected upon the story of the exodus with these words: "Many times he delivered them, but they were rebellious in their purposes and were brought low through their iniquity" (Psalm 106.43).

How often we say to ourselves, "If I could just see some miraculous display of God's power, then I would know I could trust Him." But the truth is that the exodus did not breed a people of faith; it bred a people of contempt, complaining, and rebellion. Faith that demands proof is not really faith. Faith must be based upon faith and not sight. And while we think that great sight will breed great faith, think again. The story of the exodus gives a different testimony.

Covenant and the Law

After delivering the people of God from Egypt, the Lord brought them to a place of covenant, to Mount Sinai. On the mountain of God, the Lord revealed to Moses His intentions with these people.

> *The Lord called to him out of the mountain, saying, "Thus you shall say to the house of Jacob, and tell the people of Israel: You yourselves have seen what I did to the Egyptians, and how I bore you on eagles' wings and brought you to myself. Now therefore, if you will indeed obey my voice and keep my covenant, you shall be my treasured possession among all peoples, for all the earth is mine; and you shall be to me a kingdom of priests and a holy nation. These are the words that you shall speak to the people of Israel." (Exodus 19.3-6)*

The people of God were to enter into a special relationship with Him based upon a few criteria.

The covenant of God can be summarized in three basic concepts. First, they were to worship the Lord only and have no other gods before Him. Second, they were to obey Him fully. Third, when they disobeyed, there were to repent and to seek forgiveness through the sacrificial system.

If the people lived in faithful relationship to God under this covenant, then they would experience certain blessings. They would be a treasured possession of God living in blessings unequaled, and they would be a kingdom of priests. Since a priest is "a mediatory agent between humans and God" (*Merriam-Webster*), then a nation of priests would be a mediatory agent between all of mankind and God. In other words, the nation of Israel was to have a priestly function of representing God to all the nations. Unfortunately, they never understood or embraced this function. They were too enamored with enjoying the special blessings of being a treasured people to ever get too consumed about sharing that blessing with other nations.

Understanding the Law

One of the most difficult portions of the entire Bible to understand properly is the Old Testament law. Beginning with Exodus and continuing through Deuteronomy, the Lord laid out some very hard to understand and difficult to apply rules and expectations. As we read the Old Testament laws through New Testament eyes, we often pick and choose which ones are still relevant for today.

There was a man in one of the churches I served who had very strong feelings about tattoos. He felt they were sinful, and he based his opinion on one verse in Leviticus.

> *You shall not make any cuts on your body for the dead or tattoo yourselves: I am the Lord. (Leviticus 19.28)*

He was also one of these former military guys who felt strongly about being clean cut. He was against men having long hair or facial hair of any kind. But the verse in Leviticus that preceded the verse about tattoos taught that we are not to trim our beards.

> *You shall not round off the hair on your temples or mar the edges of your beard. (Leviticus 19.27)*

By what right did he hold firmly to the teachings of verse 28 but ignore the teachings of verse 27?

In the absence of a well thought out framework through which to handle the law of the Old Testament, and particularly which elements of that law are still valid for New Testament believers, many believers simply pick and choose which ones they want to obey. The law becomes little more than our way of living the way we want to and trying to force others to live the way we want them to live. Not only is that poor theology, but it only gives further testimony to the unbelieving world that the Bible cannot be trusted or relied upon to lead a person to know the Creator. There must be a better way.

Two New Testament verses guide our understanding of the Old Testament covenant law. The first is found in Paul's letter to the churches of Galatia.

Now before faith came, we were held captive under the law, imprisoned
until the coming faith would be revealed. So then, the law was our
guardian until Christ came, in order that we might be justified by
faith. But now that faith has come, we are no longer under a guardian, for
in Christ Jesus you are all sons of God, through faith. (Galatians 3.23-
26)

The ESV translates the Greek word *paidagogos* with the word "guardian." The
Greek word is truly impossible to translate into English because it derives from
a cultural reality in the Roman world, and our culture has no equivalent. The
paidagogos was

A guardian and guide of boys. Among the Greeks and the Romans, the
name was applied to trustworthy slaves who were charged with the duty of
supervising the life and morals of boys belonging to the better class. The
boys were not allowed so much as to step out of the house without them
before arriving at the age of manhood. (Thayers)

The law was a tutor to lead us to Christ. It was put in charge of our spiritual
development so that we would find maturity in Christ. Now that faith has
come, we are no longer under the supervision of the law.

The other New Testament teaching about the law that will impact our
application of the Old Testament law is found in the letter to the Hebrews.

For if that first covenant had been faultless, there would have been no
occasion to look for a second....In speaking of a new covenant, he makes
the first one obsolete. And what is becoming obsolete and growing old is
ready to vanish away. (Hebrews 8.7 and 13).

As the new covenant fulfilled the old, the old is now obsolete. Does this mean
that God no longer cares about holiness or about loving our neighbor?
Absolutely He does. Those ideas are clearly affirmed in the New Testament.
But, it does mean that the age of grace is a new age and much of the old age of
the law has been replaced.

So, if the old covenant has been replaced and its job of leading us to Christ has
been accomplished, then of what value is the Old Testament law? To help
answer this question, let's break down the Old Testament law into three
categories.

Ceremonial Law

Some of the laws of the Old Testament regard ways in which God's people were to relate to Him in the old covenant. Detailed procedures were given to Moses that were to guide how the people lived in covenant relationship to God. These included such ceremonies as the sacrifices and offerings, the feast days and festivals, the cleanliness codes and the priestly duties. These requirements guided the people and the priests as they worshipped a holy God despite their sinfulness.

In addition, they guided the people to understand how a person was ceremonially unclean and how to obtain cleanliness. For instance, a woman was ceremonially unclean during her menstrual cycle or after giving birth. Persons with leprosy or who had recently touched a dead body were also unclean. See Leviticus 13-15 for other examples of the cleanliness laws.

However, these portions of the Old Testament law have been fulfilled in Christ. This is the reason that no one brings a turtle dove to church or why a priest does not examine a person's house to see if the mildew has been removed. The New Testament teaches us that our cleanliness has been achieved once and for through the sacrifice of Jesus.

The New Testament teaches that we are no longer under the sacrificial system of the law in several places.

> *And every priest stands daily at his service, offering repeatedly the same sacrifices, which can never take away sins. But when Christ had offered for all time a single sacrifice for sins, he sat down at the right hand of God, waiting from that time until his enemies should be made a footstool for his feet. For by a single offering he has perfected for all time those who are being sanctified. (Hebrews 10.11-14)*

Christ is the once and for all sacrifice, and it is through His sacrifice that we are made right with God and forgiven. We are no longer under the sacrificial law.

Likewise, the New Testament teaches that the dietary code of the law has been fulfilled in Christ (see Acts 10.9-16 and Mark 7.19), that the festivals of the law are no longer valid (see Colossian 1.16-17), and even that the law of circumcision no longer means anything (see Galatians 6.15). All of these things were a mere shadow of the things to come, which was Christ.

Christ has fulfilled the ceremonial law.

Civil Law

Some of the Old Testament laws guided the theocratic government. A theocracy is a form of government where a state is governed by immediate divine guidance. God spoke specific laws to Moses about how the nation of Israel was to be governed.

Many of these laws were case law. Case law is a specific example of problems along with a given solution. For example, if a man was found slain and it was not known who killed him, what should be done? Deuteronomy 21.1-9 gives the process by which the elders and judges were to use to deal with this problem. There are a host of case laws in the Old Testament.

Much of these laws were regulations regarding how the people of God were to govern themselves. They involved specific punishments, often the death penalty, that were to be administered under certain guidelines to deal with violators. The primary motivation of the law was to keep the people of God pure, to "purge the evil" from among them (see Deuteronomy 21.21).

However, the people of God no longer live in a theocracy. In the new covenant, the Kingdom of God is not of this world, involves people of all nations, and Jesus is the only King. As such, these applications and case laws are no longer applicable to God's people.

One of the biggest Scriptural reasons for not living under the legal law of the Old Testament is the way Jesus dealt with and applied the legal law. In John 8, the Pharisees tried to trap Jesus into stoning a woman caught in adultery, as the law of the Old Testament demanded. Did Jesus enforce the legal law? No, He shared grace with the woman and commanded her to go on her way and to sin no more. Even Jesus did not affirm the legal law of the Old Testament.

Moral Law

The bulk of the Old Testament law falls into a third category: moral law. Moral law is the definition of that which is morally right and wrong. These moral definitions transcend cultures and historical periods. They have always been morally right, and they will always be morally right. For example, it has always been morally wrong to lie, and it always will be morally wrong to bear false witness against another. It has always been morally wrong to shed innocent blood, and it will always be wrong to murder. It has always been wrong to commit adultery, and it will always be wrong to commit adultery. The moral law is God's revelation of His heart and character, and therefore, remains consistent across both covenants.

The biggest confirmation about the constancy of moral law is the affirmation of such in the New Testament. Whereas the New Testament never affirms the ceremonial or sacrificial laws of the Old Testament, it constantly affirms the moral teachings of the Old Testament. The "sin lists" of the New Testament, where the New Testament writers described sinful behavior or attitudes, affirms the moral law of the Old Testament. For example, Romans 1.29-32, Galatians 5.19-21, 1 Peter 4.3 and other similar passages list sinful behaviors like envy, murder, greed, disobedience to parents, and lying and other behaviors that are consistent with Old Testament law.

Applying the Law

The moral laws are the elements of the Old Testament law that are still valid for New Testament believers. So, one interpretive task for the student of the Bible is to determine which portions of the Old Testament law fit into which category and how they relate to New Testament believers. There will always be cultural issues that will press us uncomfortably as we try to apply and understand these distinctions.

One of those key issues today is the issue of homosexuality. While many would have us to believe that this and other sexual standards just need to come of age, they fit into the moral law section of the Old Testament and are affirmed as sinful behavior in the New Testament (see Romans 1.26-27). Therefore, we should continue to understand them as sinful.

Another example is what to do with the Sabbath. Is the Sabbath part of the moral law or part of the ceremonial law? I believe it is part of the ceremonial law that has been replaced by the new covenant (see Colossians 2.16-17). The same is true of "putting on your best clothes to go to church." This might have been valid for Old Testament priests, but it is very hard to find a New Testament passage that affirms this.

There are two reasons why it is so crucial that the student of the Bible have a well thought out theology regarding the Old Testament law. First, it prevents inconsistent legalism, where Old Testament laws are randomly chosen and enforced more by one's personal preferences than by any theological standards. Second, it prevents libertinism and the abuse of grace. While some want to embrace grace and throw out all of the Old Testament law, this is not consistent with the teachings of our Lord or the teachings of the apostles.

The Tabernacle

In addition to the giving of the law on the mountain of God, the Lord gave detailed instructions to Moses regarding the building of the Tabernacle.

 The Tabernacle was the mobile house of worship for the people of God during the wilderness journey. There were three tabernacles, or dwellings, where God met with His people in the Old Testament. The first was the tent of meeting, described in Exodus 29.42, where the Lord met with Moses. The second was the Sinaitic Tabernacle, which was built in accordance with the Lord's instructions to Moses in Exodus 25-40. The final Tabernacle was the dwelling place built by David to house the ark before the Temple was completed. It is described in 2 Samuel 6.17.

The Tabernacle of the wilderness wanderings was surrounded by a large curtain or fence which enclosed the outer court, an area 150 feet by 75 feet. Inside that area was the 45 by 15 foot tent of meeting which housed the holy place and the holy of holies. The holy of holies contained the ark of the testimony. The ark was an oblong chest containing the two tablets of stone, a pot of manna, and Aarons' rod.

The outer holy place was the larger chamber of the tabernacle and housed the table for the showbread, the golden candlestick, and the golden altar of incense. The outer court held the altar for the burnt offering.

Over 400 years later, Solomon would build the Temple on the same pattern as the Tabernacle. The Scriptures tell us that the pattern of the Tabernacle and the Temple are based upon the true tabernacle in Heaven (see Hebrews 9.23-24).

Kadesh Barnea: The Faith Crisis

After the Lord revealed the law to Moses on the mountain,

> The LORD our God said to us in Horeb, 'You have stayed long enough at this mountain....See, I have set the land before you. Go in and take possession of the land that the LORD swore to your fathers, to Abraham, to Isaac, and to Jacob, to give to them and to their offspring after them.' (Deuteronomy 1.6, 8)

After an eleven day journey (see Deuteronomy 1.2), the people arrived at Kadesh Barnea. Here, the Lord instructed Moses to send in twelve spies to explore the land and to investigate the best way to capture the land. When the spies returned, they gave wonderful testimonies of the land, agreeing with the Lord that it did flow with milk and honey.

However they also discovered that the people who inhabited the land were powerful and the cities were fortified and very large. While two of the spies, Caleb and Joshua, encouraged the people to trust the Lord to give to them the land that He promised, the people sided with the ten spies who testified that it would be impossible to take the land (see Numbers 13).

As punishment, the Lord declared that none of the people who had seen the signs of the exodus would be allowed to enter the land of promise.

> None of the men who have seen my glory and my signs that I did in Egypt and in the wilderness, and yet have put me to the test these ten times and have not obeyed my voice, shall see the land that I swore to give to their fathers. (Numbers 14.22-23)

The people were condemned to wander for 40 years, one year for every day the spies explored the land. Only Joshua and Caleb would enter the land.

The rest of the exodus journey is the story of these 40 years of wandering that were the result of refusing to believe in the Lord's promise.

The story of Kadesh Barnea is a powerful one. It reminds us that the Lord often brings us to moments of faith, where we have to act in faith upon the promises of the Lord. While we see the obstacles and all the many reasons why the land of promise could never become our own, we must act in faith that the Lord will do what He has promised to do. The shameful testimony of Kadesh Barnea is that a group of people who had seen God's marvelous hand in so many miraculous ways still refused to trust in the Lord.

The story of the exodus ended with the people at the edge of the land of promise. The generation that left Egypt died in the wilderness because of their lack of faith. Even Moses did not enter the land of promise because of his lack of faith in the word of the Lord.

The Pentateuch

The first five books of the Old Testament are called the Pentateuch. The word is the combination of two Greek words which mean "five scrolls."

The book of Genesis covers the story from creation through the life of Joseph.

The book of Exodus tells the story of the deliverance from Egypt and the giving of the law to Moses on the mountain.

The third book, Leviticus, focuses on the rules and regulations regarding the priests and the sacrifices along with instructions about the feasts and special days like the Day of Atonement.

The book of Numbers tells the story of the wanderings from Sinai to Kadesh Barnea and to the edge of the land of promise.

The book of Deuteronomy, which means "second law," is Moses' address to the people as they gathered on the east side of the Jordan River, preparing to enter the land of promise. It recounts many of the events already covered, including some of the laws (including the Ten Commandments), and finishes with a clear challenge to remain faithful to the covenant after entering the land of promise.

> *See, I have set before you today life and good, death and evil. If you obey the commandments of the LORD your God that I command you today, by loving the LORD your God, by walking in his ways, and by keeping his commandments and his statutes and his rules, then you shall live and multiply, and the LORD your God will bless you in the land that you are entering to take possession of it. But if your heart turns away, and you will not hear, but are drawn away to worship other gods and serve them, I declare to you today, that you shall surely perish. You shall not live long in the land that you are going over the Jordan to enter and possess. I call heaven and earth to witness against you today, that I have set before you life and death, blessing and curse. Therefore choose life, that you and your offspring may live, loving the LORD your God, obeying his voice and holding fast to him, for he is your life and length of days, that you may dwell in the land that the LORD swore to your fathers, to Abraham, to Isaac, and to Jacob, to give them. (Deuteronomy 30.15-20)*

The Barbaric Old Testament

Before we leave the exodus story, we should wrestle with the fact that some parts of the story seem quite barbaric to our modern ears. God's wrath was often poured out in the form of plagues or snakes or even dramatic natural events. The death penalty was prescribed for disobedient children. Women and children of the enemies were killed in cold blood. It is no wonder that some have concluded that the God of the Old Testament cannot be the God of the New Testament. Is there any compatibility between grace and law?

How do we answer these claims, especially when our hearts see the apparent contradiction? Some of the problem is that God was dealing with a primitive people in a primitive age. There was no police force or judicial system, no medical team, and no standing army.

It is also helpful to remember the concept of progressive revelation. Progressive revelation means that the Lord revealed Himself to His people progressively over a period of 1500 years. In years past, He spoke through the law and the prophets. Finally, He has spoken fully in Christ.

Making it Profitable

The Scriptures become living and active when we find ourselves in the story, and the exodus story is one of the greatest places in all of the Bible to do just that. Just like the Lord found Israel enslaved in Egypt, so He found us enslaved to sin. Just like the Lord delivered Israel through the Passover lamb, so He delivered us through the blood of Jesus. And just like the Lord entered into a special covenant with Israel, so He has entered into a covenant of grace with us.

This story comes alive in our souls as we come to experience it with our souls. Will you be content to simply understand the story or will you set your sights on something deeper, encountering the God of the exodus in your own faith journey?

I hope you will go deeper, and take the time this week to invest in your relationship with Christ by developing the spiritual disciplines of daily Bible reading, meditation, and Scripture memory.

Daily Bible Readings

The daily readings for this act compare an Old Testament reading with a New Testament reading. The New Testament book of Hebrews is the best commentary on the book of Leviticus, so I have paired relevant sections.

Suggested Memory Verses

I am the LORD your God, who brought you out of the land of Egypt, out of the house of slavery. You shall have no other gods before me. (Exodus 20.2-3)

Now this is the commandment, the statutes and the rules that the LORD your God commanded me to teach you, that you may do them in the land to which you are going over, to possess it, that you may fear the LORD your God, you and your son and your son's son, by keeping all his statutes

*and his commandments, which I command you, all the days of your
life, and that your days may be long. (Deuteronomy 6.1-2)*

*Hear, O Israel: The LORD our God, the LORD is one. You shall love
the LORD your God with all your heart and with all your soul and with all
your might. And these words that I command you today shall be on your
heart. You shall teach them diligently to your children, and shall talk of
them when you sit in your house, and when you walk by the way, and
when you lie down, and when you rise. (Deuteronomy 6.4-5)*

*Know therefore that the Lord your God is God, the faithful God who keeps
covenant and steadfast love with those who love him and keep his
commandments, to a thousand generations. (Deuteronomy 7.9)*

*And now, Israel, what does the Lord your God require of you, but to fear
the Lord your God, to walk in all his ways, to love him, to serve the Lord
your God with all your heart and with all your soul, and to keep the
commandments and statutes of the Lord, which I am commanding you
today for your good? (Deuteronomy 10.12-13)*

*See, I have set before you today life and good, death and evil. If you obey
the commandments of the LORD your God that I command you today, by
loving the LORD your God, by walking in his ways, and by keeping his
commandments and his statutes and his rules, then you shall live and
multiply, and the LORD your God will bless you in the land that you are
entering to take possession of it. (Deuteronomy 30.15-16)*

Day One: Exodus 12.1-14 and Hebrews 9.11-28

_S:_ _____

_____
_____
_____
_____
_____
_____
_____

_O:_ _____

_____
_____
_____
_____
_____
_____
_____

_A:_ _____

_____
_____
_____
_____
_____
_____
_____

_P:_ _____

_____
_____
_____
_____
_____
_____
_____

Day Two: Exodus 20.1-17 and Galatians 3.10-25

S:
_____
_____
_____
_____
_____
_____
_____
_____

O:
_____
_____
_____
_____
_____
_____
_____
_____

A:
_____
_____
_____
_____
_____
_____
_____
_____

P:
_____
_____
_____
_____
_____
_____
_____
_____

Day Three: Leviticus 16 and Hebrews 10.1-18

_S:_ _____

_____
_____
_____
_____
_____
_____

_O:_ _____

_____
_____
_____
_____
_____
_____

_A:_ _____

_____
_____
_____
_____
_____
_____

_P:_ _____

_____
_____
_____
_____
_____
_____

Day Four: Numbers 13.17-14.35 and Hebrews 3.12-19

S:

_____

_____

_____

_____

_____

_____

_____

O:

_____

_____

_____

_____

_____

_____

_____

A:

_____

_____

_____

_____

_____

_____

_____

P:

_____

_____

_____

_____

_____

_____

_____

Day Five: Deuteronomy 4.1-14 and Hebrews 5.11-6.12

S:

O:

A:

P:

Day Six: Deuteronomy 30.1-20 and 1 Peter 2.9-12

S:

O:

A:

P:

One of the largest figures in the entire biblical narrative has just left the stage. Because of his disobedience to the Lord during the forty years of wandering in the wilderness, Moses did not enter the land of promise. But by no means did he leave the story in disgrace.

Moses is a prominent figure, not only in the memory of the Jewish people, but also in the future salvation story. It was Moses who appeared with Elijah on the Mount of Transfiguration with Jesus (see Luke 9.28-36), and many believe that Moses was one of the "two men" who were at the empty tomb and the ascension of Jesus (see Luke 24 and Acts 1). In addition, it seems quite clear that Moses is one of the two witnesses during the unfolding of history's finale in Revelation 11. He might not have entered the land of promise, but he certainly looms large in the salvation story.

Joshua

The next key figure in the story of biblical history is Joshua. Joshua, born into the slave conditions of Egypt, was more than just another traveler on the journey. He was the servant of Moses and had the unique privilege of joining Moses on the mountain when he received the law. As one of the twelve spies sent into the land at Kadesh Barnea, only he and Caleb encouraged the people to trust the Lord and enter the land in faith. As a result, these two were the only adults who survived the forty years of wandering and who were allowed to enter the land of promise.

The Lord selected Joshua to succeed Moses before Moses' death, and he turned out to be an exceptional leader of God's people. While he does not jump off the biblical pages like Moses, Abraham, or David, his ministry was equally important. He led the people into the land of promise and served as a military, political, and spiritual leader.

We can only imagine the fear and uncertainty that filled the camp of the children of Israel as they heard of the death of Moses. Just like he appeared, he mysteriously disappeared. The Scriptures tell us that the Lord buried him, and the people never knew the location of his tomb. The people grieved for the loss of a giant of a leader for thirty days. Afterwards, the Lord gave His instructions to the new leader.

> *After the death of Moses the servant of the* LORD, *the* LORD *said to Joshua the son of Nun, Moses' assistant, "Moses my servant is dead. Now therefore arise, go over this Jordan, you and all this people, into the land that I am giving to them, to the people of Israel. Every place that the sole of your foot will tread upon I have given to you, just as I promised to Moses. From the wilderness and this Lebanon as far as the great river, the river Euphrates, all the land of the Hittites to the Great Sea toward the going down of the sun shall be your territory. No man shall be able to stand before you all the days of your life. Just as I was with Moses, so I will be with you. I will not leave you or forsake you. Be strong and courageous, for you shall cause this people to inherit the land that I swore to their fathers to give them. Only be strong and very courageous, being careful to do according to all the law that Moses my servant commanded you. Do not turn from it to the right hand or to the left, that you may have good success wherever you go. This Book of the Law shall not depart from your mouth, but you shall meditate on it day and night, so that you may be careful to do according to all that is written in it. For then you will make your way prosperous, and then you will have good success. Have I not commanded you? Be strong and courageous. Do not be frightened, and do not be dismayed, for the* LORD *your God is with you wherever you go."* (Joshua 1.1-9)

A Second Exodus

After the reminder that fruitfulness and blessing are connected to faithfulness to the covenant, Joshua was commanded to lead the people into the Promised Land. In many ways, the key events of the exodus were recreated as this new generation learned to trust in the Lord. This was a "do-over" as they got a second chance to step out in faith.

Before they entered the land, they sent in spies to explore the land. However, this time, they only sent in two spies instead of twelve. Symbolically, they left the unbelieving ten behind.

After being sheltered by Rahab, the spies returned with a dramatically different report.

> *Truly the Lord has given all the land into our hands. And also, all the inhabitants of the land melt away because of us. (Joshua 2.24)*

No longer were the Hebrews afraid because of the powerful cities.

Another parallel was the dramatic river crossing. Just like the exodus began with a miraculous water crossing of the Red Sea, so the entrance into the land began with a miraculous water crossing of the Jordan River. In the exodus, it was the rod of Moses, raised high that parted the waters. In the second exodus, it was the Ark of the Covenant that led the way. Both were acts of faith for the waters did not stop flowing until the feet of the priests who were carrying the ark stepped into the water.

Just like Moses led the people in a worship experience right after the miraculous crossing of the Red Sea, Joshua led the people to erect a memorial with twelve stones taken from the river's bottom. These stones were to be an everlasting memorial to their children. When their children asked, "What do these stones mean," they were to tell them the story of the river crossing.

After the river crossing, the men who had not been circumcised during the wilderness wanderings were circumcised. Then, they celebrated the Passover for the first time in the Promised Land. After these things, the manna stopped, and for the first time, they ate some of the produce of the land.

Just like in the exodus story, there was an immediate faith crisis that confronted the people. Kadesh Barnea forced the people of God to choose to live by faith or to live by fear. With the second exodus, the faith crisis came in the form of the first place of battle: Jericho.

The Battle of Jericho

This might be one of the best known stories of the Bible by our children, and because we know the story so well, it is hard to allow ourselves to feel the shock.

Imagine being part of a newly formed group that was going to march in and take a new territory by storm. You would be charged up and ready to go. The dramatic river crossing would strengthen your faith in the cause. The testimony of the spies would only stoke the flames within. By now, even the sight of the fortified city of Jericho could do nothing to dampen your excitement. All you are waiting for now is for the military leader to lay out the battle plans and to blow the attack horn.

With all that testosterone flowing in the camp, imagine how the plan of the Lord, as revealed to Joshua, must have sounded.

> *You shall march around the city, all the men of war going around the city once. Thus shall you do for six days. Seven priests shall bear seven trumpets of rams' horns before the ark. On the seventh day you shall march around the city seven times, and the priests shall blow the trumpets. And when they make a long blast with the ram's horn, when you hear the sound of the trumpet, then all the people shall shout with a great shout, and the wall of the city will fall down flat, and the people shall go up, everyone straight before him. (Joshua 6.3-5)*

What faith it must have taken to believe in such a ridiculous plan. Every night, around the campfire, they licked the wounds of embarrassment after being mocked by the guards on the wall throughout the day's march. Surely the people wrestled with whether or not they could trust in such a far-fetched plan. But the people persevered, and the people trusted in the plan of the Lord. Instead of the sting of defeat that their forefathers felt, they experienced the first taste of victory in their new home.

The Promised Land

It is important to consider the nature of the land of promise, particularly if we are going to accurately interpret and apply some of the promises given to God's people during this period to our own lives. There is a parallel between the Promised Land of the old covenant and the abundant life of the new covenant, but the parallels are not exact. The blessings of the Promised Land are similar but significantly different than the blessings of the new covenant.

In the Old Covenant

Under the old covenant, the Promised Land was a land of blessing that was both national and geographical.

By national and geographical, I mean that the blessings of the Promised Land were given to the nation of Israel as God's people and were limited to the geographical area we know as Israel. As such, the nation was blessed with expanded borders, military success, economic prosperity, and political freedom. When they were faithful to the covenant, God blessed them with prosperity and protection. The land flowed with milk and honey (a sign of prosperity), the crops were abundant, and there was plenty of rain. They were protected from their enemies, and were not oppressed or invaded by foreign armies.

Consider the following statement by Moses as he spoke about the blessings the people would experience in the land of promise.

> *Blessed shall you be in the city, and blessed shall you be in the field. Blessed shall be the fruit of your womb and the fruit of your ground and the fruit of your cattle, the increase of your herds and the young of your flock. Blessed shall be your basket and your kneading bowl. Blessed shall you be when you come in, and blessed shall you be when you go out. The LORD will cause your enemies who rise against you to be defeated before you. They shall come out against you one way and flee before you seven ways. The LORD will command the blessing on you in your barns and in all that you undertake. And he will bless you in the land that the LORD your God is giving you. (Deuteronomy 28.3-8)*

A marvelous description of the land of promise.

But, if the people abandoned the covenant, God promised that He would revoke the blessings. He would remove the prosperity of the abundant crops and adequate rainfall. He would remove His protection, and marauding armies would invade them. And ultimately, if they did not repent, He would remove them from the Promised Land.

Even though the people of God would ultimately be removed from the land of promise, and their fellowship with God was broken, they did not cease to be the people of God. God disciplines the children that He loves, and His discipline is a sign of our relationship to Him (see Hebrews 12.5-8). Even so, it is a dreadful thing to fall into the disciplining hand of the Lord.

In the New Covenant

As wonderful as the old covenant sounds, praise God we are no longer under it. The blessings of the old covenant were tied to their ability to fulfill the covenant, something that we now know is impossible to do in our flesh. No one can be made right with God through works of the law (see Romans 3.20). Israel lost the blessings of the Promise Land, and God removed them in 586 BC.

But under the new covenant, there is a new kind of blessing for those in covenant with the Lord and Savior Jesus Christ by grace through faith. Christ has come that we might have abundant life (see John 10.10).

While the old covenant was national and geographical, the new covenant extends to all people of faith, regardless if they are physical descendants of Abraham or not (see Galatians 3.6-14). The new covenant extends to people of all nations. In fact, the new covenant is creating a new nation, the Kingdom of God, where people from every tribe and every tongue will gather around the throne in worship of Christ.

The basic premise of the Promised Land remains. When we are walking in obedience to Christ, He blesses us with abundant life. When we rebel against His lordship, He disciplines us as a Father who loves us (see Hebrews 12.3-11).

But there are significant differences between the Promised Land and the abundant life. The abundant life is not a promise of economic prosperity, physical health, or material abundance. God may bless us with these, but they are not promised to us. While there is great blessing and prosperity for those who trust in the Lord, that blessing is primarily of the soul and not the body. In other words, we experience these blessings most abundantly in our souls and not in our check books.

The New Testament speaks of a life in Christ that requires endurance and perseverance (see Hebrews 12.1-2), a life that groans within a world that is locked in bondage to decay (see Romans 8.18-25), and a life that holds fast to a future hope when Christ returns to make all things right.

The new covenant is new, and completely different from the old. The new covenant is based upon what God has done on our behalf through Christ. In the new covenant, God recognizes that we could never fulfill the demands of the law. In the new covenant, God indwells the believer and changes the Christian from the inside out. In the new covenant, the rewards and blessings are not of this world.

Are there blessings in trusting in Christ? Yes, but the blessings are not of this world. The blessings are the treasures that our hearts and souls long for, the real treasures of life. The blessings of living in Christ are the blessings of joy, love, hope, contentment, and peace. These are the treasures of the abundant life in Christ.

So, when we read about the Promised Land, we can hear God speak to us about covenant faithfulness. We can hear God call us to confession and repentance so that we can live under the shadow of His wings of protection and blessing. But we also hear that we live in a fallen world that is held in bondage to decay. We also hear that what we long for is the Promised Land that will only be known when Christ returns. We hear Christ call us to abandon the treasures of this world and to lay up for ourselves treasure in heaven. We hear that to love the things of this world is idolatry. We hear that the greatest blessing is to be found in Christ and to share in His calling.

Listen to how the apostle Paul described the abundant life of Christ. He did not talk about economic prosperity or freedom from oppression. He wrote of something greater.

> *But whatever gain I had, I counted as loss for the sake of Christ. Indeed, I count everything as loss because of the surpassing worth of knowing Christ Jesus my Lord. For his sake I have suffered the loss of all things and count them as rubbish, in order that I may gain Christ and be found in him, not having a righteousness of my own that comes from the law, but*

*that which comes through faith in Christ, the righteousness from God that
depends on faith—that I may know him and the power of his resurrection,
and may share his sufferings, becoming like him in his death, that by any
means possible I may attain the resurrection from the dead. Not that I
have already obtained this or am already perfect, but I press on to make it
my own, because Christ Jesus has made me his own. Brothers, I do not
consider that I have made it my own. But one thing I do: forgetting what
lies behind and straining forward to what lies ahead, I press on toward
the goal for the prize of the upward call of God in Christ Jesus.
(Philippians 3.7-14)*

The treasures of the new covenant are not of this world.

Land Taken, Not Given

There is something in our soul that rejoices when a group of slaves find
freedom and prosperity. We can rejoice when the people of God know blessing
and prosperity because of their faithfulness to a faithful God. Marvelous stories
of parting waters and angelic visitors do our hearts good. But, it doesn't take
too long before we begin to read some very disturbing stories.

The Sin of the Amorite

The land of promise first shows up on the pages of the Bible in Genesis 12.
Abraham was called to leave his homeland and to go to a land that the Lord
would show Him. However, the Lord told Abraham, "To your offspring, I will
give this land" (Genesis 12.7).

Shortly thereafter, a famine forced Abraham to leave the region. Why didn't
God just give the land to Abraham right then? Why make His chosen people go
through the oppression in Egypt?

There are two key answers to that question. First, it was very important for the
people of God to be shaped by the exodus experience. Remember, it was a
salvation type, a foreshadowing of our salvation in Christ. The dramatic
redemption, the Passover lamb, the ratification of the covenant, and so much
more shaped the people of God and prepared the Jews for the coming Messiah.
If God had simply given the land to Abraham and his family, God's people
would have missed that.

The second answer is found in the words God spoke to Abraham.

> *As for yourself, you shall go to your fathers in peace; you shall be buried in a good old age. And they shall come back here in the fourth generation, for the iniquity of the Amorites is not yet complete. (Genesis 15.15-16)*

Unfortunately, the Lord did not share any more information with Abraham, but these words give us the understanding that the time had not yet come for the Lord to judge the Amorites for their sin. Just like the Israelites were removed from the land because of their sin in 586 BC, so were the Amorites removed from their land. However, at this point, the time of judgment for the Amorites had not yet come.

The Ban

The Amorites did not simply vacate the land when Israel entered the land of promise. They were forcibly removed. The commands of God to Joshua are some of the most difficult parts of the Old Testament to comprehend and to interpret. For instance, consider the Lord's commands to Joshua regarding the town of Jericho.

> *"And the city and all that is within it shall be devoted to the LORD for destruction. Only Rahab the prostitute and all who are with her in her house shall live, because she hid the messengers whom we sent. But you, keep yourselves from the things devoted to destruction, lest when you have devoted them you take any of the devoted things and make the camp of Israel a thing for destruction and bring trouble upon it. But all silver and gold, and every vessel of bronze and iron, are holy to the LORD; they shall go into the treasury of the LORD." So the people shouted, and the trumpets were blown. As soon as the people heard the sound of the trumpet, the people shouted a great shout, and the wall fell down flat, so that the people went up into the city, every man straight before him, and they captured the city. Then they devoted all in the city to destruction, both men and women, young and old, oxen, sheep, and donkeys, with the edge of the sword. (Joshua 6.17-21)*

The word translated "devoted to the Lord" is the Hebrew word *cherem*. It means "a thing devoted, dedicated, or banned" (*Brown-Driver-Briggs*).

What lies before us is the single greatest moral problem in the book of Joshua. Why did the Lord command the Israelites to kill not only the enemy's soldiers, but also the seemingly innocent women and children? In addition, the Lord commanded the destruction of all of the livestock. All items of value (including the gold, silver, bronze, and iron items) were to be deposited into the treasury of the Tabernacle.

How do we reconcile this barbaric story with the grace of God?

A few insights might help us as we wrestle with understanding the ban. First, the Lord was working to establish a people for His own possession, a holy people, a royal priesthood to represent the Lord to the nations of the world. It was important that the Promised Land be inhabited by a faithful people group, worshipping only the Lord. If there remained a pagan population within the boundaries of the Promised Land, then the children of Israel would intermarry and certainly begin to worship the gods of the land. This was the warning given by Moses years before:

> *When the LORD your God brings you into the land that you are entering to take possession of it, and clears away many nations before you, the Hittites, the Girgashites, the Amorites, the Canaanites, the Perizzites, the Hivites, and the Jebusites, seven nations more numerous and mightier than yourselves, and when the LORD your God gives them over to you, and you defeat them, then you must devote them to complete destruction. You shall make no covenant with them and show no mercy to them. You shall not intermarry with them, giving your daughters to their sons or taking their daughters for your sons, for they would turn away your sons from following me, to serve other gods. Then the anger of the LORD would be kindled against you, and he would destroy you quickly. (Deuteronomy 7.1-4)*

Notice, the reason for the ban (or total destruction) was to prevent them from making treaties with the inhabitants of the land and to prevent intermarriage. Intermarriage would almost certainly lead to worshipping other gods which would lead to the destruction of Israel.

This was exactly what happened. The people failed to drive out all of the nations, and many remained as a thorn in their sides. Ultimately, because Israel began to worship the false gods of the Canaanites, they were removed from the land of promise by the Lord.

The danger of syncretism, which is "the combination of different forms of belief or practice" (*Merriam-Webster*), has always threatened the people of God and still does. If the enemy is not able to get the righteous to forsake the covenant with the Lord, then the enemy will try to corrupt the covenant by deceiving the people into combining true Yahweh worship with other false gods. This hybrid worship has always been offensive to the Lord whether it was the golden calf during the exodus, the Baal worship in the Promised Land, or the materialism of Western Christianity. God is a jealous God who will not share the stage with another.

We might be tempted to think that we would be able to preserve pure Yahweh worship even among those who don't. We would like to think that our faith is strong enough, but the Scriptures tell us that "Bad company ruins good morals" (1 Corinthians 15.33). It was important to create a pure nation with whom the task of representing the Lord to the world could be entrusted.

Whether we understand the importance of the ban or not, it was very important to the Lord. In fact, those who broke the ban were punished by death. Achan took a beautiful robe, some coins, and a wedge of gold from the ruins of Jericho, and it cost him and his whole family their lives. They had to be removed from the people of God because, in the words of the Lord, "You cannot stand before your enemies until you take away the devoted things from among you" (Joshua 7.13). Their future victories were dependent upon their holiness.

Thorns in Their Sides

Unfortunately, the story of the conquest of the land of promise did not end well. As Joshua neared the end of his life, he delivered his famous farewell address to the people. Along with encouraging them to choose whom they would serve, he also said to them,

> *For the LORD has driven out before you great and strong nations. And as for you, no man has been able to stand before you to this day. One man of you puts to flight a thousand, since it is the LORD your God who fights for you, just as he promised you. Be very careful, therefore, to love the LORD*

your God. For if you turn back and cling to the remnant of these nations remaining among you and make marriages with them, so that you associate with them and they with you, know for certain that the LORD your God will no longer drive out these nations before you, but they shall be a snare and a trap for you, a whip on your sides and thorns in your eyes, until you perish from off this good ground that the LORD your God has given you. (Joshua 23.9-13)

At the end of his life, there still remained parts of the Promised Land which had not been conquered. There were still battles to fight and land to claim. If the people failed to win the full victory, these unconquered areas would remain a "thorn" among them. These are the same words that Moses said to them years before.

But if you do not drive out the inhabitants of the land from before you, then those of them whom you let remain shall be as barbs in your eyes and thorns in your sides, and they shall trouble you in the land where you dwell. (Numbers 33.55)

And this would be the continual story of the people of God. Never fully conquering the land of promise, they never fully experienced the promises of the land. Ultimately, it would bring about their downfall, and they would be removed from the land.

Once again, the application of the biblical story is so powerful. As the Lord calls us into a covenant relationship with Him and invites us into abundant life, we hear His call to repent from our sinful thoughts, attitudes, and behaviors. Whenever we make a treaty with any of these and allow them to remain, they become a thorn in our side. Of course, we get to avoid the painful work of driving out our enemies, but we do not get to enjoy the freedom either. We cannot peacefully co-exist with sin. As the saying goes, we will either have too much religion to enjoy our sin or too much sin to enjoy our religion.

Judges

Joshua died at the age of 110, and his death ushered in the next chapter of the story: the period of the judges.

At this time, it is improper to even speak of the "nation of Israel," for they were anything but. The land was divided amongst the twelve tribes, but there was no sort of centralized government. Not only did the twelve tribes fail to work together, they often fought amongst themselves. Each tribe exercised leadership over their own territory, but there quickly came a need to band together to face larger enemies. The Philistines, their neighbors within the land, whom they failed to drive out, became their primary nemesis during this period.

During this time frame, the Lord raised up key leaders who united some of the tribes to defeat a common enemy. These leaders were called "judges." While this might conjure up images of judicial figures in black robes, these leaders were charismatic leaders who exercised military, spiritual, and political leadership. There are thirteen judges listed in the book of Judges, and they covered a period of 410 years. Since they entered the land in 1400 BC and the first king was crowned in 1050 BC, some of the rules of the judges had to be concurrent. The book of Judges describes this period, and one of its primary purposes was to show that Israel's spiritual condition determined its political and material situation.

The Cycle of the Judges

There are many well-known and interesting stories told in this book of the Bible, including the stories of Gideon, Samson, and Deborah. The names changed, but the basic plot remained the same. So much so, that many scholars refer to it as the "cycle of the judges" because all of the stories follow the same plot. It is most succinctly described in Judges 2.

> *And they abandoned the LORD, the God of their fathers, who had brought them out of the land of Egypt. They went after other gods, from among the gods of the peoples who were around them, and bowed down to them. And they provoked the LORD to anger. They abandoned the LORD and served the Baals and the Ashtaroth. So the anger of the LORD was kindled against Israel, and he gave them over to plunderers, who plundered them. And he sold them into the hand of their surrounding enemies, so that they could no longer withstand their enemies. Whenever they marched out, the hand of the LORD was against them for harm, as the LORD had warned, and as the LORD had sworn to them. And they were in terrible distress. Then the LORD raised up judges, who saved them out of the hand of those who*

*plundered them. Yet they did not listen to their judges, for they whored
after other gods and bowed down to them. They soon turned aside from
the way in which their fathers had walked, who had obeyed the
commandments of the LORD, and they did not do so. Whenever the LORD
raised up judges for them, the LORD was with the judge, and he saved
them from the hand of their enemies all the days of the judge. For
the LORD was moved to pity by their groaning because of those who
afflicted and oppressed them. But whenever the judge died, they turned
back and were more corrupt than their fathers, going after other gods,
serving them and bowing down to them. They did not drop any of their
practices or their stubborn ways. So the anger of the LORD was kindled
against Israel, and he said, "Because this people have transgressed my
covenant that I commanded their fathers and have not obeyed my voice, I
will no longer drive out before them any of the nations that Joshua left
when he died, in order to test Israel by them, whether they will take care
to walk in the way of the LORD as their fathers did, or not." So the LORD
left those nations, not driving them out quickly, and he did not give them
into the hand of Joshua. (Joshua 2.10-23)*

Throughout this period, the cycle continued to repeat itself. The Israelites
stopped obeying the Lord's commands and began to worship other gods. As a
result, the Lord sent invading armies into the land to plunder them and to
discipline them. The people cried out in great distress, so the Lord raised up a
judge to deliver them. As long as the judge lived, the people followed the judge
and lived in faithfulness to the Lord. However, as soon as the judge died, they
returned to their corrupt ways. This five step cycle (disobedience, judgment,
repentance, deliverance, freedom) was repeated over and over throughout this
period.

Understanding the cycle does more than just illuminate history; it speaks to our
own spiritual walk, too. So many times, we too live in the cycle of sin,
oppression and discipline, repentance, forgiveness, and then return to our sin
again. We need to learn the lesson of the judges, and learn to maintain our
freedom by remaining faithful to the Lord in times of freedom. For some
reason, there is always a strong temptation to forsake the Lord when times are
good, during times of blessing. Moses warned them and us of this very thing.

*When you eat and are full, then take care lest you forget the Lord, who
brought you out of the land of Egypt, out of the house of slavery.
(Deuteronomy 6.11-12)*

Often, the times of God's greatest victories in our lives can become the beginning of our falling away.

Making It Profitable

Richard Foster's book, *Celebration of Discipline,* is one of the most influential books about the spiritual disciplines. If you have any desire to deepen your walk with Christ, his book is a must read. As you consider whether or not to extend your understanding of the Bible into experiencing the Christ of the Bible through developing the spiritual disciplines, I offer you a quote from his book about meditation.

> *The discipline of meditation was certainly familiar to the authors of Scripture. The Bible uses two different Hebrew words to convey the idea of meditation, and together they are used some 58 times. These words have various meanings: listening to God's word, reflecting on God's works, rehearsing God's deed, ruminating on God's law, and more. In each case, there is stress upon changed behavior as a result of our encounter with the living God. Repentance and obedience are essential features in any biblical understanding of meditation. (Foster, 15)*

Will you make meditation a part of your spiritual development? One way to do that is to journal as you read Scripture. Take the time to write down one verse each day that stands out to you in your daily readings. Think deeply about that verse and what God might be saying to you through it. Capture His voice on paper and then think about it as you go through your day.

Daily Bible Readings

The daily Bible readings for this week cover the major events during the period of conquest and the period of the judges. 400 years of biblical history and two books of the Bible cannot be adequately consumed in only a week. But, we can start.

What can the Lord teach you each day this week? How will the Lord correct you? How will God use these passages of the Bible to train you in righteousness? How will the Lord use His words to equip you for the good work He created you to do?

The only way to find out is to invest the time and energy in the spiritual disciplines of daily Bible reading, mediation, Scripture memory, and prayer.

Suggested Memory Verses

Be strong and courageous, for you shall cause this people to inherit the land that I swore to their fathers to give them. Only be strong and very courageous, being careful to do according to all the law that Moses my servant commanded you. Do not turn from it to the right hand or to the left, that you may have good success wherever you go. (Joshua 1.6-7)

This Book of the Law shall not depart from your mouth, but you shall meditate on it day and night, so that you may be careful to do according to all that is written in it. For then you will make your way prosperous, and then you will have good success. (Joshua 1.8)

And if it is evil in your eyes to serve the LORD, choose this day whom you will serve, whether the gods your fathers served in the region beyond the River, or the gods of the Amorites in whose land you dwell. But as for me and my house, we will serve the LORD. (Joshua 24.15)

Day One: Joshua 1.1-9

S:

_____
_____
_____
_____
_____
_____
_____

O:

_____
_____
_____
_____
_____
_____
_____

A:

_____
_____
_____
_____
_____
_____
_____

P:

_____
_____
_____
_____
_____
_____
_____

Day Two: Joshua 6

_S:_ _____

_____

_____

_____

_____

_____

_____

_O:_ _____

_____

_____

_____

_____

_____

_____

_A:_ _____

_____

_____

_____

_____

_____

_____

_P:_ _____

_____

_____

_____

_____

_____

_____

Day Three: Joshua 7

S:

_____

_____

_____

_____

_____

_____

O:

_____

_____

_____

_____

_____

_____

_____

A:

_____

_____

_____

_____

_____

_____

P:

_____

_____

_____

_____

_____

_____

Day Four: Joshua 24

S:
_____
_____
_____
_____
_____
_____
_____

O:
_____
_____
_____
_____
_____
_____
_____

A:
_____
_____
_____
_____
_____
_____
_____

P:
_____
_____
_____
_____
_____
_____
_____

Day Five: Judges 2

S:

O:

A:

P:

Day Six: Judges 15

S: _____

_____

_____

_____

_____

_____

_____

O: _____

_____

_____

_____

_____

_____

_____

A: _____

_____

_____

_____

_____

_____

_____

P: _____

_____

_____

_____

_____

_____

_____

Ultimately, the loose confederation of the twelve tribes during the period of the judges were replaced with a centralized government united under one king. More than just a dramatic change in the form of government, it was a dramatic shift in their understanding and practice of their relationship to God. As can be expected, this change was not sudden or painless. Therefore, the Lord raised up a special person to lead His people during this chapter of their story.

Samuel

Samuel was a transitional figure, the key leader as the twelve tribes transitioned into a united kingdom. More than just the last in a long line of judges, Samuel was the first in a long line of prophets. Of course, there had been prophets in the biblical narrative before this time, but Samuel was the first of the prophets who represented God in the presence of the kings. He was the voice of God to the king, a model that Elijah and others would follow.

Samuel was one of a few special men in the Bible with dramatic birth stories. Like Sarah and Rebekah, his mother was unable to have children, but the Lord opened Hannah's womb, and Samuel was born.

As a young child, the Lord called Samuel into service. His experience as a young child hearing the audible voice of the Lord is a favorite Bible story for children, and he joined Abraham, Jacob, and Moses as important figures with dramatic call experiences.

Samuel's life and ministry is recorded in 1 Samuel. In the beginning, he led the people as a judge similar to the judges before him. However, his ministry dramatically changed when the people cried out for a king. After Samuel anointed the first king of Israel, his role changed to that of a prophet, speaking for the Lord and calling the king to live faithfully to the covenant of the Lord.

The People Ask For A King

Was it God's will for Israel to have a king? Did the Lord intend for His people to be organized under a united government or did He intend for the period of the judges to continue indefinitely?

Moses certainly expected the people to ask for a king after they entered the land.

> *When you come to the land that the LORD your God is giving you, and you possess it and dwell in it and then say, 'I will set a king over me, like all the nations that are around me,' you may indeed set a king over you whom the LORD your God will choose. One from among your brothers you shall set as king over you. You may not put a foreigner over you, who is not your brother. Only he must not acquire many horses for himself or cause the people to return to Egypt in order to acquire many horses, since the LORD has said to you, 'You shall never return that way again.' And he shall not acquire many wives for himself, lest his heart turn away, nor shall he acquire for himself excessive silver and gold. And when he sits on the throne of his kingdom, he shall write for himself in a book a copy of this law, approved by the Levitical priests. And it shall be with him, and he shall read in it all the days of his life, that he may learn to fear the LORD his God by keeping all the words of this law and these statutes, and doing them, that his heart may not be lifted up above his brothers, and that he may not turn aside from the commandment, either to the right hand or to the left, so that he may continue long in his kingdom, he and his children, in Israel. (Deuteronomy 17.14-20)*

His words of warning turned out to be alarmingly accurate. However, the question remains, was the request for a king a godly request? Was this part of God's plan?

To answer this question, let us examine 1 Samuel 8 where the people asked Samuel to appoint a king. Samuel had aged, and his sons were not doing a good job as judges over the land. They sought dishonest gain and accepted brides. So, the elders of Israel asked Samuel to "appoint for us a king to judge us like all the nations" (1 Samuel 8.5). This request displeased Samuel, so he sought the Lord in prayer.

> *And the LORD said to Samuel, "Obey the voice of the people in all that they say to you, for they have not rejected you, but they have rejected me from being king over them. According to all the deeds that they have done,*

from the day I brought them up out of Egypt even to this day, forsaking me and serving other gods, so they are also doing to you. Now then, obey their voice; only you shall solemnly warn them and show them the ways of the king who shall reign over them." So Samuel told all the words of the LORD to the people who were asking for a king from him. He said, "These will be the ways of the king who will reign over you: he will take your sons and appoint them to his chariots and to be his horsemen and to run before his chariots. And he will appoint for himself commanders of thousands and commanders of fifties, and some to plow his ground and to reap his harvest, and to make his implements of war and the equipment of his chariots. He will take your daughters to be perfumers and cooks and bakers. He will take the best of your fields and vineyards and olive orchards and give them to his servants. He will take the tenth of your grain and of your vineyards and give it to his officers and to his servants. He will take your male servants and female servants and the best of your young men and your donkeys, and put them to his work. He will take the tenth of your flocks, and you shall be his slaves. And in that day you will cry out because of your king, whom you have chosen for yourselves, but the LORD will not answer you in that day." (1 Samuel 8.7-18)

The Lord was displeased with the people's request. The people were rejecting God as their king, preferring a tangible leader like other nations to a theocracy with judges and prophets.

Unfortunately, there were serious consequences to their request. The Lord explained the downside to having king. A king would require a standing army with required military service. The monarchy would take the best of the land, both produce and citizens, to support and serve the interests of the king. The king would tax the land, heavily at times.

Despite these warnings, the people insisted on having a king. "We also may be like all the nations, and that our king may judge us and go out before us and fight our battles" (1 Samuel 8.20).

The people's desire for a king was rooted in two concerns. First, they wanted to be like all the other nations. Israel was the only nation operating as a theocracy, waiting for the Lord to raise up the next judge. They may have envied the organization of their enemies. For whatever reason, they longed to be like everyone else. Just like the Israelites, our desire to be like others can take us out of our distinct calling and the distinct blessings God has prepared for us.

They also wanted a king to fight their battles. Even though the Lord proved His might and power through the wilderness wanderings, the conquest of Jericho, and even recently in the battle with the Philistines, there were certain requirements that made it difficult to live with God as the One who fought your battles. The people quickly realized that victory was related to righteousness. They would experience victory if they were living in faithfulness to the covenant. If they had a king, they could experience victory and not have to worry about living faithfully to the Lord, which is what they would try for the next five centuries.

Israel is not the only ones who have tried to experience the blessings of God without submitting to the demands of the King of Kings. People have trusted in their wealth, and nations have trusted in the power of their military, but the Scriptures are clear.

> *Blessed is the nation whose God is the LORD, the people whom he has chosen as his heritage! The LORD looks down from heaven; he sees all the children of man; from where he sits enthroned he looks out on all the inhabitants of the earth, he who fashions the hearts of them all and observes all their deeds. The king is not saved by his great army; a warrior is not delivered by his great strength. (Psalm 33.12-16)*

Israel ultimately discovered that their request for a king, and their attempt to live outside of the kingship of the Lord, would lead them to ruin.

United Monarchy

300 years after arriving in the land of promise, the people asked for a king, and Samuel anointed for them their first king. For a brief period, the people of God were united under one king, united as one nation. But, this united kingdom of Israel soon divided. After 300 years of division, Israel knew almost 120 years of unity. Unfortunately, it did not last, and a century of unity was followed by another 335 years of division.

Saul

The first king of Israel was Saul. He ruled for 42 years from 1052 to 1010 BC. The short version is that Saul was a failure as a king. After a few successful military campaigns, two major events demonstrated the weaknesses within Saul.

The first event took place when Saul gathered with his army at Gilgal preparing for a battle with the Philistines. Samuel instructed Saul to wait for him to arrive at the battlefield to offer the burnt offering. Saul waited for seven days, the time set by Samuel, but Samuel did not arrive. So, Saul offered the burnt offering in his stead. While his reasons were understandable (his army was growing impatient and beginning to scatter), Samuel confronted him with a more powerful truth. Saul had disobeyed the command of the Lord given to Saul through Samuel. Samuel said to Saul,

> But now your kingdom shall not continue. The LORD has sought out a man after his own heart, and the LORD has commanded him to be prince over his people, because you have not kept what the LORD commanded you. (1 Samuel 13.14)

Saul's days were numbered.

The second event was like the first, only this time it occurred after a battle. Through Samuel, the Lord gave specific instructions to Saul regarding the impending battle with the Amalekites. The *ban* was to be observed, and everything was to be destroyed. However, Saul spared not only the king of the Amalekites, but also the best of the cattle and everything that was good.

When confronted by Samuel for his disobedience, he tried to justify his actions by saying that he spared the best of the sheep and cattle to sacrifice to the Lord. But Samuel replied,

> Has the LORD as great delight in burnt offerings and sacrifices, as in obeying the voice of the LORD? Behold, to obey is better than sacrifice, and to listen than the fat of rams. For rebellion is as the sin of divination, and presumption is as iniquity and idolatry. Because you have rejected the

word of the LORD, *he has also rejected you from being king. (1 Samuel 15.22-23)*

This was the final rejection for Saul, and in the very next chapter, Samuel anointed the new king of Israel, a shepherd boy.

David

Unlike the first king who was head and shoulders above the rest, David was such an unlikely candidate to be the next king that his own father didn't vote for him. Literally. When Samuel came to Jesse's house to find the next king, Jesse brought all of the brothers out for the audition except for David. But the Lord's anointing fell on the youngest, as it had in so many of the biblical stories. God's heart favors the least of these.

In stark contrast to Saul, David was a success as a king. In fact, David became the model king for centuries to come. He was successful as a battlefield commander and as a politician. More importantly, he was successful in leading the nation to remaining faithful to the covenant.

David authored many of the psalms, the Old Testament book of worship. For instance, Psalm 119 is the longest psalm in the Bible and a beautiful testimony of his love and devotion to the law. So strong was David in his passion for the ways of the Lord that the Scriptures described him as a man after God's own heart (see Acts 13.22).

Story after story demonstrates his faith in the Lord and his courage in the face of opposition. The beloved story of David and Goliath is but one where he trusted so strongly in God's power to deliver that he courageously faced a giant of a warrior armed with nothing but a slingshot and his faith.

David's faith journey was not an easy one. Although he was anointed as the next king in 1 Samuel 16, he did not ascend to the throne until sixteen chapters later in 2 Samuel 2. He spent this interim time hiding in caves and running from Saul who wanted to kill his successor. During this time, David learned how to trust in the Lord for victory and provision. He experienced the Lord as his shield and shepherd, and he resisted the urge to kill Saul on a couple of occasions because he did not want to raise his hand against the Lord's anointed.

We forget that between calling and service there is often a period of preparation. The apostle Paul was called on the road to Damascus, but his service did not begin until three years of preparation were completed. In a culture where we hear, "Don't tell me about the labor, just show me the baby," we need to remember that the baby only comes after the labor. Preparation must precede service. David was who David was because of his years of preparation trusting in the Lord to protect and deliver him. Our lives of service will reflect our time of preparation. Don't despise the periods of preparation. Our fruitfulness depends upon it.

However, for all of the strengths of David's life and character, there was one obvious and famous mistake that plagued the rest of his life: his adultery with Bathsheba. While this mistake has been repeated throughout all of history, it was devastating for David's ministry. As a result, great calamity came upon David's house as a consequence and judgment for his sin. In fact, the rest of David's life was in total chaos because of this sin.

According to Nathan the prophet, the judgments on David were threefold: the child that resulted from the affair would die, the sword would never depart from his house, and another man would take one of his wives in a very public affair. The rest of David's story is a sad affair of sibling conflict, rebellious children, and constant fighting between David and his sons who wanted to take the throne by force. Forgiveness had come, but the consequences were brutal.

David's story is a powerful lesson to all about the destructiveness of sin.

Solomon

David would eventually marry Bathsheba and have a son, Solomon. David declared that out of all his sons, Solomon was to succeed him as king.

Whereas Saul was a total failure and David was an almost total success, Solomon's reign was a mixed bag. He was given the opportunity to ask the Lord for anything, and he asked for...

...an understanding mind to govern your people, that I may discern between good and evil, for who is able to govern this your great people. (1 Kings 3.9)

As a result, Solomon was considered the wisest king in Israel's history.

Whereas the book of Psalms demonstrates David's passion for the Lord and for His law, the book of Proverbs, authored by Solomon, demonstrates Solomon's passion for wisdom. In the most famous of Solomon's wise actions, he mediated a conflict between two women who both claimed to be the mother of the same child. He ordered that the child be cut in two knowing that the true mother would rather see the child live than cut in two. All of Israel was in awe because of Solomon's wisdom.

The most important accomplishment of Solomon's reign was the building of the Temple in Jerusalem. David wanted to build it, but the Lord refused. That task was reserved for Solomon. After working for seven years to complete the Temple, Solomon led the nation in a massive dedication ceremony. After his prayer of dedication, the Lord responded to Solomon,

When I shut up the heavens so that there is no rain, or command the locust to devour the land, or send pestilence among my people, if my people who are called by my name humble themselves, and pray and seek my face and turn from their wicked ways, then I will hear from heaven and will forgive their sin and heal their land. Now my eyes will be open and my ears attentive to the prayer that is made in this place. For now I have chosen and consecrated this house that my name may be there forever. My eyes and my heart will be there for all time. (2 Chronicles 7.13-16)

Solomon's Temple would be the house of worship for the Israelites from 960 BC until it was destroyed by the Babylonians in 586 BC.

Despite the wisdom of Solomon, his greatest mistake was his foolishness. Despite all of his wisdom and all of his counsel in the Proverbs about avoiding the pitfalls of lust, Solomon's greatest sin was his love for foreign women. Solomon, the wisest man in the world, had 700 wives of noble birth and 300 concubines. The vast majority of wives led Solomon away from pure Yahweh worship, and he allowed them to worship their foreign gods in Israel. Towards the end of his life, this sad commentary is presented about a very wise man:

For when Solomon was old his wives turned away his heart after other gods, and his heart was not wholly true to the LORD his God, as was the heart of David his father. For Solomon went after Ashtoreth the goddess of the Sidonians, and after Milcom the abomination of the Ammonites. So Solomon did what was evil in the sight of the LORD and did not wholly follow the LORD, as David his father had done. (1 Kings 11.4-6)

Summary

The lives of the "Big Three" can be summarized as follows: Saul was the first king, but a rebellious king. David had a passion for worship and law, but his sin with Bathsheba brought chaos and confusion into the land. Solomon had a passion for wisdom, but his many wives led him astray.

Or, it could be stated: Saul, no heart; David, whole heart; Solomon, half-heart.

Making It Profitable

The stories of Samuel, Saul, David, and Solomon are a rich part of the Scriptures that encourage us on our own journey of faith. By learning from their ways of faith, and by their mistakes, we can learn how to follow God faithfully and obediently.

But, these can only be profitable to us today if we take the time to read them and to listen to God's voice. Hopefully this chapter has helped you to understand this part of the story of God's relationship with His people, but I hope that you will take the time to make this section of Scripture profitable to you. Instead of reading the next chapter of this book, I encourage you to take the next week to complete the following daily readings, to journal using the SOAP method, and to memorize one of the suggested memory verses.

Daily Bible Readings

The daily readings for this week are taken from the books of the Bible that tell the story of Samuel, Saul, David, and Solomon. These readings capture some of the major moments of their lives. But please don't read them just to understand their stories. Read them with your journal open. Ask the Spirit to highlight one Scripture verse from each daily reading. Take a moment to write down a few observations. Ask the Lord how this might apply to your life, how this might teach you, correct you, or prepare you for good works. And then spend some time talking to God in prayer. Try to walk away from your daily reading time with one truth that you can be in conversation with God all day long.

Suggested Memory Verses

If my people who are called by my name humble themselves, and pray and seek my face and turn from their wicked ways, then I will hear from heaven and will forgive their sin and heal their land. (2 Chronicles 7.14)

For the eyes of the Lord run to and fro throughout the whole earth, to give strong support to those whose heart is blameless toward him. You have done foolishly in this, for from now on you will have wars. (2 Chronicles 16.9)

Has the LORD as great delight in burnt offerings and sacrifices, as in obeying the voice of the LORD? Behold, to obey is better than sacrifice, and to listen than the fat of rams. For rebellion is as the sin of divination, and presumption is as iniquity and idolatry. Because you have rejected the word of the LORD, he has also rejected you from being king. (1 Samuel 15.22-23)

Create in me a clean heart, O God, and renew a right spirit within me. Cast me not away from your presence, and take not your Holy Spirit from me. Restore to me the joy of your salvation, and uphold me with a willing spirit. (Psalm 51.10-12)

How can a young man keep his way pure? By guarding it according to your word. With my whole heart I seek you; let me not wander from your commandments! I have stored up your word in my heart, that I might not sin against you. (Psalm 119.9-11)

Your word is a lamp to my feet and a light to my path.(Psalm 119.105)

Day One: 1 Samuel 3

_S:_ _____

_____

_____

_____

_____

_____

_____

_____

_O:_ _____

_____

_____

_____

_____

_____

_____

_A:_ _____

_____

_____

_____

_____

_____

_____

_P:_ _____

_____

_____

_____

_____

_____

_____

Day Two: 1 Samuel 14

_S:_ _____
_____
_____
_____
_____
_____
_____
_____

_O:_ _____
_____
_____
_____
_____
_____
_____
_____

_A:_ _____
_____
_____
_____
_____
_____
_____

_P:_ _____
_____
_____
_____
_____
_____
_____

Day Three: 1 Samuel 17

S:

_____
_____
_____
_____
_____
_____
_____
_____

O:

_____
_____
_____
_____
_____
_____
_____
_____

A:

_____
_____
_____
_____
_____
_____
_____

P:

_____
_____
_____
_____
_____
_____
_____

Day Four: 1 Samuel 11-12

S: _____

_____
_____
_____
_____
_____
_____
_____

O: _____

_____
_____
_____
_____
_____
_____
_____

A: _____

_____
_____
_____
_____
_____
_____

P: _____

_____
_____
_____
_____
_____
_____

Day Five: 1 Kings 3

S:
_____
_____
_____
_____
_____
_____
_____

O:
_____
_____
_____
_____
_____
_____
_____

A:
_____
_____
_____
_____
_____
_____
_____

P:
_____
_____
_____
_____
_____
_____
_____

Day Six: 2 Chronicles 6-8

S:
_____
_____
_____
_____
_____
_____
_____

O:
_____
_____
_____
_____
_____
_____
_____

A:
_____
_____
_____
_____
_____
_____
_____

P:
_____
_____
_____
_____
_____
_____
_____

After 120 years of united bliss, division rocked the people of God. Moses led the children of Israel out of bondage and slavery. Joshua led them into the land of promise. After 350 years of following the judges raised up by the Lord, the people cried out for a king. Despite the Lord's warnings, the people insisted on having a king like other nations who could fight their battles for them. The first king, Saul, was a colossal failure. The second king, David, was a success despite the serious consequences from his sin with Bathsheba. The third king, Solomon, was a partial success, and it was this partial success that led to the division of the kingdom.

Divided Monarchy

One of the most confusing aspects of Old Testament history is keeping up with all the names of people, places, and nations. It doesn't help matters that two names keep appearing when referring to the people of God. At times, they are referred to as Israel, and at other times they are referred to as Judah. It is important to remember that these are not synonyms for the same nation; they are two different names for two different nations.

The Death of Solomon

For all of Solomon's strengths, one of his weaknesses was his penchant for building projects. The Temple might have been his most important achievement, but his palace was probably a greater architectural achievement. It took 13 years to build, but more importantly, it took a lot of labor. To build all of his projects, not only did he tax the nation heavily, but he also instituted corvée, or forced labor, upon his own people. Little more than slave labor camps, this was the work force that built all of Solomon's wonderful projects. Needless to say, after the king's death, the people were tired, and the idea of a mutiny was beginning to grow.

What adds spice to this story is the prophecy of Ahijah. Jeroboam, a man of
standing who was in charge of a large workforce for the king, was walking
alone in Jerusalem one day. The prophet took hold of the new cloak he was
wearing and tore it into twelve pieces. Then he said to Jeroboam,

> Take for yourself ten pieces, for thus says the LORD, the God of Israel,
> "Behold, I am about to tear the kingdom from the hand of Solomon and
> will give you ten tribes." (1 Kings 11.31)

The prophecy was disturbing to Solomon, no doubt, so Jeroboam was banished
from Israel.

Solomon's son, Rehoboam, became king at Solomon's death. Almost
immediately, he was forced to deal with a crisis. The people assembled before
Rehoboam with a simple request.

> Your father made our yoke heavy. Now therefore lighten the hard service
> of your father and his heavy yoke on us, and we will serve you. (1 Kings
> 12.4)

In other words, the people were tired of the taxes and the *corvée*, and they
wanted relief. To deal with the crisis, Rehoboam sought advice from two
groups. The first group was the older advisors who had served with his father.
They agreed with the people and advised Rehoboam that if he would serve the
people, they would always serve him. The second group of advisors was his
young friends who told Rehoboam to take control of the situation by making
tougher demands of the people to force their loyalty.

Unfortunately, he listened to his young friends. The result was that the
frustrated masses looked for another leader, another king. And Jeroboam just
happened to be the crowd favorite.

The Divided Kingdom

Up until this point, we have been able to talk about the people of God as one
group. But when the nation divided, there were two nations who both
considered themselves to be the people of God.

The two southern tribes of Judah and Benjamin remained under the leadership
of Rehoboam to form the nation of Judah. The capital city, Jerusalem, and the

Temple were part of the southern kingdom. In addition, the Davidic line passed through the tribe of Judah.

The northern ten tribes broke away to form their own nation, the nation of Israel under the kingship of Jeroboam. They built a center of worship to break all of its ties with Jerusalem and the Temple.

The story of the divided kingdom is told in the Old Testament books of First and Second Kings and First and Second Chronicles. Sometimes the two nations fought with each other, and sometimes they fought alongside each other.

For each king of both nations, the Bible gives a summary statement of their reign. Either they "did evil in the eyes of the Lord" or they "did what was right in the sight of the Lord."

Of the 19 kings of Israel, the northern kingdom, only one is described as righteous. Of the 20 kings of Judah, the southern kingdom, only eight are described as righteous. So, only 5% of the kings of Israel were righteous and only 40% of the kings of Judah were righteous. Taken together, only 26% of the kings were righteous.

Unfortunately, the warnings of the Lord regarding the people's request for a king were right. The monarchy was a colossal failure. Evidently, living like everyone else was not the path to the abundant life.

Bright Lights in a Dark Land

The 335 years of the divided monarchy, while dominated by poor leadership and false worship, did have its bright lights. For example, despite growing up in the wicked home of Ahaz, who not only failed to live righteously before the Lord but who also set up altars to false gods on every street corner, King Hezekiah was quite different. He led the people on a campaign of spiritual renewal. He reopened the Temple, which involved not only repairing the neglected sanctuary but also restoring the priesthood and the collection of tithes. He observed the Passover for the first time in years, and he put the Levites back to work.

His greatest contribution was his contribution of faith. Towards the end of his reign, he faced a huge crisis of faith. The Assyrian army was on the march. They had already marched through Israel both conquering and destroying everything in sight. When Sennacherib, the king of Assyria, set his sights on Jerusalem, surely the heart of Hezekiah was filled with fear.

However, the Lord sent the prophet Isaiah to Hezekiah with a powerful word of hope. Even though Sennacherib had Hezekiah caught up like a "bird in a cage" (a statement from Sennacherib's own journal), the Lord miraculously delivered Judah. The angel of the Lord put to death 185,000 soldiers during the night. When Sennacherib awoke, he immediately broke camp and returned to Assyria. Because of Hezekiah's faith, the people were saved (see 2 Kings 18-19 for the complete story).

Another bright light was Josiah. Another young king who was raised in a wicked home, Josiah became king at the tender age of eight. He loved the Lord and followed the path of David. Like Hezekiah, he led the nation in a period of spiritual renewal complete with the necessary Temple cleaning to rid the sanctuary of the unclean things of his father and grandfather.

During the remodeling, the lost law of the Lord was found by the High Priest. Imagine a period of history so spiritual void that even the High Priest did not know where the law of the Lord was kept. Upon reading the law, Josiah was greatly disturbed because he knew that he and the people had not been living in faithfulness to the covenant. Josiah repented and led the people in faithful obedience to the law. Because of his humility and repentance, the Lord did not send the impending judgment upon His people during the reign of Josiah. Josiah also celebrated again the Passover in the restored Temple.

The Story Gets Confusing

Until now, the history of the Old Testament and the books of the Bible that tell that story followed a linear path. The story could be easily followed simply by reading the books of the Bible in order. After 2 Chronicles, that is no longer true. While the story continues chronologically with Ezra and Nehemiah, the majority of the rest of the Old Testament overlaps the period of history that has just been told in the books of Samuel, Kings, and Chronicles. For that reason, it is imperative that these historical events be firmly understood so that the other books of the Bible can be properly "shelved" in their correct location.

If we think of the Bible as "one story" with many chapters, then the outline of that story might look like this:

- Chapter 1: The people were enslaved in Egypt

- Chapter 2: Moses led the people out of Egypt

- Chapter 3: Joshua led the people into the Promised Land

- Chapter 4: The 12 tribes lived in the Promised Land as a loose confederation of tribes under the leadership of judges.

- Chapter 5: The 12 tribes united under one king

- Chapter 6: The kingdom divided into two separate nations

- Chapter 7: The Lord sent the prophets to warn His people of impending judgment

- Chapter 8: The Lord removed His people from the Promised Land because of their unfaithfulness to the covenant. They spent 70 years in captivity in Babylon. This period is called the exile.

- Chapter 9: The people of God returned to Judah to rebuild Jerusalem and the Temple.

While most of the chapters unfold chronologically, chapter 7 is an exception. The period of the prophets was not confined to the divided kingdom, nor did it stop when the exile began.

The period of the Old Testament prophets actually began with Samuel. Their ministry continued through the united kingdom, through the divided monarchy, into the exile, and through the return of the people to Jerusalem.

So, the chronological time period of chapter 7 actually coincides with chapters 4-9. So, the key to understanding the prophets is to learn which prophets of the Old Testament are associated with which chapter of the Old Testament story.

If we add the writing prophets to our outline, it might look like this:

- Chapter 1: The people were enslaved in Egypt

- Chapter 2: Moses led the people out of Egypt

- Chapter 3: Joshua led the people into the Promised Land

- Chapter 4: The 12 tribes lived in the Promised Land as a loose confederation of tribes under the leadership of judges.

- Chapter 5: The 12 tribes united under one king

- Chapter 6: The kingdom divided into two separate nations

- Chapter 7: The Lord sent the prophets to warn His people of impending judgment (Obadiah, Joel, Jonah, Amos, Hosea, Micah, Isaiah, Nahum, Habakkuk, Zephaniah, Jeremiah, Ezekiel)

- Chapter 8: The Lord removed His people from the Promised Land because of their unfaithfulness to the covenant. They spent 70 years in captivity in Babylon. This period is called the exile. (Daniel, Jeremiah, Ezekiel)

- Chapter 9: The people of God returned to Judah to rebuild Jerusalem and the Temple (Haggai, Zechariah, Malachi)

The Exile

The message of the prophets, even going back as far as Moses, was fairly simple. If the people refused to live in faithfulness to the covenant, then the Lord would remove them from the land of promise. This judgment upon His people was executed in two stages. The first stage was the fall of Israel; the second stage was the fall of Judah. In both instances, the Lord used another nation as an instrument of judgment.

In 721 BC, the Lord raised up Assyria in judgment over Israel. Assyria was a ruthless nation, dealing harshly with its conquered peoples. Assyria's method of dealing with captives to prevent any future resistance or attempts to reorganize and cast off Assyrian rule was to move the captive citizens of one place to another conquered territory.

So, not only were many Israelites removed from the geographical land known as Israel, but Israel was also repopulated by the Assyrians with captives from other lands. Over time, the Jews that were left behind intermarried with these misplaced peoples. After years of this practice, the "pure Jews" of Judah grew to hate the "half-breeds" of the north. This resentment and hatred was still in force hundreds of years later at the birth of Christ. The people of this regions came to be known as the Samaritans.

The judgment continued after the fall of Israel. In 605 BC, the Lord raised up Babylon under the rule of Nebuchadnezzar to conquer Judah. This conquest was carried out in stages. In 605 BC, the leading citizens were taken back to Babylon. Daniel was among this group. In 586 BC, the city of Jerusalem was destroyed, along with the Temple, and the vast majority of its citizens were carried off in exile to Babylon. It lasted 70 years from the first conquest of 605 BC until they were freed to return home in 536 BC by Cyrus, King of Persia.

The Prophets

Perhaps the most underused and misunderstood portion of the Old Testament is the prophetic books. Even though they represent 16 of the 39 books, a whopping 41% of the Old Testament, most Christians rarely, if ever, read them. They seem like a bunch of grumpy old men who do nothing but complain and issue words of woe. Admittedly, they can be depressing to read, but they are part of the inspired word of God and are profitable for teaching, correction, training, and equipping. Each of the prophets had a unique slant to the same basic message, and many had very creative ways of sharing the word from the Lord.

It is important to remember that some of the most important prophets do not have whole books dedicated to their name. For instance, Nathan, Elijah, and Elisha were extremely important prophetic figures, but their stories are told in the historical books.

The basic role of the prophet was to serve as a spokesperson for the Lord. We tend to think of the predictive element of prophecy, but this was a minority of their message. In fact, only 2% of Old Testament prophecy was Messianic (foretelling the coming of Jesus), less than 5% was about the new covenant age, and less than 1% was related to events still yet to come (the second coming of Christ). Over 90% of the material of the prophets was related to the historical events surrounding the prophet. The prophet was speaking for the Lord to His people in the prophet's own time.

While each ministry was unique, their calls were basically the same. If we use Ezekiel's call as an example, we see that a prophet was one who was chosen by God (Ezekiel 2.3), sent to a rebellious people (Ezekiel 2.4), instructed not to fear (Ezekiel 2.6), and commanded to speak only the words of the Lord (Ezekiel 2.7). Unfortunately, although the people should listen, they would not (Ezekiel 3.5-7).

Jeremiah

In each major section of the story of God's relationship with His people, I have chosen a leading figure to represent each act of the story. I chose Jeremiah to represent the prophetic section for several reasons.

First, Jeremiah's life spanned both the period of the divided kingdom and the period of the exile. Unlike many prophets whose ministry spanned only a few years, Jeremiah's covered more than 50 years. Also, while each prophet is unique, Jeremiah is illustrative of the prophetic ministry, perhaps more so than some of the more distinctive prophets.

Jeremiah was chosen by God to be a prophet before he was even born.

> *Before I formed you in the womb I knew you, and before you were born I consecrated you; I appointed you a prophet to the nations. (Jeremiah 1.5).*

Like the ministries of Ezekiel, Amos, and the others, his ministry was not easy. His message was one of judgment.

> *I will declare my judgments against them, for all their evil in forsaking me. They have made offerings to other gods and worshiped the works of their own hands. But you, dress yourself for work; arise, and say to them everything that I command you. Do not be dismayed by them, lest I dismay you before them. (Jeremiah 1.16)*

Such a burden was his calling that it even brought him to despair. At one point, he even wished that he had never been born. He longed to quit preaching his message of judgment, but he could not.

If I say, "I will not mention him, or speak any more in his name," there is in my heart as it were a burning fire shut up in my bones, and I am weary with holding it in, and I cannot. (Jeremiah 20.9)

Jeremiah was a prophet from birth, burdened and gifted with a special call.

Two of Jeremiah's prophecies are worthy of special attention. The first is found in Jeremiah 13. The Lord instructed Jeremiah to purchase a linen belt and to wear it around his waist. Then he was to take that belt and bury it among the rocks. When he was commanded to dig up the belt, he found that it was ruined and completely useless. Then the Lord spoke these beautiful words to Jeremiah,

For as the loincloth clings to the waist of a man, so I made the whole house of Israel and the whole house of Judah cling to me, declares the LORD, that they might be for me a people, a name, a praise, and a glory, but they would not listen. (Jeremiah 13.11)

In chapter 18, Jeremiah visited a potter's house and observed as the potter fashioned a lump of clay into a vessel. When the vessel was marred in the potter's hand, the potter formed it into another pot, shaping it as seemed best to him. After watching this, the word of the Lord came to Jeremiah saying,

O house of Israel, can I not do with you as this potter has done? declares the LORD. Behold, like the clay in the potter's hand, so are you in my hand, O house of Israel. If at any time I declare concerning a nation or a kingdom, that I will pluck up and break down and destroy it, and if that nation, concerning which I have spoken, turns from its evil, I will relent of the disaster that I intended to do to it. And if at any time I declare concerning a nation or a kingdom that I will build and plant it, and if it does evil in my sight, not listening to my voice, then I will relent of the good that I had intended to do to it. Now, therefore, say to the men of Judah and the inhabitants of Jerusalem: 'Thus says the LORD, behold, I am shaping disaster against you and devising a plan against you. Return, everyone from his evil way, and amend your ways and your deeds.' "But they say, 'That is in vain! We will follow our own plans, and will every one act according to the stubbornness of his evil heart.' (Jeremiah 18.6-12)

Jeremiah was the prophet to whom the Lord revealed that the exile was going to last 70 years (see Jeremiah 25.11). He was one of the few who were commanded to write down his words, and even by Daniel's time, they were considered sacred text. During the exile, he encouraged the people to seek the welfare of the city, and he even modeled this by purchasing a field in Babylon. It was during the exile that Jeremiah spoke some of the most encouraging words of the Lord.

For I know the plans I have for you, declares the LORD, plans for wholeness and not for evil, to give you a future and a hope. (Jeremiah 29.11).

Lamentations

The book of Lamentations is a book about laments. The author, the prophet Jeremiah, wrote about the destruction of Jerusalem. It is a book of grief, a funeral dirge over an irrevocable past.

Isaiah

One of the other Major Prophets, Isaiah is the most quoted Old Testament prophet in the New Testament.

The most distinguishing characteristic of Isaiah is the messianic portions of his prophecy. Many sections of Isaiah speak of a "servant," and one of the complicated interpretive issues of Isaiah is deciding about whom is the prophet speaking. Ironically, this is the exact question of the Ethiopian official in Acts 8. "About whom, I ask you, does the prophet say this, about himself or about someone else?" (Acts 8.34).

Without a doubt, some of them are speaking about the coming messiah. For instance Isaiah 53 (the passage read by the Ethiopian and applied to Jesus by Philip) and Isaiah 61 (the passage read by Jesus in Luke 4 and applied to Himself) are both messianic. Others seem to be speaking about a person who was a servant of the Lord during the historical period of Isaiah, and scholars still debate about a few. These "Suffering Servant" passages are unique to Isaiah.

Ezekiel

Ezekiel was called to dramatically demonstrate his messages. For instance, he was instructed by the Lord to lie on his side one day for each year the Lord would bear the sin of Israel, 390 days (Ezekiel 4.5)! He even role played the exile by packing his bags and escaping through a hole in the wall of Jerusalem (Ezekiel 12.5).

In addition, he had wonderful visions. One of the most significant is the vision of the Glory of the Lord leaving the Temple in Jerusalem (Ezekiel 10). Even the death of his wife was part of Ezekiel's message and ministry (Ezekiel 24.15-27). And of course, who can forget the valley of dry bones being brought back to life by the Spirit of the Lord (Ezekiel 37)?

Daniel

Daniel is a unique prophetic book because it is told in story form. Daniel was among the leading citizens carried off to Babylon by King Nebuchadnezzar in 605 BC. He resisted the attempts the mold him into a good Babylonian citizen and remained faithful to the Lord. As a result, the Lord blessed him and made his life fruitful.

The first six chapters of Daniel are filled with the favorite stories of the fiery furnace, the lion's den, and a few dreams by the king. In the last six chapters, Daniel's visions get more complicated. They speak of the history that would unfold between the life of Daniel and the life of Christ, but also speak to end time events. In fact, Daniel is one of the most important books in trying to understand eschatology, or the study of the end times.

Hosea

Hosea is the first of the twelve Minor Prophets. They are not considered Minor Prophets because they were of less importance but because their writings were shorter than Jeremiah, Isaiah, or Ezekiel.

Hosea's distinctive characteristic is his family. Hosea was called by God to marry a prostitute. In this marriage, he would act out the relationship of God to an unfaithful people.

When the LORD first spoke through Hosea, the LORD said to Hosea, "Go, take to yourself a wife of whoredom and have children of whoredom, for the land commits great whoredom by forsaking the LORD." (Hosea 1.2)

His children were named Jezreel ("God sows"), Lo-Ruhamah ("not loved"), and Lo-Ammi ("not my people"). The names of his three children told the story of God planting His people in the Promised Land, but because of their adultery, they would be removed from that land. Peter used this imagery when he wrote,

Once you were not a people, but now you are God's people; once you had not received mercy, but now you have received mercy. (1 Peter 2.10)

Joel

The prophecy of Joel is a short encouragement for the people to repent and to experience the renewal of God's blessings. He told the people to "Rend your hearts and not your garments" (Joel 2.13). In other words, don't just go through the outward signs of repentance (tearing a garment was a visible, outward demonstration of grief) without returning to the Lord with the whole heart.

It was the prophecy of Joel where the coming day of the Lord was revealed, a day where God would pour out His Spirit among His people. "Even on the male and female servants in those days I will pour out my Spirit (Joel 2.29). According to Peter, this day was fulfilled on the Day of Pentecost when the Spirit fell upon the church (Acts 2.17).

Amos

Amos was a fruit picker turned prophet by the call of God. His prophecy began with God's judgment on the nations because of their wickedness. Unfortunately, God would also judge the nations of Israel and Judah.

Amos spoke of the people's hollow worship where they went to the northern houses of worship, Bethel and Gilgal, to sin (Amos 4.4). In fact, the Lord "despised their religious feasts" (Amos 5.21). He spoke against the wealthy who oppressed the poor (Amos 4.1). It was Amos who cried out those famous words quoted by Martin Luther King, "Let justice roll down like waters, and righteousness like an ever-flowing stream" (Amos 5.24).

Obadiah

Obadiah is one of the shortest of the Minor Prophets, only 21 verses long. It is a prophecy against Edom for their mistreatment of Judah.

> *But do not gloat over the day of your brother in the day of his misfortune; do not rejoice over the people of Judah in the day of their ruin; do not boast in the day of distress. (Obadiah 12)*

Jonah

The story of Jonah is one of the most well known in all of the Old Testament. Jonah was called to preach a message of judgment to the hated city of Nineveh, the capital of Assyria. Normally, a person would enjoy preaching a word of doom against their enemy, but Jonah knew that the Lord was full of mercy.

> *For I knew that you are a gracious God and merciful, slow to anger and abounding in steadfast love, and relenting from disaster. (Jonah 4.3)*

He knew that the Lord would forgive them if they repented, and he didn't want his enemies forgiven.

So, Jonah tried to run away from the Lord, but the Lord caught up to him on a ship sailing for Tarshish. Tossed overboard by his traveling companions, the Lord sent a great fish to swallow Jonah.

After repenting and being vomited on to dry land, Jonah went to Ninevah with the message. The city did repent, and Jonah did resent it. The book ends with the prophet wrestling to understand that the Lord is compassionate to all nations. He is the God of second chances.

Micah

The basic prophetic message against God's people continues with Micah. One of the most significant prophecies regarding the Messiah is found in Micah.

> *But you, O Bethlehem Ephrathah, who are too little to be among the clans of Judah, from you shall come forth for me one who is to be ruler in Israel, whose origin is from of old, from ancient days. (Micah 5.2).*

This is how the religious leaders of Jerusalem directed Herod to the birthplace of the Jesus (Matthew 2.6).

Nahum

Nahum is another short book among the Minor Prophets. Like Jonah, it was another prophetic word against Nineveh. The nation of Assyria was famous for its ruthless treatment of its enemies. The "bloody city" (Nahum 3.1) would be destroyed by the God of righteousness.

Hidden in this short book is the vision of one who speaks the good news of deliverance from the enemies. "Behold, upon the mountains, the feet of him who brings good news, who publishes peace!" (Nahum 1.15). The apostle Paul drew upon this imagery in Romans when he wrote,

> *And how are they to preach unless they are sent? As it is written, "How beautiful are the feet of those who preach the good news!" (Romans 10.15)*

Habakkuk

Even though we have a hard time spelling or pronouncing the prophet's name, his message is extremely relevant and powerful.

The prophet began with a simple question, "How long will the Lord allow injustice to continue among His people?" The answer: not very long. The Lord was in the process of raising up the Babylonians as an instrument of judgment. But this only brought up more questions.

> *You who are of purer eyes than to see evil and cannot look at wrong, why do you idly look at traitors and are silent when the wicked swallows up the man more righteous than he? (Habakkuk 1.13).*

In other word, how could God use a wicked nation like Babylon to judge His people? God's answer was that He would also judge the Babylonians in due time. Regarding these visions, the Lord said to the prophet,

> *For still the vision awaits its appointed time; it hastens to the end—it will not lie. If it seems slow, wait for it; it will surely come; it will not delay. (Habakkuk 2.3).*

Zephaniah

During the spiritual renewal of Josiah's reign, the Lord sent a message through the prophet Zephaniah. Though the Lord would not carry out the judgment during the time of Josiah (due to his righteousness, humility, and repentance), the judgment was still coming. After the judgment would come restoration.

> *The LORD your God is in your midst, a mighty one who will save; he will rejoice over you with gladness; he will quiet you by his love; he will exult over you with loud singing. (Zephaniah 3.17)*

Haggai

Haggai is one of the few prophets who ministered after the exile was over. His words were spoken to the people who had returned to Jerusalem to rebuild the city and the Temple. He encouraged the people to recommit themselves to the task of rebuilding the Temple and renewing themselves to the covenant of God.

Thus says the LORD of hosts: "These people say the time has not yet come to rebuild the house of the LORD." Then the word of the LORD came by the hand of Haggai the prophet, "Is it a time for you yourselves to dwell in your paneled houses, while this house lies in ruins?" (Haggai 1.2-4)

Zechariah

Like Haggai, Zechariah was also a post-exilic prophet. Zechariah was entrusted with two basic prophetic words. First, he joined Haggai in encouraging Israel to complete the rebuilding of the Temple. Second, he also spoke prophetically of the coming Messiah. Zechariah spoke of both the first coming of the Messiah and the second coming of the Messiah. He is considered by many to be the most messianic prophet of the entire Old Testament.

Malachi

Not only is Malachi the last book of the Old Testament, it also covers some of the last chronological events of the Old Testament story.

A post-exilic prophet, Malachi served as a spiritual leader after Nehemiah returned to Persia around 434 BC. His life and ministry were intertwined with the lives and ministries of Ezra and Nehemiah. He encouraged the people to use the completed Temple to its fullness by worshiping the Lord with faithfulness and holiness. While Malachi is most known for the encouragement to "Bring the full tithes into the storehouse, that there may be food in my house" (Malachi 3.10), its value is far greater than just a book to teach stewardship to the church.

Conclusion

Long before the Israelites ever set foot in the land of promise, the Lord said through Moses,

If you forget the LORD your God and go after other gods and serve them and worship them, I solemnly warn you today that you shall surely

*perish. Like the nations that the L*ORD *makes to perish before you, so shall you perish, because you would not obey the voice of the L*ORD *your God. (Deuteronomy 8.19-20)*

These words played out in full. The people entered the land, but they forgot the Lord. They worshipped other gods and forgot the covenant. Therefore, as prophesied, the Lord removed them from the land of promise. He exiled them.

However, the Lord was compassionate. He was and is a loving God who restores and redeems. Despite the wickedness of the people, the Lord gave His people another chance to live in the land of promise. A remnant would return.

Making It Profitable

The message of the Old Testament prophets continues to yield fruit for the body of Christ today. Though their message was rooted in the historical exile, their message of warning and judgment is still valid for today. Even the New Testament warns the people of God to walk in obedience less they experience the wrath of God. Consider,

For if we go on sinning deliberately after receiving the knowledge of the truth, there no longer remains a sacrifice for sins, but a fearful expectation of judgment, and a fury of fire that will consume the adversaries. Anyone who has set aside the law of Moses dies without mercy on the evidence of two or three witnesses. How much worse punishment, do you think, will be deserved by the one who has spurned the Son of God, and has profaned the blood of the covenant by which he was sanctified, and has outraged the Spirit of grace? For we know him who said, "Vengeance is mine; I will repay." And again, "The Lord will judge his people." It is a fearful thing to fall into the hands of the living God. (Hebrews 10.26-31)

Just like the people of God in the Old Testament were warned about the impending judgment should they cast aside the law of Moses, so too are the new covenant believers warned of the impending judgment of God should they cast aside the Lordship of Christ.

Therefore, the warnings of the Old Testament prophets continue to be relevant today. They should not be ignored by believers but diligently listened to and obeyed.

Daily Bible Readings

I encourage you to take the time this week to meditate upon the message of the prophets and what the Lord might be saying to you today. Don't just skip to the next chapter because you want to avoid the heavy message of judgment. Remember, the Scriptures are intended to be profitable for correction just as much as they are for encouragement.

Suggested Scripture Memory Verses

For I know the plans I have for you, declares the LORD, plans for wholeness and not for evil, to give you a future and a hope. (Jeremiah 29.11)

He gives power to the faint, and to him who has no might he increases strength. Even youths shall faint and be weary, and young men shall fall exhausted; but they who wait for the LORD shall renew their strength; they shall mount up with wings like eagles; they shall run and not be weary; they shall walk and not faint. (Isaiah 40.29-31)

Listen to me, O house of Jacob, all the remnant of the house of Israel, who have been borne by me from before your birth, carried from the womb; even to your old age I am he, and to gray hairs I will carry you. I have made, and I will bear; I will carry and will save. (Isaiah 46.3-4)

Remember the former things of old; for I am God, and there is no other; I am God, and there is none like me, declaring the end from the beginning and from ancient times things not yet done, saying, "My counsel shall stand, and I will accomplish all my purpose," (Isaiah 46.9-10)

But he was wounded for our transgressions; he was crushed for our iniquities; upon him was the chastisement that brought us peace, and with his stripes we are healed. All we like sheep have gone astray; we have turned every one to his own way; and the LORD has laid on him the iniquity of us all. (Isaiah 53.5-6)

Rend your hearts and not your garments. Return to the LORD, your God, for he is gracious and merciful, slow to anger, and abounding in steadfast love; and he relents over disaster. Who knows whether he will not turn and relent, and leave a blessing behind him, a grain offering and a drink offering for the LORD your God? (Joel 2.13-14)

Take away from me the noise of your songs; to the melody of your harps I will not listen. But let justice roll down like waters, and righteousness like an ever-flowing stream. (Amos 5.23-24)

For still the vision awaits its appointed time; it hastens to the end—it will not lie. If it seems slow, wait for it; it will surely come; it will not delay. (Habakkuk 2.3)

They shall be mine, says the LORD of hosts, in the day when I make up my treasured possession, and I will spare them as a man spares his son who serves him. Then once more you shall see the distinction between the righteous and the wicked, between one who serves God and one who does not serve him. (Malachi 3.17-18)

Day One: Isaiah 1

_S:_ _____
_____
_____
_____
_____
_____
_____

_O:_ _____
_____
_____
_____
_____
_____
_____

_A:_ _____
_____
_____
_____
_____
_____
_____

_P:_ _____
_____
_____
_____
_____
_____
_____

Day Two: Isaiah 5

S:

_____

_____

_____

_____

_____

_____

_____

O:

_____

_____

_____

_____

_____

_____

_____

A:

_____

_____

_____

_____

_____

_____

_____

P:

_____

_____

_____

_____

_____

_____

_____

Day Three: Jeremiah 13

S: _____
_____
_____
_____
_____
_____
_____

O: _____
_____
_____
_____
_____
_____
_____

A: _____
_____
_____
_____
_____
_____
_____
_____

P: _____
_____
_____
_____
_____
_____
_____

Day Four: Ezekiel 3

S:

_____
_____
_____
_____
_____
_____
_____

O:

_____
_____
_____
_____
_____
_____
_____

A:

_____
_____
_____
_____
_____
_____
_____

P:

_____
_____
_____
_____
_____
_____
_____

Day Five: Amos 4

S:
_____
_____
_____
_____
_____
_____
_____

O:
_____
_____
_____
_____
_____
_____
_____

A:
_____
_____
_____
_____
_____
_____
_____

P:
_____
_____
_____
_____
_____
_____
_____

Day Six: Micah 5

_S:_

_O:_

_A:_

_P:_

9 | ACT 6 | NEHEMIAH AND THE RETURN

The previous act of the story of God's relationship with His people ended in darkness. God removed His people from the land of promise because they refused to obey the Lord and to worship Him alone. After years and years of warnings to repent, judgment finally came through the Babylonian army, and Jerusalem was destroyed.

We can only imagine the despair that was felt by God's people. In our own national history, the period of the Great Depression might give us some insight into their condition. Hope was lost, and the despair was overwhelming. Their 854 year identity as the people of God, led by His presence resting on the Ark of the Covenant, was over. The Lord had finally turned His back on them.

Of course, while the majority of the people of God were unfaithful to the covenant, there was always a righteous remnant, however small it might have been. For those who truly mourned over the unrighteousness of the nation, for those whose spirit was broken to see the Temple of the Lord destroyed, for those who still lived by the words of the covenant, the exile was exceedingly harsh. However, for these, there was hope.

Even the prophets, with their harsh words of judgment, often spoke words of hope to the righteous remnant.

> *I will restore the fortunes of my people Israel, and they shall rebuild the ruined cities and inhabit them; they shall plant vineyards and drink their wine, and they shall make gardens and eat their fruit. I will plant them on their land, and they shall never again be uprooted out of the land that I have given them. (Amos 9.14-15).*

> *In that day the remnant of Israel and the survivors of the house of Jacob will no more lean on him who struck them, but will lean on the LORD, the Holy One of Israel, in truth. A remnant will return, the remnant of Jacob, to the mighty God. For though your people Israel be as the sand of the sea, only a remnant of them will return. Destruction is decreed,*

overflowing with righteousness. For the Lord GOD of hosts will make a
full end, as decreed, in the midst of all the earth. (Isaiah 10.20-23)

I will gather the remnant of my flock out of all the countries where I have
driven them, and I will bring them back to their fold, and they shall be
fruitful and multiply. (Jeremiah 23.3)

The message of hope was constantly mixed in with the message of judgment.

A remnant would return.

Cyrus, King of Persia

The prophet Habakkuk was right to struggle with his questions. How could the
Lord be silent while the wicked were swallowing up the more righteous
(Habakkuk 1.13)? The Lord's answer to Habakkuk's question was even more
prophetic. Babylon would be judged because it plundered many nations and
built up itself by unjust gain. The mighty Babylon fell to the Persian Empire in
539 BC.

As king, Cyrus reversed the policy of the Babylonians. Instead of hording
captive people, the Persians allowed the people to return to their homeland.

The opening words of the book of Ezra reveal the hand of the Lord through this
moment in history.

> *In the first year of Cyrus king of Persia, that the word of the LORD by the*
> *mouth of Jeremiah might be fulfilled, the LORD stirred up the spirit of*
> *Cyrus king of Persia, so that he made a proclamation throughout all his*
> *kingdom and also put it in writing: "Thus says Cyrus king of Persia:*
> *The LORD, the God of heaven, has given me all the kingdoms of the earth,*
> *and he has charged me to build him a house at Jerusalem, which is in*
> *Judah. Whoever is among you of all his people, may his God be with him,*
> *and let him go up to Jerusalem, which is in Judah, and rebuild the house*
> *of the LORD, the God of Israel—he is the God who is in Jerusalem. And let*
> *each survivor, in whatever place he sojourns, be assisted by the men of his*
> *place with silver and gold, with goods and with beasts, besides freewill*
> *offerings for the house of God that is in Jerusalem." (Ezra 1.1-4)*

With these dramatic words, the Lord once again proved that He is the God of
the Nations. He not only stirred up Assyria and Babylon as tools of judgment,

but He also stirred the heart of a pagan king to allow and equip His people to return to Jerusalem to rebuild the Temple. Equally startling, Jeremiah had prophesied seventy years earlier that Babylon would be judged and that the people would return. Furthermore, Isaiah prophesied that Cyrus would be the one who would allow the Temple to be rebuilt.

There were four kings who dominated the rule of Persia over the people of God: Cyrus, Darius, Xerxes, and Artaxerxes. All four are found throughout the story of Ezra, Nehemiah, Daniel, and Ester

Three historical books and four prophetic books tell the story of the exile. The historical narrative is told through the lives of Ezra, Nehemiah, and Esther. The prophetic ministry was shared through the prophetic lives of Haggai, Zechariah, Malachi, and Daniel.

Daniel and Esther provide a different perspective on the return than do the other books. They remained in the Babylonian territory under Persian rule.

Daniel's life and ministry actually began before the exile as he was one of the first captives removed from Jerusalem by Nebuchadnezzar. His post-exilic ministry was confined within the Babylonian territory. Even though he was not one of the returning Jews, his writing does inform our understanding of this period in biblical history. Likewise, Esther was one of the Jews who remained in the Babylonian territory, and her life became entangled with the Persian king, Xerxes, who reigned after Cyrus.

Ezra

The book of Ezra tells the story of the return to Jerusalem. Close to 50,000 people returned to the ruined city, and promptly began the work of rebuilding the Temple. It would not be an easy task. The locals who had inhabited the area in the absence of the Jews were not particularly excited about the rebuilding of the Temple or Jerusalem.

In addition to their opposition, the passing of Cyrus and the rise of Xerxes proved another stumbling block. Both Xerxes, and his son Artaxerxes, were encouraged by the opponents of the Jews to halt the work on the Temple.

This opposition continued even until the reign of Darius, but the Temple project was allowed to continue when it was discovered in the archives that Cyrus had authorized it. After much hard work, the Temple was completed in 515 BC, and immediately, the Passover was celebrated for the first time since the exile.

Many times in the history of Israel, the celebration of the Passover was one of the first marks of restoration. The Passover was celebrated after Joshua led the people across the Jordan River (Joshua 5.10). Both Hezekiah and Josiah celebrated the Passover after they led the nation in spiritual renewals (2 Chronicles 30 and 35). And the Passover was the meal observed by Jesus just before the ultimate restoration.

One of the interesting elements of this segment of biblical history is the lack of a single key figure during the rebuilding of the Temple. Zerubbabel, the governor of Judah, and Joshua, the high priest, were the key figures during this period, but their presence did not loom large over this particular event in history. From a story teller's perspective, the building of the Temple just seemed to happen. The focus of the return was not so much on the rebuilding of the Temple but on the renewal of the covenant and the rebuilding of the walls.

Ezra, the priest, led another group of returnees well after the Temple had been rebuilt. In 458 BC, Ezra returned with an imperial decree to gather the items needed to furnish the Temple. He led the nation in restoring the covenant and biblical worship. His first major challenge in leading the people to faithfulness was to address the issue of mixed marriages. While this term is used in our society to talk about marriages among people with different racial backgrounds, the mixed marriages of Ezra's day were spiritually mixed: the Jews had married people from other nations who worshipped other gods.

For they have taken some of their daughters to be wives for themselves and for their sons, so that the holy race has mixed itself with the peoples of the lands. And in this faithlessness the hand of the officials and chief men has been foremost. (Ezra 9.2)

Over 800 years earlier, Moses had warned the people about the risk of marrying people who worship other gods. This was Solomon's downfall, and Ezra did not want the people to commit the same mistake. So, he led the nation in purifying itself by sending away the wives and children from marriages with foreign women. Ezra's call was drastic, sacrificial, but necessary.

Nehemiah

During the same period as Ezra's ministry, Nehemiah was a cupbearer to King Artaxerxes. He heard a report from some Jews who had returned for Jerusalem that the walls of the city were still in disarray. This caused him great grief, and this grief caught the attention of the king. According to the custom of the Persian rulers, it was not proper to show sadness in the royal courts; so, Nehemiah was very much afraid because his sadness had been noticed by the king. When asked, he boldly shared the reason for his grief.

> I said to the king, "Let the king live forever! Why should not my face be sad, when the city, the place of my fathers' graves, lies in ruins, and its gates have been destroyed by fire?" (Nehemiah 2.3)

He asked the king for permission to return to Jerusalem, to lead the effort to rebuild the walls, and for permission to obtain the necessary supplies required to do the task. This was a bold request, but the gracious hand of the Lord was upon him, and the king granted his request. More than just a passing phrase, the "hand of the Lord" played a prominent role in the Ezra/Nehemiah story. For instance, it was the hand of the Lord which caused Ezra and Nehemiah to receive the favor of the king, and it was the hand of the Lord which granted them safe travel.

Upon returning to Jerusalem, Nehemiah inspected the walls of Jerusalem and led the people in the difficult task of rebuilding the destroyed walls. Despite opposition from the locals, the walls were completed in only 52 days in 445 BC (Nehemiah 6.15).

However, rebuilding the walls of Jerusalem was more than just a construction project. It was a faith restoration project. After the walls were rebuilt, Ezra the priest stood before the people and read the law of the Lord from daybreak until noon for seven days. In response, the people confessed the sins of their fathers and their own.

During the days of Ezra and Nehemiah, there was renewed spiritual fervor and dedication to the covenant of God.

Esther

Few contemporary short stories could match the book of Esther for excitement, ironic plots twists, and high drama.

The story took place during the reign of Xerxes, King of Persia (486 to 464 BC). Xerxes was the grandson of Cyrus and the son of Darius, so Esther's stories took place during the general period after the Temple was rebuilt but before the walls were rebuilt.

A certain scribe named Mordecai was raising his niece, Esther, in the region of Susa in the far eastern part of the old Babylonian Empire. The king was looking for a new wife, and Esther caught his eye. Under the council of Mordecai, she did not reveal to the king her Jewish ancestry.

One day, Mordecai overheard some palace guards discussing their plan to assassinate the king. He shared this with Esther who told the king, and the plot was foiled. Though credited with saving the king's life, no reward was given to Mordecai.

However, the king's second in command, Haman, hated Mordecai because he refused to bow to Haman. This so angered Haman that he developed a plan to slaughter all of the Jews and confiscate their treasures for the king. A date was set and publicized by Haman when the massacre was to take place.

When Mordecai found out about the plot, he told Esther that she must tell the King about the plot so that it could be stopped. However, no one, not even the queen, was allowed to approach the king without an invitation, and an invitation had not been given in the past thirty days. Then, Mordecai spoke these challenging words of faith to Esther.

*For if you keep silent at this time, relief and deliverance will rise for
the Jews from another place, but you and your father's house will perish.
And who knows whether you have not come to the kingdom for such a time
as this? (Esther 4.14)*

For such a time as this, Esther asked the Jews to pray and fast on her behalf.
Miraculously, when she approached the king, she found favor in his eyes.
Esther, along with Ezra and Nehemiah, were all major characters during this
time period who received favor from pagan kings to accomplish God's plans.

However, instead of telling the king about the plot to kill the Jews, she invited
the king and Haman to a banquet in their honor. After a successful banquet, she
invited them both to a second banquet.

But before the second banquet took place, the king had a sleepless night. He
ordered the book of chronicles, the record of his reign, to be read to him so that
he might fall asleep. As the story was being read, he realized that Mordecai had
never been honored for preventing the plot to kill the king. So, he commanded
Haman to lead Mordecai through the town on the king's horse proclaiming all
the good he had done. This only intensified Haman's hatred for Mordecai.

Towards the end of the second banquet, the king was so honored that he
offered to grant the queen any request up to half of the kingdom. Esther's
request was simple, "Let my life be granted me…for we have been sold, I and
my people, to be destroyed, to be killed, and to be annihilated" (Esther 7.3).
Upon hearing of the plot to kill the queen and her people, the Jews, the king
demanded the death of the man who devised such a plan. Remember, at this
point, no one knew that Esther was a Jew.

Haman was hanged in the place of Mordecai, and the slaughter of the Jews was
avoided. The events are still remembered annually during the Feast of Purim.

Esther is a story of faith, and a story of the sovereignty of God over the kings
of the world. However, the name of God does not appear in the story of Esther,
a fact which caused many rabbis to debate its inclusion in the canon of the Old
Testament.

The Period of Silence

As the stories of Ezra, Nehemiah, and Esther conclude, so does the historical narrative of the Old Testament. The walls of Jerusalem were finished in 445 BC, and the next historical event in the biblical story was the birth of Christ.

What happened to the people of God during the 400 years in between? They are often called "the silent years" because the canonical Scriptures are simply silent about these events. However, despite the Scriptural silence, there are some significant developments during this period that are important to readers of the Bible.

Alexander the Great

The story of the Old Testament ended with the people of God under Persian rule, but that situation did not last long. The victory of Persia over Babylon in 539 BC was followed by Greece's victory over Persia in 331 BC. Alexander the Great took the throne of Greece at the young age of 20, and by his death at only 32 years of age, he had conquered much of the known world.

The most lasting impact of Alexander's domination was the Hellenization (the spread of Greek culture) of the conquered regions. Not only did he unite his territory under one government, he also spread a united culture throughout the world. The Greek world view, complete with its language and religion, began to influence the entire world. He commanded that everyone everywhere should speak Greek, think Greek, write Greek, and live Greek.

So persuasive were his efforts, that three centuries later when the text of the New Testament was written, mostly by Hebrews, it was written in Greek. It was the Greek pantheon of gods that provided the backdrop for the early church as they shared Jesus Christ, the Messiah, the one and only Son of the one and only true God.

Antiochus Epiphanes

While Alexander spread the Greek culture around the world, another Greek king impacted the story of God's people. Antiochus Epiphanes was a demented and evil ruler bent on the destruction of the Jews. He outlawed the Sabbath, circumcision, and even the possession of the Hebrew Scriptures. All of these were punishable by death. In 167 BC, he even sacrificed a pig on the altar of the Temple in Jerusalem. Most scholars understand this to be the "abomination of desolation" prophesized by Daniel (Daniel 11.31). More importantly, Antiochus serves as a "type" of the antichrist that will appear in the end times.

The Maccabean Rebellion

So horrible was the rule of Antiochus, it caused a rebellion among the Jews led by Mattathias. He led the Jews on a campaign of guerrilla warfare aimed at ridding Jerusalem of the hated Greek ruler. Upon his death, his son Judas Maccabaeus, also called Judas the Hammer, took over. His war was so successful, that he gained two major concessions from the Greeks: religious freedom for the Jews and the reopening of the Temple for sacred worship.

The Feast of Hanukkah, or the Festival of Lights, commemorates the cleansing of the Temple after the Maccabean revolt.

Roman Rule

The relative freedom of the people of God lasted for but a few years. In 63 BC, General Pompey of the ever spreading Roman Empire conquered Palestine. The rule of Rome overshadowed the people of God from this day forward through the end of the New Testament period.

Synagogues

With the destruction of the Temple, the people of God needed a place to gather to study the law and to worship. During the exile, these local places of worship and study became formalized as "synagogues," a Greek word meaning "assembly." They were a place of prayer, Scripture reading, and sermons. So prominent were the synagogues in the life of God's people during the exile, they continued the practice even after returning to Jerusalem. The synagogue became the local expression of the Jewish faith. In fact, being "put out of the synagogue" was one of the Jew's greatest fears (for example, see John 9.22).

Jesus began His ministry in the synagogue, and the apostles began sharing the gospel in the synagogues.

Pharisees

Another result of Antiochus' horrible reign was the formation of several spiritual renewal groups within Jewish life. One of these groups was the Pharisees, so named from the Hebrew word *parash* which means "to separate." This group focused on keeping the Jewish faith pure from the encroachment of the Greek gods so prevalent in the Hellenization of Judea. Unfortunately, by the time of Christ, this group had deteriorated into a legalistic and prideful religious group, but it had noble and righteous beginnings.

Wisdom Literature

With the close of the Old Testament story, all of the books of the Old Testament have been addressed with the exception of one final category: the wisdom literature. These five books of the Hebrew Scriptures are a category all to themselves, and include Job, Psalms, Proverbs, Song of Solomon, and Ecclesiastes. The wisdom literature generally address how to live a godly life.

Psalms

The Book of Psalms is often called the worship book of the Bible. If a person wants to learn how to pray, there is no better book in the Bible to study. By reading and praying through the Psalms, a disciple can develop a biblical prayer life. The book of Psalms, or book of songs, contains 150 psalms written by a variety of authors. About two thirds of the psalms are ascribed to David. There are seven basic types of psalms.

> *The Psalms of Praise focus on worshipping and praising the Lord.*
> *"O LORD, our Lord, how majestic is your name in all the earth! You have set your glory above the heavens." (Psalm 8.1)*

The Psalms of Wisdom describe the path to wisdom: meditating on God's word. "Blessed is the man who walks not in the counsel of the wicked, nor stands in the way of sinners, nor sits in the seat of scoffers; but his delight is in the law of the LORD, and on his law he meditates day and night." (Psalm 1.1-2)

The Psalms of Lament are the expressions of people who were hurting and who brought their pain before the Lord. "Hear my prayer, O LORD; let my cry come to you! Do not hide your face from me in the day of my distress! Incline your ear to me; answer me speedily in the day when I call!" (Psalm 102.1-2)

A few of the Psalms are Messianic and describe the coming Messiah. "The LORD says to my Lord: 'Sit at my right hand, until I make your enemies your footstool.' The LORD sends forth from Zion your mighty scepter. Rule in the midst of your enemies!" (Psalm 110.1-2)

The Psalm of Penitence demonstrates genuine contrition and repentance. "Have mercy on me, O God, according to your steadfast love; according to your abundant mercy blot out my transgressions. Wash me thoroughly from my iniquity, and cleanse me from my sin! For I know my transgressions, and my sin is ever before me." (Psalm 51.1-3)

The Psalms of Imprecation, or cursing, call down God's holy wrath on the author's enemies. "Let their own table before them become a snare; and when they are at peace, let it become a trap. Let their eyes be darkened, so that they cannot see, and make their loins tremble continually. Pour out your indignation upon them, and let your burning anger overtake them." (Psalm 69.22-24)

The Psalms of Thanksgiving praise the Lord for all of His good gifts. "For this I will praise you, O LORD, among the nations, and sing to your name." (Psalm 18.49)

Proverbs

The book of Proverbs is a collection of wise sayings and instructions for living a useful and effective life. The collection was primarily authored by Solomon though some of the proverbs are attributed to others. They cover a wide variety of subjects and are almost impossible to categorize.

Ecclesiastes

The book of Ecclesiastes is the personal journal of King Solomon. It is so named because of the Greek translation of the Hebrew word for "teacher," which is the first word of the book.

Two competing world views are presented in Ecclesiastes: the world under heaven and the world under the sun. Living life under the sun is meaningless, but a life that fears the Lord will not be. The conclusion of the matter? "Fear God and keep his commandments, for this is the whole duty of man" (Ecclesiastes 12.13).

Song of Solomon

The Song of Solomon, also called the Song of Songs, is a collection of love poems celebrating the experiences of a lover and his beloved as they taste the beauty, power, agony, and joys of human sexual love. The songs are an exchange between the king and his bride.

Some have questioned whether or not this collection belongs in the sacred Scriptures. As the people of God have struggled with that question through the ages, this book of the Bible has been treated primarily as an allegory of God's love relationship with His people. No doubt, the Bible does use the analogy of marriage to describe the church's relationship as the bride of Christ. But, there is little in the book itself to support the idea that it was meant to be read allegorically. It is better to accept is as a celebration of love between a husband and a wife.

Job

The book of Job deals with the problem of evil and suffering. The setting for the story is in the patriarchal period, before the law was given to Moses.

Job was a righteous man, who unknowingly played a part in a debate between the Lord and Satan. Satan's challenge was that Job only worshipped the Lord because of the good things the Lord had given to him. If these gifts were to be taken away, Satan argued, Job's affections would change.

The Lord allowed Satan to afflict Job in every way but he was not allowed to take his life. Job remained faithful despite the losses with these words of faith,

> *Naked I came from my mother's womb, and naked shall I return. The LORD gave, and the LORD has taken away; blessed be the name of the LORD. (Job 1.21)*

However, his friends shared their wisdom with Job. They were convinced that these evil things happened to Job because of some secret sin. Through it all, Job defended his righteousness. Eventually, the pain finally got to Job, and he began to question God's fairness. He felt that if God would examine his life, He would see that these horrible things were unfair for such a righteous man.

In the last few chapters, the Lord finally spoke, but it is not what Job wanted to hear.

> *Who is this that darkens counsel by words without knowledge? Dress for action like a man; I will question you, and you make it known to me. Where were you when I laid the foundation of the earth? Tell me, if you have understanding. (Job 38.2-4)*

What follows is a beautiful poetic description of God's power and wisdom. So overwhelming was the picture of God's sovereignty, Job's only response was "I have uttered what I did not understand, things too wonderful for me, which I did not know" (Job 42.3). God's basic message to Job was, "Don't question how I manage the universe that I created."

Even though the Lord restored the fortunes of Job, Job's questions were never answered. He never knew of the cosmic challenge. The Lord called him to faith and to trust in the sovereign, powerful, and wise rule of the Lord.

Conclusion

Thus ends the historical narrative of relationship of God with His people before the birth of the Messiah. However, let's look at it from another angle before we turn our attention to the New Testament.

We can also view the Old Testament as theological history. The story began with God's creative act in forming the world. Sin twisted God's plan for His creation, and He began His plan of redemption by choosing a people and inviting them into a covenant relationship.

However, the people were never able to maintain the covenant. They couldn't obey the laws, and the temptation to worship other gods was too great. Even with the forgiveness offered freely by God through the sacrificial system, the problem of sin was too great. Something had to be done about sin itself, or this horrible cycle of sin, judgment, and repentance would continue forever.

The story of the New Testament is really the answer to the problem of the Old Testament. What can be done about the problem of sin? Can sinners obey the rules and become righteous enough? No. Will forgiveness be enough to keep them faithful? No. Can they be disciplined into faithfulness? No. Something dramatic had to be done with the problem of sin.

The people walking in darkness needed to see a great light. And that Light of the World would change everything.

Making It Profitable

Daily Bible Readings

The wisdom literature of the Old Testament is some of the best portions to read. The worship literature of Psalms helps believers express their praise and prayers to the King of Kings. The practical wisdom of Proverbs still cannot be beat for its value. And while there is so much good to be found in this section, one week of daily readings forces us to make choices. For this week's daily readings, I have focused on the Psalms and the Proverbs.

Suggested Scripture Memory Verses

And do not be grieved, for the joy of the LORD is your strength. (Nehemiah 8.10)

Naked I came from my mother's womb, and naked shall I return. The LORD gave, and the LORD has taken away; blessed be the name of the LORD. (Job 1.21)

Blessed is the man who walks not in the counsel of the wicked, nor stands in the way of sinners, nor sits in the seat of scoffers; but his delight is in the law of the LORD, and on his law he meditates day and night. He is like a tree planted by streams of water that yields its fruit in its season, and its leaf does not wither. In all that he does, he prospers. (Psalm 1.2-3)

Now I know that the LORD saves his anointed; he will answer him from his holy heaven with the saving might of his right hand. Some trust in chariots and some in horses, but we trust in the name of the LORD our God. (Psalm 20.6-7)

For you, O Lord, are good and forgiving, abounding in steadfast love to all who call upon you. Give ear, O LORD, to my prayer; listen to my plea for grace. In the day of my trouble I call upon you, for you answer me. (Psalm 86.5-7)

Search me, O God, and know my heart! Try me and know my thoughts! And see if there be any grievous way in me, and lead me in the way everlasting! (Psalm 139.23-24)

The fear of the LORD is the beginning of knowledge; fools despise wisdom and instruction. (Proverbs 1.7)

Trust in the LORD with all your heart, and do not lean on your own understanding. In all your ways acknowledge him, and he will make straight your paths. (Proverbs 3.5-6)

A soft answer turns away wrath, but a harsh word stirs up anger. (Proverbs 15.1)

Good sense makes one slow to anger, and it is his glory to overlook an offense. (Proverbs 19.11)

Two are better than one, because they have a good reward for their toil. For if they fall, one will lift up his fellow. But woe to him who is alone when he falls and has not another to lift him up! (Ecclesiastes 4.9-10)

Set me as a seal upon your heart, as a seal upon your arm, for love is strong as death, jealousy is fierce as the grave. Its flashes are flashes of fire, the very flame of the LORD. (Song of Songs 8.6)

Day One: Psalm 1

_S:_ _____

_____

_____

_____

_____

_____

_____

_O:_ _____

_____

_____

_____

_____

_____

_____

_A:_ _____

_____

_____

_____

_____

_____

_____

_P:_ _____

_____

_____

_____

_____

_____

_____

Day Two: Psalm 23

_S:_
_____
_____
_____
_____
_____
_____
_____
_____

_O:_
_____
_____
_____
_____
_____
_____
_____
_____

_A:_
_____
_____
_____
_____
_____
_____
_____
_____

_P:_
_____
_____
_____
_____
_____
_____
_____
_____

Day Three: Psalm 51

_S:_ _____

_____
_____
_____
_____
_____
_____
_____

_O:_ _____

_____
_____
_____
_____
_____
_____
_____

_A:_ _____

_____
_____
_____
_____
_____
_____
_____

_P:_ _____

_____
_____
_____
_____
_____
_____
_____

Day Four: Psalm 119

S:
_____
_____
_____
_____
_____
_____
_____

O:
_____
_____
_____
_____
_____
_____
_____

A:
_____
_____
_____
_____
_____
_____
_____

P:
_____
_____
_____
_____
_____
_____
_____

Day Five: Proverbs 1

S:

O:

A:

P:

Day Six: Proverbs 3

S: _____
_____
_____
_____
_____
_____
_____
_____

O: _____
_____
_____
_____
_____
_____
_____
_____

A: _____
_____
_____
_____
_____
_____
_____

P: _____
_____
_____
_____
_____
_____
_____

To this point, the story of God's relationship with His people has spanned from creation to the period of silence after the rebuilding of the walls of Jerusalem. And yet, the entire story has been moving, slowly, but methodically towards the moment when God would act in history unlike any other moment.

From the beginning, God spoke to His people through various ways and various prophets, through burning bushes and pillars of fire, through dreams and even animals. But this time, it would be different. This time, God would enter His creation Himself. God would become flesh and dwell among His own people. It was the moment that all of creation had been groaning for, and it would forever split time. As the apostle Paul wrote,

> But when the fullness of time had come, God sent forth his Son, born of woman, born under the law. (Galatians 4.4)

Finally, the time had come.

John the Baptist

It is hard to underestimate the ministry of John the Baptist. Only two of the four gospels tell of the birth of Christ, but all four tell of John's ministry. In the words of Jesus, "Among those born of women none is greater than John" (Luke 7.28). The entire Jewish nation was waiting for the prophecy of Malachi to be fulfilled.

> Behold, I will send you Elijah the prophet before the great and awesome day of the Lord comes. (Malachi 4.5)

Everyone knew that before the Messiah would come, a prophet in the spirit of Elijah who would prepare the way. Jesus told His followers that John was the one spoken of by Malachi (Luke 7.27).

We are accustomed to the story of John, but we forget the significance of his ministry. The last prophet to speak the words of the Lord was Malachi, over 400 years earlier. Jerusalem and the people of God had been through a famine of the word of the Lord. The prophetic voice was silent.

Then, suddenly, the word of the Lord returned in dramatic fashion. John, a voice crying in the wilderness, burst on the scene with a message of preparation. He preached a baptism of repentance for the forgiveness of sins so that the people would be prepared for the coming Messiah.

Two significant moments stand out in the ministry of John. The first was his ministry of baptism. Scholarship seems divided over the place and role of baptism in the first century. John was certainly not the first to baptize. Converts to the Jewish faith were often baptized, and even other religious movements had ceremonial washings.

Regardless, it is important to remember that the baptism of John was different than today's Christian baptism. John's baptism was of repentance from sins so that they might believe in the One who was to come, Jesus (see Acts 19.1-6). Christian baptism is a confession of both repentance from sin and a demonstration of one's faith in the death, burial, and resurrection of Christ. It is very important that the church make that distinction today as we lead people through the act of baptism.

The second significant moment in the ministry of John was his declaration of Jesus as "The Lamb of God, who takes away the sin of the world!" (John 1.29). John not only preached of the coming Messiah, he personally identified Him with this statement.

More importantly, not only did he identify Jesus as the Messiah, but he also identified the role of the Messiah. The Messiah would not be a military ruler bringing political freedom to Jerusalem. Instead, the Messiah would be a sacrificial lamb. This lamb, in the image of the Passover lamb or the lamb on the Day of Atonement, would not only forgive sins but would also take away sins. Though much blood had been spilt on the Temple altar, they were powerless to actually take away sin. Jesus' blood did just that.

Further, John used the powerful image from two of the most sacred of days for the Jewish people: the Passover and the Day of Atonement. He was framing the life and ministry of Jesus as the fulfillment of these two celebrations.

Gospel before the Gospels

When we speak of the life of Christ, we use the term "gospel." Literally, the term gospel means "good news."

Very quickly, the word gospel became associated with the story and message of Christ, the Messiah. The term gospel became synonymous with a correct, biblical understanding about the person of Christ and His atoning death. The gospel, or the orthodox understanding of who Jesus was and what His life meant, existed before the story of Christ was written down. These written down stories about the life of Jesus tell the gospel story, and therefore, have come to be labeled as the gospels. However, the gospel message pre-existed the books of Matthew, Mark, Luke, and John.

In fact, in one of the earliest letters from the apostle Paul, perhaps as early as 55 AD, years before the gospel of Mark was written, Paul gave specific teachings to the churches of Galatia to reject false teachings. He wrote,

> I am astonished that you are so quickly deserting him who called you in the grace of Christ and are turning to a different gospel—not that there is another one, but there are some who trouble you and want to distort the gospel of Christ. But even if we or an angel from heaven should preach to you a gospel contrary to the one we preached to you, let him be accursed. (Galatians 1.6-8)

If we understand Paul's point, then we will understand that an orthodox understanding of the life of Christ pre-existed the written gospel stories. "The gospel" was already set long before it was written. There was and is a difference between the gospel and the written accounts of this gospel story.

The Four Gospels

There are four books in the Bible that tell the story of the life of Christ, and each presents the story with a different perspective and with different emphasis.

If we were to ask four people to tell us the story of "9/11," the tragic moment when the airplanes hit the world trade towers on September 11, 2001, each would tell the story from a different perspective with a different emphasis. The secretary who escaped the towers before they collapsed would tell of the fear and chaos as she exited the building. The fireman's widow would tell of the courage and bravery of her husband's last moments. The news anchor would concentrate on the facts and details while the Secretary of Defense would focus on the implications of national defense.

The story of each would be accurate, and none of the four would invent facts. However, they would include and exclude information from their account that would coincide with their perspective and the emphasis they wished to make.

The four gospel writers present the story of Christ in four different ways, through four different lenses, each presenting the story with their own perspective and their own emphasis.

Matthew

Matthew, more than any other gospel writer, was interested in the Jewishness of Jesus. He more frequently quoted from the Old Testament to illustrate how various facets of Jesus' life either fulfilled Old Testament predictions or recapitulated Old Testament themes. He displayed more interest than the other writers in matters relating to the Jewish law and customs, Jewish national privilege, and the relation between Israel and faith in Jesus. The first gospel was addressed primarily to Jews to convince them that Jesus was indeed the long awaited Messiah.

Mark

The second gospel account is the shortest of the four. Over 90% of the gospel of Mark is contained in either Matthew or Luke, and was most likely a source used by both. Mark's gospel was written with a fast moving style and is primarily concerned with relating the actions of Jesus though he does not neglect the teachings of Jesus. At least five times, Mark used Aramaic phrases, but also translated them into Greek. This indicates that he was not writing for Jewish readers. He often gave Latin equivalents for terms and amounts.

Therefore, it seems that Mark was writing to inform action oriented Romans of the gospel of Jesus Christ.

Luke

The third gospel is the first part of a two volume work, referred to by scholars as "Luke/Acts." These two books together comprise the largest block of material by a single New Testament author, even more than Paul.

His is the only gospel addressed to a particular person, Theophilus. However, since the name means "lover of God," many have wondered if this is more symbolic than a proper noun. The description of Theophilus as "most excellent" would only be appropriate if applied to a Gentile of considerable social or political standing in the community. Luke's stated purpose of researching and writing the gospel was so that Theophilus might know the certainty of the things he had been taught.

It appears that Luke wrote his gospel to a high ranking Gentile who had heard about Jesus but needed to know more about Him. In the book of Acts, there are two figures who might be either the intended Theophilus or who would be the kind of person Theophilus might have been.

The first is Cornelius, the Gentile Roman centurion who was converted to the Christian faith. His story not only takes one entire chapter to tell, but Peter retells the story several times while explaining his actions of accepting Gentiles into the church. In fact, it is Cornelius' salvation that brings the first real crisis to the early church: the salvation of the Gentiles. This new convert would certainly need to know more about the person of Christ, and this gospel would explain in detail the life and ministry of Jesus to a new convert.

King Agrippa is another possible Theophilus. Contrary to Cornelius, Agrippa was not a convert to Christianity but rather a skeptic. He heard the gospel story but warned Paul, "In a short time would you persuade me to be a Christian?" (Acts 26.28). Agrippa was a high ranking Gentile who needed more evidence to convince him before he would put his faith in Christ. The gospel of Luke may have been written to do just that.

Another important fact to consider about Luke is that he was not an eyewitness to the life of Christ. Instead, he was an eyewitness to the birth and expansion of the Christian church. As a traveling companion of Paul, he witnessed firsthand the spread of the gospel through the ends of the earth. He understood the importance of having a written gospel to educate both new converts and skeptics.

John

The fourth gospel is altogether different and probably the last of the four to be written.

One distinguishing characteristic of the gospel of John is the organization of the gospel story around the seven signs. These miraculous signs all pointed to the fact that Jesus was in fact the Messiah. The seven signs are: turning the water into wine at the wedding of Cana (John 2.11), the healing of the royal official at Capernaum (John 4.54), the healing at the pool of Bethsaida (John 6.2), the feeding of the 5000 (John 6.14), restoring the sight to a man born blind (John 9.16), the raising of Lazarus from the dead (John 11.47), and the resurrection (John 20.30).

John's gospel contains fewer stories, and the events in the life of Christ are accompanied by longer dialogue and teaching sections. His gospel is more poetic and theological in its presentation. For instance, the birth narrative in the fourth gospel is a theological birth story.

> *The Word became flesh and dwelt among us, and we have seen his glory, glory as of the only Son from the Father, full of grace and truth.(John 1.14).*

Nothing is mentioned about the historic events surrounding the birth, but John's presentation of the birth narrative provides us with the best understanding of what exactly happened when the babe was wrapped in swaddling clothes and put in the manger.

The Synoptic Problem

No presentation of the gospels would be complete without a discussion about the synoptic problem.

The scholar Griesbach, who died in 1812, was the first to use the term "synoptic" in reference to the first three gospels (Harrison, 142). The term is taken from the Greek which means, "to see together" or "the same view." Matthew, Mark, and Luke presented and organized the story of Christ in very much the same way. They order the events the same, and often use the exact same words and phrases. In fact, they have more in common with each other than they do in difference.

For instance, 93% of Mark, 58% of Matthew, and 41% of Luke share a close affinity with each other. Only 7% of Mark, 42% of Matthew, and 59% of Luke is peculiar to each gospel account (Harrison, 143). More interesting than this is the amount of commonality between Matthew and Luke when they presented material absent from Mark.

However, it is not only the surprising degree of agreement that has created the synoptic problem, but it is also the differences between them that has birthed the questions. Sometimes they use similar language, grammar, and word order when they present common material. However, at other times, they locate events in different cities and in a different chronology. How can the similarities and differences be explained?

For example, when Jesus taught His disciples how to pray, the three gospel writers presented Jesus' teaching in different ways.

And when you pray, do not heap up empty phrases as the Gentiles do, for they think that they will be heard for their many words. Do not be like them, for your Father knows what you need before you ask him. Pray then like this: "Our Father in heaven, hallowed be your name. Your kingdom come, your will be done, on earth as it is in heaven. Give us this day our daily bread, and forgive us our debts, as we also have forgiven our debtors. And lead us not into temptation, but deliver us from evil. For if you forgive others their trespasses, your heavenly Father will also forgive you, but if you do not forgive others their trespasses, neither will your Father forgive your trespasses. (Matthew 6.7-15)

And whenever you stand praying, forgive, if you have anything against anyone, so that your Father also who is in heaven may forgive you your trespasses. (Mark 11.25-26)

Now Jesus was praying in a certain place, and when he finished, one of his disciples said to him, "Lord, teach us to pray, as John taught his disciples." And he said to them, "When you pray, say: "Father, hallowed be your name. Your kingdom come. Give us each day our daily bread, and forgive us our sins, for we ourselves forgive everyone who is indebted to us. And lead us not into temptation." (Luke 11.1-4)

What is immediately striking is that Mark did not present the actual Lord's Prayer, but the other two gospels did. However, Matthew and Luke introduced the prayer differently. In Luke, Jesus taught His disciples to pray in response to their question, but Matthew omitted that request. The actual phrases of the prayers are similar but different.

The question of the synoptic problem is how to explain the similarities in such a way as to also explain the differences. In searching for a solution, a few foundational principles will guide the way.

Jesus Repeated His Teachings

The teaching ministry of Jesus spanned three years and dozens of cities and villages. It is quite illogical to think that Jesus never repeated the same material. On the other hand, it would be quite logical to think that Jesus had a core message that He shared with each village and synagogue in which He taught. Naturally, while the content of His message remained the same, the presentation of that message would vary from occasion to occasion depending upon the audience.

The different presentations of the same material by the gospel writers may be nothing more than the recordings of different teaching events. After all, how many times did Jesus teach His followers about prayer? In comparison, how many sermons and devotionals will a typical pastor preach on prayer during a three year period?

Two Source Theory

While the fact that Jesus often taught on the same subject might explain the differences between the gospel accounts, it does not explain their word for word similarities. Though a variety of theories have been offered to solve this problem, the two source theory still presents the best explanation.

According to this theory, Mark wrote his gospel first. Both Matthew and Luke had a copy of Mark before them when they researched and wrote their gospels. This explains why over 90% of Mark is contained in both Matthew and Luke. It also explains why Matthew and Luke follow Mark's order.

However, it does not explain the similarities between Matthew and Luke. For instance, why did both Matthew and Luke present the Lord's Prayer when Mark did not? After comparing the common material between Matthew and Luke that is absent from Mark, many scholars believe that both Matthew and Luke had access to another common source. Whether this source was written or oral remains in question.

Because a German scholar was the first to postulate the idea, the German word for source, *quelle,* has been used to designate this possible source. For simplicity, the letter "Q" has been used to identify this missing source.

Of course, both Matthew and Luke added their own material and repackaged both Mark and Q in their gospel. So, the writing of the synoptic gospels might have gone something like this: Mark wrote his gospel first. Matthew used Mark, Q, his own experiences, and his own research to craft his gospel. Luke used Mark, Q, and his own research to craft his gospel. This helps to explain the similarities as well as their distinctive characteristics.

Challenging the Jesus Story

"Who was this man called Jesus?" The answer to this question has changed the world. More importantly, the question itself has mobilized the forces of hell to stop the spread of this incredible story.

Not surprisingly, one of the tactics that the opponents to the gospel story have used to stop it has been lies. From the beginning, those who did not believe in Jesus as the Messiah spread lies about the events of His life to keep others from putting their faith in the person of Jesus. Even on resurrection morning, the chief priests and elders of the Jewish faith devised a plan to explain away the empty tomb. They instructed the soldiers to say,

"His disciples came by night and stole him away while we were asleep."
They bribed the soldiers, and "this story has been spread among the Jews
to this day." (Matthew 28.12-15)

Two thousand years later, the story of Jesus is still questioned, both from those outside of the Christian faith and also from those within the Christian faith. Any reader of the Bible needs to be aware of at least some of the primary ways that the story of Jesus has been and still is being questioned today.

Pseudo Gospels

I remember the first time that I heard that the four gospels of the New Testament were not the only written accounts of the life of Jesus. Initially, I was shocked and felt betrayed, like some great secret of the church had been revealed. Once the initial shock wore off, the existence of other "gospel" stories really made sense.

Just like the priests and elders at the empty tomb circulated false stories about the empty tomb, the Enemy tried to spread other lies about this Jesus. Scholars call these false stories about the life of Christ, "pseudo gospels." The most famous are *The Gospel of Thomas*, *The Gospel of Peter*, and *The Gospel of Judas*.

These and other pseudo-gospels contain fanciful stories from Jesus' childhood where he cursed his playmates who disagreed with Him and the like. Some of their material is innocuous, but much of it is unorthodox. This is why the early church rejected them and did not include them in the canonical Scriptures.

Jesus Seminar

Another attempt to cast doubt on the Jesus story has come from within the camp of Christian scholars. In 1985, a scholar named Robert Funk gathered about 100 biblical scholars with the goal of determining exactly what the historical Jesus did or did not say or do.

To decide, each of the scholars brought their years of research and knowledge to the room. They were each given four colored beads. They examined the reported words of Jesus in each of the gospel accounts, and each scholar cast in one of their beads as to their opinion of the historicity of each word. If they thought that Jesus did say that word, they tossed in a red bead. If they thought Jesus probably said something like that word, they tossed in a pink bead. If they thought Jesus did not say that word but the passage does contain the ideas of Jesus, they tossed in a grey bead. If they thought that Jesus did not say the word and the passage was the product of later admirers or even a different religious tradition, they tossed in a black bead.

Or, to put in another way: red (that's Jesus), pink (sounds like Jesus), grey (well, maybe), black (there's been some mistake).

When the beads were counted, the highest number of beads would win (with a weighted scoring system). Afterwards, a color coded Jesus Seminar edition of the gospels was published in *The Five Gospels: What Did Jesus Really Say*. For instance, the only "red" words in their version of the Lord's Prayer are "our Father."

The same scholars have done the same with the acts of Jesus, and have tried to create much doubt as to the historicity of the biblical Jesus. It should come as no surprise that the god of this world would spread such disinformation within the church to try to persuade people to disbelieve in the person of Jesus.

Demythologizing the New Testament

One of the most influential New Testament scholars was Rudolf Bultmann. Despite many positive additions to the field of biblical scholarship, he also presented the idea of demythologizing the New Testament, particularly the story of Jesus. According to Bultmann, the basic message of Jesus, what he called the *kerygma*, was couched in mythological terms by His followers. The important task is to demythologize the *kerygma* to arrive at the core message of the Christ.

Because of the highly subjective nature of this task, one's presuppositions determine what must be stripped away. Therefore, since the scholastic community has been a slave of the enlightenment for decades, anything supernatural that could not be explained through the scientific method was stripped away from the *kerygma*. So, the miracle stories and the casting out of demons was questioned. Some scholars went so far as to question the resurrection and the incarnation. The answer to "Who is this Jesus" was reduced to little more than just a good teacher.

But the supernatural was more than just the packaging of the gospel message. The gospel itself is a supernatural story, with the God of creation becoming flesh and dwelling among mankind. The resurrection was a supernatural event, but even more importantly, every salvation is a supernatural event where a soul is brought to new life in Christ through the regenerating work of the Spirit of God. To strip away the supernatural from the gospel is to deplete the gospel of its essence, which is a supernatural Savior.

The Story of Jesus

But enough of how different people have tried to twist or deny the story of Jesus. Let's look at the story of Jesus as told by the gospel writers. It would be impossible to give an introduction to the gospels in a single book surveying the entire Bible, but a few significant aspects of the gospels need to be addressed.

Incarnation

With the exception of Mark, all of the gospel stories begin with an examination of how Jesus came into the world. Matthew wrote of the angel coming to Joseph in a dream and with the visit of the Magi. Luke told of the angel visiting Zechariah, Mary, and the shepherds. But, it is John who gave the theology behind the birth of Christ.

In the beginning was the Word, and the Word was with God, and the Word was God. He was in the beginning with God. All things were made through him, and without him was not any thing made that was made. In him was life, and the life was the light of men. The light shines in the darkness, and the darkness has not overcome it. There was a man sent from God, whose name was John. He came as a witness, to bear witness about the light, that all might believe through him. He was not the light, but came to bear witness about the light. The true light, which enlightens everyone, was coming into the world. He was in the world, and the world was made through him, yet the world did not know him. He came to his own, and his own people did not receive him. But to all who did receive him, who believed in his name, he gave the right to become children of

God, who were born, not of blood nor of the will of the flesh nor of the will of man, but of God. And the Word became flesh and dwelt among us, and we have seen his glory, glory as of the only Son from the Father, full of grace and truth. (John 1.1-14)

What happened on that "Christmas" morning? The Word became flesh and dwelt among us.

The miracle of the incarnation is the most amazing miracle story contained in the entire Bible, more amazing than the crossing of the Red Sea, more amazing than the ax head floating on the water, more amazing than raising Lazarus from the dead, and, with all due respect, even more amazing than the resurrection. How amazing that the God of all creation would enter His own creation in the form of a human, in humility.

How did this happen? Christians throughout the ages have argued this. What was the exact nature of the union of His divinity and His humanity? The truth is that all of this is far too wonderful for us to comprehend. It is a miracle that we accept in faith.

Miracles

Of course, if the miracle of creation and the miracle of the incarnation can be accepted as historical fact, then the miracles of Jesus are really nothing at all. If God can speak and light came into being, then restoring the sight of a man born blind is child's play. But, more important than the acceptance of the miracles as historical is to understand the role of the miracle stories in the gospel narratives. The miracles were signs giving evidence to the nature of Jesus.

Now Jesus did many other signs in the presence of the disciples, which are not written in this book; but these are written so that you may believe that Jesus is the Christ, the Son of God, and that by believing you may have life in his name. (John 20.30-31)

Unfortunately, while they sometimes led people to faith, they most often did not. In fact, many times, the miraculous actions of Jesus were more stumbling blocks than stepping stones to faith. Like the miraculous period of the exodus, the miraculous period of the life of Christ actually bred rebellion rather than faith. Even though people demanded a sign, and the most wonderful sign of all was given to them (the sign of Jonah, the resurrection), they still refused to believe. As Jesus said, "Blessed are those who have not seen and yet have believed" (John 20.29).

Parables

Jesus often used parables to teach His disciples. While they are simple and beautiful stories, they are far from simple to understand. Some have called them "earthly stories with a heavenly meaning," but this is too easy of a summary. Most biblical scholars insist that each parable has only one meaning. Surely, this is a reaction to the many in church history who have treated the parables as allegories. Allegories are symbolic stories where each element of the story stands for something else.

The best known allegorical treatment of a parable is Augustine's explanation of the Parable of the Good Samaritan.

> *A certain man went down from Jerusalem to Jericho; Adam himself is meant; **Jerusalem** is the heavenly city of peace, from whose blessedness Adam fell; **Jericho** means the moon, and signifies our mortality, because it is born, waxes, wanes, and dies. **Thieves** are the devil and his angels. **Who stripped him**, namely, of his immortality; and **beat him**, by persuading him to sin; and **left him half-dead**, because in so far as man can understand and know God, he lives, but in so far as he is wasted and oppressed by sin, he is dead; he is therefore called, **half-dead**. The **priest** and **Levite** who saw him and passed by, signify the priesthood and the ministry of the Old Testament which could profit nothing for salvation. **Samaritan** means Guardian, and therefore the Lord Himself is signified by this name. The **binding of the wounds** is the restraint of sin. **Oil** is the comfort of the good hope; **wine** the exhortation to work with fervent spirit. The **beast** is the flesh in which he deigned to come to us. The **being** set upon the beast is belief in the incarnation of Christ. The **inn** is the church, where travelers returning to their heavenly country are refreshed after pilgrimage. The **morrow** is after the resurrection of the Lord. The **two pence** are either the two precepts of live, or the promise of this life and that which is to come. The **innkeeper** is the Apostle (Paul). The supererogatory payment is either his counsel of celibacy, or the fact that he worked with his own hands lest he should be a burden to any of the*

weaker brethren when the Gospel was new, though it was lawful for
him "to live by the Gospel" [from Questions Evangeliorum, *II, 19].*

As you can see, the problem with allegorizing the parables is that the point is often missed. Because the allegories can take such fanciful directions, they very quickly lose their moorings to their contexts. In reaction, biblical scholars insist that parables have one main point.

While this is a good principle to follow, it must be observed that Jesus Himself did not follow it. In fact, on only two occasions did Jesus interpret His own parables: the Parable of the Soils and the Parable of the Weeds. In both instances, He allegorized the story with each element of the story standing for something else. Sure, it can be said that Jesus can take liberties that an ordinary Bible student cannot. However, it is difficult to rule out a way of reading the Bible as "never allowable" when Jesus Himself used it.

Regardless, the primary key to understanding the parables of Jesus is the context. Why did Jesus tell the story? Was He asked a question and then told the parable in response? Did He observe something and tell the story in response? How did the gospel writer arrange the presentation of the parable? Careful attention to these questions will lead the Bible student to the right interpretation.

Resurrection

One final issue from the gospels needs our attention. The life of Christ would mean nothing without the death and resurrection of Christ. In fact, Paul taught that if Jesus lived and taught everything that He did, and even died on the cross for our sins, but was not raised from the dead, then our faith is in vain and we are still in our sins (see 1 Corinthians 15.17). It was the resurrection that finished the work of redemption.

It was the resurrection that gave the Christian church the proof it needed to preach Christ as the Messiah. It was not the feeding of the 5000 or the walking on the water that convinced the world about Jesus. It was the resurrection. Paul preached the gospel in the Areopagus in Athens, and he said,

God has fixed a day on which he will judge the world in righteousness by a man whom he has appointed; and of this he has given assurance to all by raising him from the dead. (Acts 17.31)

The proof of the Christian faith is the resurrection.

But how can the resurrection be proved today, over two thousand years later? Can it be believed? Is it historical and factual? How can that question be answered?

Any historical event, whether it happened last week or two thousand years ago, can be proven using the same basic formula: eyewitness testimony, physical evidence, and the ripple effect.

For instance, how do we know that the Japanese army attacked Pearl Harbor on December 7, 1941? First, there were many people there who witnessed firsthand the attack. Many of those soldiers and civilians are still alive today, and they can give vivid accounts of that Sunday morning. Some of the eyewitnesses have passed on, but they have written down their memories in journals or in letters to their families.

Another way that we can believe in the historicity of the Pearl Harbor attack is the physical evidence. Many pictures were taken of that day, hundreds were killed, and a large portion of the United States naval forces were either damaged or destroyed. In fact, one can still visit the USS Arizona Memorial that sits over the sunken remains of one vessel. The physical evidence abounds.

But there is still another type of evidence that is compelling. As the war in Europe raged on, the United States debated their role. Some insisted that the United States should get involved and stop the expanding German army. Others insisted that the war was a European issue and that the United States should stay out of it. The bombing of Pearl Harbor was the straw that broke the camel's back. The events of that morning compelled an entire nation into World War II. Because of that event, American history, and world history, was changed forever. It rippled and changed things forever.

Can these three criteria of evidence be applied to the resurrection? Of course. First, there is massive eyewitness evidence to the resurrected Jesus. After a very public and highly publicized death, Jesus appeared alive to more than 500 people at one time, not to mention all of the private post-resurrection appearances during the forty days after His death. The most startling thing about these appearances was that He appeared in Jerusalem, the same place as His crucifixion. The same people who saw Him die, saw Him alive.

The undeniable physical evidence is the empty tomb. The easiest way for the Jews to defeat this upstart religious movement was to produce the body of Jesus. It would have ended any hope of the new church, but the Jewish leaders were powerless to do so.

Many theories have been presented to explain the empty tomb. Some have suggested that Jesus did not die on the cross; He only passed out. In the cool of the tomb, He regained consciousness and returned to "life" though He was never dead. This is called the "swoon theory."

This theory requires us to believe that the centurions, experts in crucifixion, buried a half dead man. In addition, this half dead man would be able to roll a stone away from the opening of the grave and overpower a team of guards. Then, the half dead man appeared to hundreds of people and convinced them of a resurrection.

From the beginning, the Jews told others that the disciples stole the body from the tomb. This idea is more plausible than the swoon theory, but it does not explain the resurrection appearances. And, it does not explain the ripple effect.

The resurrection of Jesus changed the world. It turned a group of fearful fishermen into a courageous group of disciples willing to die for their belief in the resurrection. While one crazy person might be willing to die, it would be hard for twelve men and many others to be willing to face that consequence. The disciples were so changed by the resurrection experience that they traveled the world telling of His resurrection.

When we look at the eyewitness evidence, the physical evidence, and the ripple effect, the resurrection remains an undeniable historical fact.

Conclusion

The entire Bible points to the story told in the four gospels. The law led people to Christ, and the church pointed people back to Christ. Christ was the answer to sin and the answer to a sin ravaged creation. The rest of the Bible will focus on telling others about this Jesus and teaching others to obey everything He commanded them.

Making It Profitable

Daily Bible Readings

Any Scripture reading plan must include a regular diet of the gospels. So this week, I want to stretch you in your daily Bible reading. I want to challenge you to read the entire book of Mark this week. The gospel of Mark is sixteen chapters long. And while that sounds long, the average reader could sit down and read the entire gospel in less than thirty minutes.

But the goal is not to finish the gospel quickly, but for the gospel to become profitable to you. The readings this week will be longer, but you will be reading a story and it will come quickly. Be looking for those Scriptures that jump off the page. Be looking for those Scriptures that the Spirit draws your attention to. In your journal, make some observations about the life of Christ. Spend time in prayer seeking the Lord to explain to you have this truth applies to your life.

Suggested Scripture Memory Verses

In the beginning was the Word, and the Word was with God, and the Word was God. He was in the beginning with God. All things were made through him, and without him was not any thing made that was made. In him was life, and the life was the light of men. (John 1.1-4)

And when Jesus heard it, he said to them, "Those who are well have no need of a physician, but those who are sick. I came not to call the righteous, but sinners." (Mark 2.17)

Fear not, little flock, for it is your Father's good pleasure to give you the kingdom. Sell your possessions, and give to the needy. Provide yourselves with moneybags that do not grow old, with a treasure in the heavens that does not fail, where no thief approaches and no moth destroys. For where your treasure is, there will your heart be also. (Luke 12.32-34)

For the Son of Man came to seek and to save the lost. (Luke 19.10)

Jesus said to them, "I am the bread of life; whoever comes to me shall not hunger, and whoever believes in me shall never thirst. (John 6.35)

The thief comes only to steal and kill and destroy. I came that they may have life and have it abundantly. (John 10.10)

I am the vine; you are the branches. Whoever abides in me and I in him, he it is that bears much fruit, for apart from me you can do nothing. (John 15.5)

If you abide in me, and my words abide in you, ask whatever you wish, and it will be done for you. (John 15.7)

Nevertheless, I tell you the truth: it is to your advantage that I go away, for if I do not go away, the Helper will not come to you. But if I go, I will send him to you. And when he comes, he will convict the world concerning sin and righteousness and judgment: concerning sin, because they do not believe in me; concerning righteousness, because I go to the Father, and you will see me no longer; concerning judgment, because the ruler of this world is judged. (John 16.7-11)

For God so loved the world, that he gave his only Son, that whoever believes in him should not perish but have eternal life. (John 3.16)

And Jesus came and said to them, "All authority in heaven and on earth has been given to me. Go therefore and make disciples of all nations, baptizing them in the name of the Father and of the Son and of the Holy Spirit, teaching them to observe all that I have commanded you. And behold, I am with you always, to the end of the age." (Matthew 28.18-20)

But I say to you who hear, Love your enemies, do good to those who hate you, bless those who curse you, pray for those who abuse you. (Luke 6.27-28)

Day One: Mark 1-3

S:

_____

_____

_____

_____

_____

_____

_____

O:

_____

_____

_____

_____

_____

_____

_____

A:

_____

_____

_____

_____

_____

_____

_____

P:

_____

_____

_____

_____

_____

_____

_____

Day Two: Mark 4-5

S:

_____

_____

_____

_____

_____

_____

_____

_____

O:

_____

_____

_____

_____

_____

_____

_____

A:

_____

_____

_____

_____

_____

_____

_____

P:

_____

_____

_____

_____

_____

_____

_____

Day Three: Mark 6-8

_S:_ _____
_____
_____
_____
_____
_____
_____
_____

_O:_ _____
_____
_____
_____
_____
_____
_____
_____

_A:_ _____
_____
_____
_____
_____
_____
_____
_____

_P:_ _____
_____
_____
_____
_____
_____
_____
_____

Day Four: Mark 9-11

_S:_
_____
_____
_____
_____
_____
_____
_____

_O:_
_____
_____
_____
_____
_____
_____
_____

_A:_
_____
_____
_____
_____
_____
_____
_____

_P:_
_____
_____
_____
_____
_____
_____
_____

Day Five: Mark 12-13

_S:_ _____

_____

_____

_____

_____

_____

_____

_O:_ _____

_____

_____

_____

_____

_____

_____

_A:_ _____

_____

_____

_____

_____

_____

_____

_P:_ _____

_____

_____

_____

_____

_____

_____

Day Six: Mark 14-16

_S:_

_O:_

_A:_

_P:_

The fulfillment of the entire Old Testament, the Lamb of God, the Messiah, the Anointed One, had just returned to heaven. Naturally, the disciples were standing around and watching the Lord as He ascended to the sky. The question in everyone's mind? "What now? If this was the Messiah, and if He has returned to the Father, what does He want us to be doing? Is He coming back? What now?"

As they were gazing into the heavens, two angels told them that Jesus would return one day in the same way that He left. In the mean time, they were to carry out the Lord's last instructions.

> But you will receive power when the Holy Spirit has come upon you, and you will be my witnesses in Jerusalem and in all Judea and Samaria, and to the end of the earth. (Acts 1.8)

But before they were to get busy telling the world about the Messiah, they were to return to Jerusalem and wait to be "clothed with power from on high" (Luke 24.49).

The book of Acts is often called "The Acts of the Apostles" because it records the actions of the apostles (and other disciples) after the ascension of the Lord. However, that name is a little misleading. A better title would be, "The Acts of the Spirit Through the Apostles" for that is exactly what the book of Acts is about. It tells of the spread of the Christian faith from Jerusalem to the ends of the earth. It tells of the birth of the church, and it tells of the beginning of the mission's movement. But more than anything, it tells the story of the power of God's Spirit in the new covenant age.

Peter (Acts 1-12)

The book of Acts centers around two key figures and the events that accompanied their lives: Peter and Saul, whose name will later be changed to Paul. Peter's section begins with the wonderful events of Pentecost.

Pentecost

The festival of Pentecost, literally "fiftieth," was celebrated on the fiftieth day from the second day of Passover. The festival was first described in Exodus 23.16 as the Feast of Harvest and also in Exodus 34.22 as the Day of the Firstfruits. The most distinguishing aspect of Pentecost is that it would be the first major sacred assembly after the Passover, after the resurrection of Jesus. With all of Jerusalem assembled in one place, the gift of the Spirit was given.

Jesus had tried to tell His disciples about the coming Spirit, but I am sure they did not comprehend its full meaning. On another feast day, Jesus said,

> On the last day of the feast, the great day, Jesus stood up and cried out, "If anyone thirsts, let him come to me and drink. Whoever believes in me, as the Scripture has said, 'Out of his heart will flow rivers of living water.'" Now this he said about the Spirit, whom those who believed in him were to receive, for as yet the Spirit had not been given, because Jesus was not yet glorified. (John 7.37-39)

The Spirit that the disciples later received was streams of living water for all who would believe. It would give life to the soul, and it would quench the soul's thirst. So many times, the Lord spoke of the coming Spirit. Once, in the midst of their sadness and grief after hearing of His impending death, He told them,

> Nevertheless, I tell you the truth: it is to your advantage that I go away, for if I do not go away, the Helper will not come to you. But if I go, I will send him to you. And when he comes, he will convict the world concerning sin and righteousness and judgment: concerning sin, because they do not believe in me; concerning righteousness, because I go to the Father, and you will see me no longer; concerning judgment, because the ruler of this world is judged. (John 16.7-11)

In many ways, the story of the church is the ongoing story of a group of believers growing in their understanding of life in the Spirit. Their entire religious orientation had changed. Before, they were living in the power of the flesh trying to obey the rules of God. Religion was working for God, working to please God, and working to gain His forgiveness.

But now, all of that had changed. Now, with the indwelling Spirit of God, they had become new creations. They were no longer working to gain God's good favor. God's good favor had been given through the atoning death of Jesus. They were no longer trying to work for God. Instead, God was working through them. It would take time for the young church to grasp all of this, just like it takes a lifetime for believers to grasp it today.

There can be no greater moment in the biblical story than the resurrection, but the Pentecost event comes in at a close second. The followers of Jesus, including the apostles and the women who followed Jesus, gathered in an upstairs room, waiting as the Lord had told them to do. They were in constant prayer, and then, on the day of Pentecost, it happened.

> *And suddenly there came from heaven a sound like a mighty rushing wind, and it filled the entire house where they were sitting. And divided tongues as of fire appeared to them and rested on each one of them. And they were all filled with the Holy Spirit and began to speak in other tongues as the Spirit gave them utterance. (Acts 2.2-4)*

So much happened in that one moment. They were each filled with the Spirit and began to speak in other tongues. They began to declare the wonders of God to all of the multinational crowd gathered for Pentecost, and miraculously, everyone could hear them speaking in their own language. Naturally, they asked, "What do these things mean?"

Peter stood before the crowd and delivered one of the greatest sermons in the entire Bible. Though the crowd thought the babbling was the result of too much early drinking, Peter explained that it was the fulfillment of Joel's prophecy: "In the last days…I will pour out my Spirit" (Acts 2.17). Then, he shared the basic gospel story to a very interested crowd.

Peter reminded everyone of the miracles and wonders that Jesus did in their presence and of His horrible death on the cross. He also reminded them that

God raised Jesus back to life and that they were all witnesses to that fact. And now that Jesus had returned to the Father, the promised Holy Spirit was poured out on His people. Now, all Israel can be assured: Jesus is both Lord and the Christ (Messiah).

The crowds were overwhelmed by Peter's sermon, but more importantly, they were overwhelmed by what they themselves had experienced. They witnessed the miracles of Jesus. They witnessed the crucifixion of Jesus, and they witnessed a living Jesus only a few days later. Peter connected the dots and laid it out in simple terms. All of these things pointed to the fact that Jesus was the Messiah, the Christ. With that obvious truth before them, the people cried out, "What shall we do?" (Acts 2.38).

Peter's answer summed up the gospel message: repent from sins, be baptized in the name of Jesus Christ for the forgiveness of sins (which is a confession of Jesus as the Messiah), and receive the Holy Spirit. The offer was good for anyone and everyone who would call upon the name of Jesus. About 3000 people accepted the message of Peter and were added to the number of disciples.

And the church was born.

Simon was one of the first disciples to confess his belief in Jesus as the Christ. As a result, Jesus changed his name to Peter and promised, "On this rock, I will build my church" (Matthew 16.18). Peter became the key leader in Jerusalem as the movement of Christ followers began to share the message boldly.

Several key events in the life of Peter set up the conflict that the church would experience as the gospel message spilled over from Jerusalem. The first major section of the book of Acts is devoted to the story of Peter and the events of his life (chapters 1-12).

The Beggar at the Temple Gate

After the incredible sermon on Pentecost, the new group of Christ followers gathered around the disciples to hear more about Jesus. They shared meals in each other's homes, and they gathered in the Temple courts to discuss the fulfillment of the Jewish faith.

While we look back on this moment as the "birth of the church," we need to remember that the disciples were not starting a new religious movement. They were not seeking converts to their new religion. They were simply preaching Jesus as the fulfillment of their Jewish faith. The promised Messiah had come. His miracles proved it. His resurrection proved it. The outpouring of the Spirit proved it. Jesus was the Messiah, and there was no reason not to preach the gospel message in the Temple courts because the whole of the law and prophets pointed to Jesus.

So, one day, Peter and John were on their way to the Temple to talk about Jesus when they met a beggar who asked for money. Instead of money, Peter healed the man in the name of Jesus Christ. The man began to dance in the Temple courts, and the crowd was amazed. Peter took this opportunity to present the gospel message again.

> *Men of Israel, why do you wonder at this, or why do you stare at us, as though by our own power or piety we have made him walk? The God of Abraham, the God of Isaac, and the God of Jacob, the God of our fathers, glorified his servant Jesus, whom you delivered over and denied in the presence of Pilate, when he had decided to release him. But you denied the Holy and Righteous One, and asked for a murderer to be granted to you, and you killed the Author of life, whom God raised from the dead. To this we are witnesses. And his name—by faith in his name—has made this man strong whom you see and know, and the faith that is through Jesus has given the man this perfect health in the presence of you all. And now, brothers, I know that you acted in ignorance, as did also your rulers. But what God foretold by the mouth of all the prophets, that his Christ would suffer, he thus fulfilled. Repent therefore, and turn again, that your sins may be blotted out, that times of refreshing may come from the presence of the Lord, and that he may send the Christ appointed for you, Jesus, whom heaven must receive until the time for restoring all the things about which God spoke by the mouth of his holy prophets long ago. (Acts 3.12-21)*

When the priests and other key Jewish leaders heard Peter speaking of Jesus as the Christ, along with the resurrection of the dead, they seized Peter and John and put them in jail. On the next day, all of the Jewish leaders convened to judge the case. They asked Peter and John, "By what power or by what name did you do this?" (Acts 4.7).

Peter preached the message of Jesus. Once again, he referenced the resurrection as the proof of Jesus as the Christ. There was no other name under heaven by which men must be saved. They insisted that Peter and John and the rest stop speaking or teaching about Jesus. However, Peter and John and the rest of the disciples counted it a privilege to suffer for Jesus, and they asked the Lord to help them share the gospel with more boldness.

Ananias and Sapphira

The story of Ananias and Sapphira might seem like an intrusion on the story line. In chapter three, Peter and John spoke about Jesus and were arrested. They were tried and released in chapter four, and in chapter five they will be arrested again for refusing to stop speaking in the name of Jesus. But, before their second arrest, Luke tells the readers the story of Ananias and Sapphira.

The disciples were living together with all things in common. They shared their resources, and there was no needy person among them. Some even sold their land or homes and brought the money to the apostles to be used to meet the needs of others. Ananias and Sapphira did this, but with a wicked twist. They sold the property, withheld a portion, and brought it to the apostles. The implication is that they claimed to bring the whole portion. Peter accused him and his wife of lying against the Holy Spirit, and they both died instantly for their guilt.

Because of this and many other miraculous signs and wonders, the people highly regarded the apostles and listened to them as teachers with authority. Because of the power of God flowing through them, they were able to both attract and instruct many people in the way of Christ.

Their teaching, and their teaching alone, was the standard of orthodoxy regarding the Christ. The people gathered and devoted themselves to the apostle's teachings, and those teaching were the orthodox gospel and the standard of truth in the church. The wonders and miracles both confirmed their message and their role as spokesmen for the Christ.

Back in Prison

Since the apostles refused to stop preaching in the name of Jesus, the Jewish leaders arrested them again and put them in the public jail. However, an angel of the Lord opened the doors of the jail and set them free. They returned to the Temple courts and continued to preach about new life in Christ.

Brought back before the religious leaders, Peter and John repeated the same message.

The God of our fathers raised Jesus, whom you killed by hanging him on a tree. God exalted him at his right hand as Leader and Savior, to give repentance to Israel and forgiveness of sins. (Acts 5.30-31)

At the trial, a Pharisee by the name of Gamaliel counseled the Sanhedrin to leave Peter and John alone.

So in the present case I tell you, keep away from these men and let them alone, for if this plan or this undertaking is of man, it will fail; but if it is of God, you will not be able to overthrow them. You might even be found opposing God! (Acts 5.38-39)

The council was persuaded by his speech, and they let Peter and John go free. The prophetic word sets up the remainder of the book of Acts as God demonstrated that the gospel was not from human origin but from God.

The Consistent Message of Peter

At each major event in Peter's life, Peter preached a consistent message: the resurrection of Jesus proved that Jesus was the Christ. He preached that message at his Pentecost, when asked about the healing of the beggar, when before the Sanhedrin the first time, and at the second trial before the Jewish religious leaders. The Jewish leaders were never able to defeat this basic truth: the people in Jerusalem had witnesses a living Jesus after a very public death, and the implications of that fact were disturbing the peace.

The Interlude of Stephen, Philip, and Saul

Stephen (Acts 6-7)

The story of Peter is put on pause while three other figures break on the scene. The first was Stephen, one of the seven who were chosen to help the apostles in the distribution of food to the widows. He was full of God's grace and power and did great wonders and signs among the people. As he spoke about Jesus in the synagogue, the synagogue leaders stirred up the people against him. Accused of speaking against the holy place of the synagogue and changing the customs of Moses, he delivered one of the greatest sermons in the entire Bible.

Stephen traced the story of God's relationship with His people from Abraham to Jesus. He described the life of Abraham, Joseph, Moses, David, and Solomon. He then accused the Jewish leaders of always resisting the Holy Spirit and of killing the Righteous One who was to come (the Messiah). While that infuriated the Jewish leaders, it was the vision of seeing Jesus standing at the right hand of God that caused them to stone Stephen to death.

The religious leaders were still trying, and still unable, to stop this uncontrollable teaching that Jesus was the Messiah and that His resurrection proved it.

Philip (Acts 8)

With the stoning of Stephen, a great persecution arose against the church in Jerusalem. It became acceptable to physically persecute those who accepted Jesus as the Messiah. Because of this great persecution, all of the Christ followers were scattered throughout Judea and Samaria. Men and women who trusted in Jesus as the Messiah were being arrested and put into prison.

It should be noted that, by chapter eight, all of the apostles and disciples were still in Jerusalem. Jesus told them to be His witnesses in Jerusalem, Judea, Samaria, and to the ends of the earth. How did God get them out of Jerusalem? Through a great persecution. Often, the Lord must use pain to get His people to obey. Sometimes, the hardest journey is going from God's good to God's best.

Philip, another one of the seven chosen in Acts 6, traveled to Samaria and preached Christ. Miraculous signs also accompanied his message. An angel of the Lord told Philip to travel on a road that led to Gaza. On the way, he met an official in the Queen of Ethiopia's court. He was reading from the prophet Isaiah in his chariot, but he did not understand what he was reading. The Spirit told Philip to approach the chariot.

Peter asked, "Do you understand what you are reading?" "How can I," he said, "unless someone guides me" (Acts 8.30-31). Philip explained that Isaiah was speaking of the Messiah as a sheep led to the slaughter. Then, Philip told the man about Jesus. He believed and was immediately baptized. Then, the Spirit of God took Philip away.

Saul (Acts 9)

At the death of Stephen, Saul held the coats of the men as they cast the stones. Saul was the one who was arresting Christians and putting them in jail, resulting in the scattering of the disciples. And now, this same Saul was on the way to Damascus, a city outside of Samaria, indicating that the gospel was on its way to the ends of the earth. Saul had with him letters to the synagogues instructing them to imprison any men or women who belonged to the Way (one of the early nicknames for Christians). However, Saul had a life changing experience along the way.

On the road to Damascus, the resurrected and glorified Jesus met Saul face to face. A bright light surrounded Saul and the traveling party, and a voice said to him, "Saul, Saul, why are you persecuting me?" "Who are you Lord?" Saul asked. "I am Jesus, whom you are persecuting" (Acts 9.4-5). Without a doubt, this was a life changing experience. He would share his testimony twice in the latter part of Acts (Acts 22.3-16 and 26.9-18).

The Lord appointed Ananias, a disciple, to welcome the blinded Saul. He was to lay his hands upon Saul that he might regain his sight and be filled with the Holy Spirit. Miraculously, this man who left Jerusalem with papers to arrest believers was now preaching in the synagogues of Damascus that Jesus was the

Son of God. In a strange twist of fate, the Jews plotted to kill Saul to silence his powerful and baffling preaching, but the disciples helped him escape.

Cornelius

With the introduction of two major themes (the gospel spreading outside of Jerusalem and the introduction of Saul), the story returns to Peter. The single most important event in the book of Acts will be the focus of the remaining section regarding Peter in Acts.

Cornelius, a gentile centurion, was a God-fearer in Caesarea. A God-fearer was one who worshipped the Jewish God but had not taken the steps to fully convert to Judaism. He was devout and a man of prayer. One day, he had a vision. An angel told him to send a man to Joppa to bring Peter back to his house.

While the men were in route, Peter also had a vision. He saw something like a large sheet being let down to earth with all kinds of animals, both clean and unclean (according to the Jewish dietary code). A voice told Peter to "kill and eat" (Acts 10.13). Peter refused because he had never eaten anything unclean, but the voice said to him, "What God has made clean, do not call common" (Acts 10.15). While Peter was contemplating the meaning of the vision, the men from Cornelius' house arrived.

When Peter arrived at Cornelius' house, Peter shared the gospel message (complete with the resurrection of Jesus). And while Peter was still speaking, the Holy Spirit came upon all who heard the message. What Peter observed would become the most perplexing problem for the early church.

> And the believers from among the circumcised who had come with Peter were amazed, because the gift of the Holy Spirit was poured out even on the Gentiles. For they were hearing them speaking in tongues and extolling God. Then Peter declared, "Can anyone withhold water for baptizing these people, who have received the Holy Spirit just as we have?" And he commanded them to be baptized in the name of Jesus Christ. Then they asked him to remain for some days. (Acts 10.45-48)

Essentially, Peter asked, "How can we not baptize these Gentiles? They have obviously been saved because they have received the Spirit." So, they were baptized in the name of Jesus. The evidence of a person being a follower of

Christ was the presence of the Spirit, and even these Gentiles had received the Spirit.

When the news reached Jerusalem that the Gentiles had received the word of God, Peter was in trouble with the other Christians. Up until that moment, the Christian movement was a Jewish movement. Salvation had come to the Jews, the people of God. If you wanted to get in on the salvation of God, then you needed to become a Jew. But now, the Gentiles were responding to the gospel.

Peter explained to the disciples in Jerusalem about his vision and his conversation with Cornelius. Peter said,

> *If then God gave the same gift to them as he gave to us when we believed in the Lord Jesus Christ, who was I that I could stand in God's way? (Acts 11.17)*

The other Christians agreed, and they praised God because He had granted even Gentiles repentance unto life.

The Peter section ends with another arrest and another miraculous deliverance from prison.

Paul (13-28)

In Act 13, the main character of the story shifts from Simon Peter to Saul, also called Paul. Saul was introduced in Acts 9, and now he takes center stage.

During a prayer meeting in Antioch, the Spirit set apart Saul (whose name will be changed to Paul in Acts 13.9) and Barnabas to be missionaries, to carry the name of Christ to the Gentiles. This is the first of what is popularly called the "Three Missionary Journeys of Paul." The first trip is described in Acts 13.1-14.27, the second journey in Acts 15.39 – 18.22, and the third journey in Acts 18.23 – 21.16.

Space does not permit a detailed account of every stop in each of his missionary journeys. In the back of many Bibles, you can find color coded maps showing the path of each missionary trip. While it might not be important to memorize the itinerary of each journey, it is important to understand the link between the book of Acts and the letters of Paul.

The book of Acts tells of Paul spreading the gospel to the churches in Galatia, Thessalonica, Ephesus, Corinth, and many others. The reader of the Bible will want to read these historical accounts when studying Paul's letters to these churches. A more detailed look at each city and church will be reserved for the next chapter.

Of course, each of the cities Paul visited were important, but a few of them are more notable than others. For instance, in Athens, Paul delivered his speech about the "unknown God" to the Areopagus (Acts 17.16-34). In Ephesus, Paul's preaching caused a counter riot by the businessmen associated with the false god, Artemis of the Ephesians (Acts 19.1-40). Furthermore, one of the most heartfelt and moving farewells takes place between Paul and the elders of the Ephesian church when they learn that they will never see Paul again (Acts 20.13-38).

The Interlude of the Jerusalem Council

Just like Peter's section was interrupted with an interlude, so is Paul's section. After the conclusion of the first missionary journey's narrative, the church dealt head on with its first crisis.

> But some men came down from Judea and were teaching the brothers, "Unless you are circumcised according to the custom of Moses, you cannot be saved." (Acts 15.1)

Remember, the Christian movement was a Jewish movement. Jesus was the fulfillment of the Jewish faith. He was the Messiah. So, naturally, the Jews who believed in Jesus thought the way to salvation was through the Jewish faith, circumcision and all.

However, the salvation of the uncircumcised Gentiles confused the disciples. They were astonished to see the uncircumcised Gentiles receiving the Spirit and salvation without first becoming Jews. As a result, there were two different brands of Christianity being spread: Paul's version, which did not require a Gentile to become a Jew in order to be saved, and another gospel which did.

This second group is often referred to as the Judaizers. While they believed that Jesus was the Messiah, they still believed that the way to be made right with God was through observing the law. They accepted Jesus as the Messiah but did not understand the new covenant of grace.

Paul and Barnabas and the elders in Jerusalem were in sharp disagreement on this issue, so a meeting was held in Jerusalem to address the issue. This meeting is often referred to as "the Jerusalem Council," though the title was not used by Paul or the elders. At the meeting, Peter again shared his experience with Cornelius. Peter's speech ended with the gospel in its simplicity, "We believe that we will be saved through the grace of the Lord Jesus, just as they will" (Acts 15.11).

With Peter's testimony, the elders in Jerusalem agreed that it was not necessary for Gentiles to become Jews in order to be saved. However, this issue did not disappear from the church. In fact, it is the cause of many of Paul's letters, particularly his letter to the churches in Galatia.

Paul in Jerusalem

Just like his Lord, Paul's life was on a collision course with Jerusalem. With his missionary journeys completed, he was compelled by the Spirit to go to Jerusalem even though he knew that prison and hardships were waiting for him. Paul's time in Jerusalem captivates six of the last eight chapters of the book of Acts. His ministry and purpose was a significant part of the story of the church. Why?

To understand that, we must take a look at what happened in Jerusalem. He was confronted with the reality of the Jerusalem Council's ruling, that he was not teaching Gentiles to become Jews in order to be saved. The Jews felt that Paul was turning his back on the Jewish faith. Though he publicly tried to explain, the people refused to accept it. In fact, the Roman authorities had to step in and restore order in the city. They arrested Paul for his own protection.

As a result, Paul was afforded the unique opportunity to explain himself and the gospel to the Sanhedrin (the Jewish ruling council), Felix (Governor of

Caesarea), Festus (Felix's successor), and King Agrippa. In fact, Paul delivered some of the most powerful sermons at his defense trials. So evangelical was his defense that Agrippa responded to his speech with these words,

> *And Agrippa said to Paul, "In a short time would you persuade me to be a Christian?" And Paul said, "Whether short or long, I would to God that not only you but also all who hear me this day might become such as I am—except for these chains." (Acts 26.28-29)*

In what could only be a divinely orchestrated chain of events, Paul exercised a Roman right during his trial before Festus: he appealed to Caesar. Every Roman citizen had the right to appeal his trial to Caesar, and that appeal had to be honored. Paul's appeal was unnecessary because King Agrippa found no guilt in Paul, but the Lord used that appeal to speak the gospel through Paul to the household of Caesar.

The last two chapters of Acts describe Paul's dangerous journey to Rome and Paul's house arrest in Rome while awaiting trial. The book ends with these open ended words.

> *He lived there two whole years at his own expense, and welcomed all who came to him, proclaiming the kingdom of God and teaching about the Lord Jesus Christ with all boldness and without hindrance. (Acts 28.30-31)*

Luke does not tell us how the story ends. Some have speculated that Luke was planning a third volume. Others have suggested that Luke died before completing the second volume. Whatever the reason, the book of Acts ends with Paul preaching in Rome and waiting for his trial.

Major Themes in Acts

The Church as a Movement

The book of Acts tells of the birth of the church, but the church of today would do well to remember that the church in Acts was a movement, not an organization. Movements are driven by passion and calling and do not allow the structure to limit its vision. Movements are larger than any one person and influence multiple organizations at the same time. There is an increasing effort today to reclaim the movement aspect of the church and to set the church free from the organization that so often stifles the Spirit of God.

The Church as a Legal Religion

Rome had limited religious freedom. Certain religions were recognized by the state, and others were not. The *religio licita* (legal religions) were free to meet and exercise their faith while those not on the list were not.

Much of the opposition to the Christian movement in Acts was focused on trying to get the Roman authorities to label Christianity as an illegal religion. In Philippi, the Christians were accused of advocating customs unlawful for Romans to accept or practice. In Thessalonica, they were accused of advocating another king besides Caesar. In Corinth, they were accused of persuading people to worship God in ways contrary to the Romans law. Paul was accused of stirring up riots all over the world.

However, not a single Roman official found fault with the Christian movement in the book of Acts. Pilate declared Jesus innocent three times in the gospel of Luke. Sergius Paulus, proconsul of Cyprus and an intelligent man, was converted. The magistrates in Philippi apologized to Paul for beating him. The proconsul of Achaia (Corinth), Gallio, judged Paul innocent of any offense against Roman law. The city clerk at Ephesus absolved him of the charge of sacrilege. Felix, Festus, and King Agrippa all found Paul innocent and declared that he could have been set free had he not appealed to Caesar. Finally, the story of Acts ends with Paul speaking freely and unhindered in Rome.

Time and time again, the Christian movement was declared innocent of any behavior that would have threatened the Roman government.

The "We" Sections

Bible readers will notice an interesting element in the narratives of Acts. In four sections, the narrative is told in first person. The narrator became part of the story, a traveling companion of Paul.

These four sections are called the "We Sections" of Acts. They include the travel to and evangelization of Philippi (Acts 16.10-17), the ministry to Troas and travel to Miletus (Acts 20.5-15), the journey from Miletus to Jerusalem (Acts 21.1-18), and the journey from Caesarea to Rome (Acts 27.1-28). Many scholars feel like these were the times when Luke was traveling with Paul.

The Spirit in Acts

The most important theme in the book of Acts is the role and activity of the Spirit within the church and within the new believers. The outline of the book is Acts 1.8, and it gives not only the geographical expansion of the gospel but also the means of the gospel expansion: the Spirit. As the story unfolds, the Spirit saturates it from beginning to end.

The book gives an experiential theology of the Spirit and not a didactic theology. In other words, it presents what the Spirit did but does not always explain what exactly it meant.

The Spirit is mentioned over 47 times in Acts in a variety of settings and with a variety of applications.

- Several times, those who quoted Old Testament Scriptures described them as the words of the Spirit speaking through the writer (1.16, 4.25, and 28.25).

- Luke summarized the story with a description of the church living in the power or fullness of the Spirit (9.31 and 13.52).

- The author described most of the key figures as being filled with the Spirit, including those gathered in the upper room (2.4), Peter (4.8), the seven chosen to care for the widows (6.3), Stephen (6.5), Saul (9.17), and Barnabas (11.24).

- It was the presence of the Spirit that marked a true believer (2.33, 2.38, 5.32, 8.15-17, 10.44-47, 11.12-15, 15.8, and 19.2-6). In fact, it was this overwhelming testimony that caused the Jewish Christians to accept Gentile Christians without requiring them to convert to Judaism.

- When confronted by the opposition, the Spirit enabled the disciples to speak with boldness (4.8, 6.10, 7.55, and 13.9).

- Often, the Spirit prompted or guided the disciples (8.29, 10.19, 11.26, 13.4, 15.26, 16.6-7, 20.22-23, 20.28).

- The Spirit interrupted moments of worship (4.31 and 13.2).

- The Spirit filled the followers of Christ and they spoke in tongues as a result (2.4, 19.6 and 10.46).

- Interestingly enough, only one time was the Spirit associated with miraculous deeds or wonders (8.39).

Speaking in Tongues

On two occasions, possibly three, the Spirit filled a believer and as a result, they spoke in tongues. Since this is outside of the some evangelical traditions, it often causes great interest among some Bible students, but also great anxiety. Therefore, it is important to take a deeper look at these few events.

First, the miracle at Pentecost is one of the three times in Acts where a miracle involving the tongue and the Spirit took place (Acts 2.4). However, what happened at Pentecost was truly unique. In fact, it was more of a miracle of hearing than anything else. People from all over the world heard in their own native language even though the believers were speaking in only one language. So, the miracle was on the hearing end and not on the speaking end.

The second time it happened was during the conversion story of Cornelius (Acts 10.46). While Peter was sharing the gospel message, the Spirit came upon all who heard it, and they began to speak in tongues.

The final time in Acts where believers spoke in tongues took place in Ephesus (Acts 19.6). Paul met some followers of John the Baptist who did not fully understand that John was pointing them to Jesus. Upon receiving the good news of Jesus, they believed. The Spirit came upon them, and they spoke in tongues and prophesied.

All of these events, including the debatable Pentecost experience, happened at crucial transitional moments in the expansion of the gospel. The first miracle enabled Peter to preach to the assembled crowds in Jerusalem. Cornelius' gift confirmed to the Jewish Christians that the Gentiles had been accepted by God. And the conversion of John's disciples to Christianity was another form of the expansion of the gospel.

The key in understanding all of these events lies in the teaching passages in the New Testament. Acts describes what happened, but the epistles explain what believers ought to expect.

Paul's teachings on the gift of speaking in tongues help us to interpret what happened in the book of Acts. First, tongues is still a valid New Testament gift (1 Corinthians 12.28). There is nothing in the Bible that indicates the cessation of this gift after the expansion of the gospel.

Second, not everyone has the gift of speaking in tongues (1 Corinthians 12.30). In fact, Paul encouraged believers to seek the gift of prophecy instead of the gift of speaking in tongues.

Third, tongues is communication from man to God and not from God to man (1 Corinthians 14.2). This means speaking in tongues is a prayer language of sorts.

Finally, the church is not to forbid the speaking in tongues, but when exercised in public, there should be an interpreter present. Absent an interpreter, the one with the gift of tongues is to keep silent in the church and speak to himself and to God (1 Corinthians 14.28).

Despite what we know about tongues, it will always remain a mystery to us. However, the mysterious and miraculous have always been in God's church, and we should not fear it just because we don't understand it. Many great spiritual truths are beyond our understand, and, in fact, counter intuitive.

Second Blessing

A related question regards the timing of the filling of the Spirit. When does the Spirit fill a believer? Some teach that the Spirit fills all believers at conversion. Others teach that there is a "second blessing" or another experience post-conversion where one is filled with the Spirit.

The historical evidence in Acts is divided. Peter promised that all who repented and believed would receive the Spirit in Acts 2.38. The Spirit filled both Cornelius (Acts 10.44) and the disciples of John at Ephesus (Acts 19.6) immediately upon conversion. So, these stories point to an immediate filling of the Spirit at conversion.

However, when the gospel came to Samaria and many responded to the gospel by being baptized in the name of Jesus, the Spirit did not come upon them. The apostles came to Samaria from Jerusalem, prayed for them, and then they received the Spirit (Acts 8.14-17). This is an obvious example of a "second blessing" type of experience.

So, which is to be normative today? Should believers rest in the fact that they have been filled with the Spirit at conversion or should they be seeking a second blessing experience?

Again, the epistles help us understand the historical account of Acts. For starters, there are no teachings in the epistles that encourage believers to receive the Spirit in some kind of second blessing. In fact, the bulk of the evidence is that all believers are indwelled with the Spirit. Paul wrote it simply.

> *You, however, are not in the flesh but in the Spirit, if in fact the Spirit of God dwells in you. Anyone who does not have the Spirit of Christ does not belong to him. (Romans 8.9).*

However, the epistles also teach that believers should "be filled with the Spirit" (Ephesians 5.18).

In summary, the normative Christian experience is that the Spirit indwells every believer at conversion. However, part of the maturing process is allowing the Spirit to fill every part of our heart, mind, body, and soul. So, the correct answer may be a both/and. Both are correct. While we do receive the Spirit at conversion, it is important to pursue a life more filled with the Spirit.

Conclusion

The book of Acts tells us of the expansion of the gospel around the world. It also tells of the work of the Spirit through the people of God. Though it often does not explain what it describes, it does paint vivid pictures of the church filled with the power of God through the indwelling Spirit.

The work of the Spirit is not limited to the first century. The same Spirit of God who indwelled the apostles in Jerusalem is still living today. The letters of the apostles were written to help new believers all over the world know and experience this reality.

Making It Profitable

Daily Bible Readings

The book of Acts is a singularly important portion of the Scriptures. Just like the gospel story, to get the full import of spread of the gospel from Jerusalem to the ends of the earth through the power of the Spirit, we really need to read the entire book of Acts.

So this week, I want to encourage you to go beyond the following daily readings and read the entire book, beginning to end, in one sitting. I know it sounds like a lot of reading, but consider the following. The average adult reads 250 words per minute. At that rate, the first chapter of Acts will take you less than 3 minutes to read. That means I am challenging you to commit to about one hour of reading this week in addition to your daily readings. In exchange for one TV show this week, you can go a long way in your goal to make the Bible profitable to you in your spiritual development.

As you complete your daily readings, continue to do the work of meditating on the Scripture so that you can hear God's voice. You will read of God's mighty acts this week, and you will see some marvelous truths being lived out in the lives of the apostles.

Don't let these truths just pass you by. Capture them in your heart by meditating upon them. Following the SOAP method, be looking for the Scriptures that stand out to you as you read each day. Write down the many things you will observe about how God moved in the early church. Spend some time each day thinking and praying about how these truths apply to you. What is God saying to you today through His Word? And don't forget the most important step of spending time in prayer, dialoguing with God about what He is saying to you.

Suggested Scripture Memory Verses

But you will receive power when the Holy Spirit has come upon you, and you will be my witnesses in Jerusalem and in all Judea and Samaria, and to the end of the earth. (Acts 1.8)

And they devoted themselves to the apostles' teaching and fellowship, to the breaking of bread and the prayers. (Acts 2.42)

This Jesus is the stone that was rejected by you, the builders, which has become the cornerstone. And there is salvation in no one else, for there is no other name under heaven given among men by which we must be saved. (Acts 4.11-12)

But Peter and John answered them, "Whether it is right in the sight of God to listen to you rather than to God, you must judge, for we cannot but speak of what we have seen and heard." (Acts 4.19-20)

But Peter and the apostles answered, "We must obey God rather than men." (Acts 5.29)

To him all the prophets bear witness that everyone who believes in him receives forgiveness of sins through his name." (Acts 10.43)

When they had preached the gospel to that city and had made many disciples, they returned to Lystra and to Iconium and to Antioch, strengthening the souls of the disciples, encouraging them to continue in the faith, and saying that through many tribulations we must enter the kingdom of God. (Acts 14.21-22)

The times of ignorance God overlooked, but now he commands all people everywhere to repent, because he has fixed a day on which he will judge the world in righteousness by a man whom he has appointed; and of this he has given assurance to all by raising him from the dead. (Acts 17.30-31)

In all things I have shown you that by working hard in this way we must help the weak and remember the words of the Lord Jesus, how he himself said, "It is more blessed to give than to receive." (Acts 20.35)

Day One: Acts 2.1-47

S:

_____
_____
_____
_____
_____
_____
_____

O:

_____
_____
_____
_____
_____
_____
_____

A:

_____
_____
_____
_____
_____
_____
_____

P:

_____
_____
_____
_____
_____
_____
_____

Day Two: Acts 5.17-42

_S:_ _____

_____

_____

_____

_____

_____

_____

_O:_ _____

_____

_____

_____

_____

_____

_____

_A:_ _____

_____

_____

_____

_____

_____

_____

_P:_ _____

_____

_____

_____

_____

_____

_____

Day Three: Acts 7

_S:_

_O:_

_A:_

_P:_

Day Four: Acts 9.1-31

_S:_

_O:_

_A:_

_P:_

Day Five: Acts 10

S:

O:

A:

P:

Day Six: Acts 15.1-35

_S:_

_O:_

_A:_

_P:_

While the gospels tell the story of Christ and the book of Acts tells of the expansion of that gospel around the world, the remaining 22 books of the New Testament are not so easily categorized. Sure, the label "epistles" is universally assigned to these books, and that designation is correct. The term epistles simply refers to a letter sent from one party to another. However, while they can all be categorized as "letters," we must be sure not to lose the incredible distinctiveness of each epistle.

The most important thing to remember about the New Testament letters is that they are all occasional documents from the first century. They were written out of the context of the author to the context of the original recipients. Sometimes the situation of the reader prompted the occasion for the letter. Perhaps there was a doctrinal error within a church or a question was posed to the author. At other times, the author created the occasion. Usually there was some kind of behavior or doctrinal error that needed to be corrected.

Unfortunately, as we study the epistles, we often know the answers but we don't know the question. Part of the work of studying the epistles is learning what the problem or issue was that prompted the letter. Then, we can better understand the answer.

Due to their occasional nature, the epistles are not first and foremost theological treatises. They are a kind of task theology, an application of the Christian faith to a specific circumstance. So, while the author provides some of their theological understanding in the letter, they do not give all of it. As a result, when the author's words are applied to a setting that is somewhat different, ours for example, the author does not have the luxury of explaining more fully his or her theological position to that new circumstance. This is the challenge of the interpreter.

Our discussion of the New Testament epistles will be divided into two main sections: the letters from Paul and the letters not known to be from Paul.

A quick note before we begin, people often wonder why the letters of the New Testament are arranged as they are. Many assume there is some theological significance to their order, but this is not true. After the gospels and Acts, the letters from Paul appear next with the non-Pauline letters following. The letters of Paul are arranged by size, longest to shortest. So much for that mystery.

Paul's Letters

1 and 2 Thessalonians

During Paul's second missionary journey, he visited the town of Thessalonica. A capital city of the region, the population was around 200,000 at the time of Paul's visit. The city had a strong Jewish community, and Paul began his ministry by reasoning with them in the synagogues, trying to prove from the Scriptures that Jesus was the Christ. After three weeks, some of the Jews and many of the God-fearing Greeks became believers. However, the Jews formed a riot mob and falsely accused Paul of treason. With so much turmoil, Paul and Silas left the city in the middle of the night. Paul's troubles were not left behind. Some of the trouble making Jews of Thessalonica followed Paul to his next stop, Berea, forcing him to leave that city, too.

Paul continued on his second missionary journey, staying at Corinth for a fruitful period of eighteen to twenty months. Timothy remained behind in Berea, but Paul sent instructions for him to join Paul in Corinth. In response to Timothy's encouraging report of the state of the church in Thessalonica, Paul wrote the letter we call 1 Thessalonians around 50 AD from the city of Corinth. During the same stay in Corinth, Paul wrote the second letter to the church, probably in the same year. Both of these represent some of the earliest of Paul's writings.

1 Thessalonians

Paul's primary reasons for writing the letter was to rejoice with them in their faithfulness. He also encouraged them to continue in the faith in the face of heavy persecution, most likely from the Jews in the community.

It appears from reading the letter that there were some in the community who were trying to undermine Paul by questioning his reputation or sincerity in the ministry. So, Paul responded to those accusations. Finally, he wrote to clarify some misunderstandings about those who had died and about the return of Jesus. These teachings about the second coming of Jesus are some of the most significant theological contributions of the entire letter.

2 Thessalonians

Paul wrote the second letter because of reports that the persecution of the believers in Thessalonica had grown worse. To make matters worse, there were some false teachers spreading the idea that the end time was already upon them, as evidenced by the increased persecution. Some had even quit their jobs to wait for the return of Jesus. So, Paul wrote to clarify about the end times, most notably teaching them about the man of lawlessness who must precede the return of Jesus.

Galatians

The Jerusalem Council did not totally put an end to the Judaizer debate. There were still Jewish believers who were insisting that one must become a Jew before they could be saved, and, more importantly, that they must live under the law of Moses to maintain their salvation. No other epistle in the New Testament confronts this problem as directly as the letter to the churches in Galatia.

Paul first visited the region of Phyrgia and Galatia during the first missionary journey. After Paul left the area and continued his travels, some Jewish believers arrived with a "different gospel" (Galatians 1.6-8). Paul described the Judaizer's gospel as really no gospel at all but just another form of the law. He defended his gospel as having come from Jesus Christ Himself and confirmed that with the results of the Jerusalem Council.

While the Judaizer debate might not rivet today's Christians to the seat of their pews, the discussion is more relevant than we might think. Most Gentile believers do not question whether we need to be circumcised in order to be saved, and we fully recognize that we are saved by grace and not by obeying the law. However, the implication reaches to our own experiences in living out our Christian faith. Paul's question to the Galatians is still valid.

> Let me ask you only this: Did you receive the Spirit by works of the law or by hearing with faith? Are you so foolish? Having begun by the Spirit, are you now being perfected by the flesh? Did you suffer£ so many things in vain—if indeed it was in vain? (Galatians 3.2-4)

In other words, do we experience the power of God in our lives because of what we are able to do for God or because of what God does in and through us by faith? Can we attain the goal of the Christian life by human effort?

Our Sunday School answer is "No," but our experiential answer is often "Yes." We still trust in the flesh to live out the Christian life, and we need to hear Paul's instructions to the contrary.

After Paul laid out the theology of the "saved by grace so live by grace" position, he applied it to real life. He wrote about our freedom in Christ and compared life in the Spirit to life in the flesh. He finished with a flourish: "For neither circumcision counts for anything, nor uncircumcision, but a new creation" (Galatians 6.15).

It remains unclear from where Paul wrote the letter, but the best suggestion is that Paul wrote the letter from Ephesus around 53 AD.

1 and 2 Corinthians

The city of Corinth was one of the greatest metropolitan cities of the ancient world. With ports on both the Aegean Sea and the Gulf of Corinth, it served as a major crossroads for travel from all points on the compass. The attention to commerce and entertainment of weary travelers did not favor the development of intellectual pursuits. People came to Corinth for a good time. The temple of Aphrodite, with its hundreds of female temple prostitutes, stood on the highest point of the city. The Isthmus games (second in popularity only to the Olympics) were held every other year in Corinth. The city was prosperous and licentious. As the capital of Achaia, it had well over half a million people living in it at the time of Paul's second missionary journey.

One can only imagine the difficulty of planting a church in Corinth. When Paul first arrived in Corinth, he reasoned with the Jews in the synagogue but was quickly removed from the synagogue. Paul had a season of fruitful ministry in Corinth, but the church he planted struggled to mature in Christ. For that reason, Paul had more written correspondence with the church in Corinth than with any other group of believers.

Only two of Paul's letters to the church in Corinth survive today, but we know that he wrote more because he referred to other letters within the two letters contained in the Scriptures. So, a brief sketch of his relationship with the church will help us to understand the depth of his communication with this church.

After 18 months of ministry in Corinth during the second missionary journey, Paul left for his next destination, Ephesus. While at Ephesus, a group of people connected to Chloe sent a report of division in the church (1 Corinthians 1.11). Then, a letter was sent to Paul with a list of several questions. While we do not have the list of questions, many of them can be deduced from Paul's responses. For instance, Paul wrote, "Now concerning the matters about which you wrote…" (1 Corinthians 7.1). In response to Chloe's report and the list of questions, Paul wrote a letter to the church in Corinth, a letter we call "First Corinthians."

This was not the first letter from Paul to the church in Corinth. 1 Corinthians 5.9 refers to a previous letter, but we do not know if the previous letter precedes the visit from Chloe's people or the list of questions. What we do know is that it preceded 1 Corinthians.

1 Corinthians was a strong letter with some harsh correction. He promised to send Timothy to check up on their progress with the threat to visit in person if they did not straighten out. However, Timothy returned with a poor report, and Paul wrote another lost letter to the church. Paul referred to it as the painful letter or letter of tears, and he regretted having sent it (2 Corinthians 2.4). The letter has not survived, but it must have been as painful to read as it was to write.

Titus delivered the letter and later delivered a good report to Paul about the resulting changes in the Corinthian congregation. Paul rejoiced, and wrote them another letter which we call Second Corinthians, but it is really the fourth letter (of which we know) to the church. This final letter prepared the congregation for a final visit from Paul.

Paul wrote both letters from Ephesus while on his third missionary journey. The time was either 55 or 56 AD.

1 Corinthians

1 Corinthians deals with a variety of issues found in many immature congregations. Paul wrote about divisions in the church, sexual immorality, conflict between members that resulted in lawsuits in the public courts, marriage, meat sacrificed to idols, the rights of an apostle to be financially supported by the ministry, the Lord's Supper, worship, spiritual gifts, and the resurrection. It seems as if the church in Corinth had every problem imaginable.

2 Corinthians

2 Corinthians is very different. It is more pastoral than confrontational. It speaks to a variety of issues, most notably the encouragement to fulfill their commitment to collect an offering for the poor saints in Jerusalem. It also contains some of the most vivid descriptions of Paul's struggles as an apostle.

Romans

Although most of Paul's letters were written to churches whose stories are told in the book of Acts, the book of Romans is a glaring exception.

Almost nothing is known of the Christian beginnings in Rome, but the New Testament does give a few hints. For instance, two key leaders in the early church were Priscilla and Aquila. Luke is silent about their conversion, but it seems possible that they were already believers when they came to Corinth from Italy (Acts 18.1-3). By the time Paul wrote his letter to Rome, their faith was being reported all over the Christian world (Romans 1.8). So, while we don't know when the gospel came to Rome, we do know that Paul was not the first one to carry it there. Despite the modern day Church of St. Peter in Rome, there is no biblical or historical evidence that Peter founded the church in Rome.

The key to understanding the date and place of writing comes from Paul's comments about the collection for the saints in Jerusalem. In both the letters to the Corinthians, the fund was in process of being collected. However, by the time Romans was written, the task had been finished (Romans 15.28). So, Romans was written after 2 Corinthians, probably in the year 57 AD. Paul probably wrote the letter from Corinth because Phoebe appears to be the bearer of the letter and is from nearby Cenchrea (Romans 16.1).

The purpose of the letter was to prepare the church for his impending visit. It appears to be a statement of the message of the gospel in preparation for missionary outreach by the Roman church. However, it is not a complete description of Paul's theology because it does not touch on some key components like the church or eschatology.

A few distinguishing characteristics of the letter should be mentioned. The book concludes with a lengthy list of names, a peculiarity for Paul. Of all of the times Paul quotes from the Old Testament, more than half of them are found in Romans. Paul used a dialogical style in the book, almost like he was debating the reader. There is not enough evidence to know if this was only a rhetorical device or if Paul had an actual person in mind. The Judaizing crisis, so prominent in other letters, is totally absent from this book. Finally, the vocabulary is full of rich theological terms which will often challenge today's readers.

Romans is a difficult book to outline. The first eight chapters deal with the nature of salvation, while the last five chapters deal with applying that salvation in life. The middle three chapters (9-11) are the hardest to understand for Paul addresses the doctrine of election with clarity and straightforwardness. Unfortunately, the scope of the doctrine of election is too large to attempt to explore in this book.

The Prison Epistles

Four of Paul's letters (Ephesians, Philippians, Colossians, and Philemon) are often designated as the "Prison Epistles" because he was in prison at the time of writing them.

Three of them (not including Philippians) are so closely linked together that they were most likely written from the same place at the same time. Tychicus delivered both the letter to the church in Ephesus and the letter to the church in Colossae (Ephesians 6.21 and Colossians 4.7). Further, Tychicus' companion on this journey was Onesimus who delivered the letter to Philemon. Therefore, these three letters are closely bound together, though the exact situation of Paul's imprisonment is unclear. Some have suggested Caesarea, others Rome, and others Ephesus, but the traditional view is the Roman imprisonment described in Acts 28.

While they were all written in the early 60s, Philippians was written at a different time than the others. In Philippians alone, Paul was confident in his impending release from prison (Philippians 1.25). It remains unclear whether this was earlier or later in the two year period of Acts 28.

Colossians

Epaphras planted the church in Colossae (Colossians 1.7), a city approximately 100 miles east of Ephesus. Apparently, Paul had neither visited the city nor preached there because he remained unknown to them.

The primary issue in Colossians was the influence of the philosophy of Gnosticism upon the church. Gnostics taught that the way to the deeper life was through gaining knowledge, specifically secret knowledge about the divine. In contrast to the threat of the Judaizers at the beginning of the church, the church struggled against the heretical teachings of Gnosticism during the latter part of the New Testament era and beyond. The emphasis of Colossians is summed up in Colossians 2.8, "See to it that no one takes you captive by philosophy and empty deceit, according to human tradition, according to the elemental spirits of the world, and not according to Christ."

Philemon

Imagine what might happen if an escaped slave ran into the apostle Paul and came to faith in Christ. To complicate matters, what if Paul knew the escaped slave's owner? What would Paul tell this slave to do? Would Paul honor his friend and tell the slave to return to his bonds, or would Paul take the opportunity to preach against the horrors of slavery and demand this new believer's freedom? This 25 verse letter is Paul's answer to that question.

Paul's response is genius. Rather than attack the institution of slavery (which he would have had little power to change), he addressed one Christian brother. He addressed the letter not only to Philemon, but also to Apphia (possibly his wife), and to the church that met in their house. This put the public spot light on Philemon and pressured him to respond appropriately to Paul's request.

Paul never told Philemon to release Onesimus from slavery, but this is the obvious implication in the letter. He instructed Philemon to take him back, no longer as a slave, but as a brother. He did not order him to do what he ought, but appealed to Philemon on the basis of love. Paul reminded Philemon that he owed Paul his very life, implying that Paul brought spiritual life in the form of the gospel to Philemon. Paul offered to repay any debt that Onesimus might owe Philemon.

Short of demanding Philemon to set Onesimus free, Paul employed every tactic to encourage Philemon to make that choice out of his love for a brother in Christ. True, the institution of slavery was never condemned by Paul, but Paul's instructions to Philemon were still radical for the cultural times.

Ephesians

There are two reasons why the book of Ephesians might not be a letter to just the church in Ephesus. First, in a few of the best manuscripts of the New Testament, the phrase "in Ephesus" is missing in Ephesians 1.1. Even though the name of no other church appears in any manuscript, the absence of "in Ephesus" suggests it might have been a circular letter.

Second, the letter appears to be addressed to a church unknown to Paul while Paul had extensive contact with the church in Ephesus. These two factors have led scholars to conclude that the book might have been an encyclical letter intended for churches in the geographical region of Ephesus. Further, it might be the "letter from Laodicea" mentioned in Colossians 4.16.

The theme of Ephesians is "in Christ." The phrase saturates the book, appearing 23 times. No other book in the New Testament describes the riches of God's grace and the joy of living in Christ with the depth of Ephesians.

Philippians

The city of Philippi was unusual because very few Jews lived there. In fact, there were not enough Jewish males in the city to have a synagogue. Luke mentions no Jewish opposition to the gospel in Acts in this predominately Gentile city. It is possible that Luke stayed in Philippi to help the group of new believers after Paul's visit on the second missionary journey.

Epaphroditus had been sent by the church in Philippi to visit Paul in prison with a love gift. After fully recovering from a serious illness, Paul sent him back to Philippi along with this letter of appreciation. The letter is affectionate, personal, and with minimum doctrinal teaching with the notable exception of a Christological Hymn (Philippians 2.5-11).

Pastoral Epistles

1 Timothy, Titus, and 2 Timothy, most likely written in that order, are commonly called the "Pastoral Epistles." Each of these books claim Paul as their author, but the genuineness of that claim has been questioned by scholars for a variety of reasons.

First, some of the events in the pastoral epistles are difficult to correlate to the account in Acts. For instance, the Acts account does not agree that Paul left Timothy behind in Ephesus. If Paul wrote these three, then he must have been released from his Roman imprisonment and made further journeys, during which time he wrote 1 Timothy and Titus. A second Roman imprisonment followed, and he wrote 2 Timothy at that time.

A second reason for questioning the authorship of Paul is the ecclesiology of the church. Some would challenge that the pastoral epistles describe an advanced church organization with clearly defined offices such as elders, bishops, and deacons. However, this degree of organization did not seem to appear during the life time of Paul.

On the other hand, there is some evidence to refute this. Paul referred to bishops and deacons in Philippians 1.1, and the church leadership structure outlined by the Ignatius (115 AD) reflected only one bishop, not the many of Paul's day. So, the argument that the ecclesiology of the pastoral epistles points to a later author is not conclusive.

A third argument raised by those who believe that Paul did not write these books is linguistic. Scholars have found 175 words used nowhere else in the New Testament. Of course, these can be explained by the subject matter of the letters without the need for a different author.

In summary, while the debate will continue, I accept that Paul wrote the pastoral epistles. Paul wrote 1 Timothy from Macedonia to Timothy who was at Ephesus. The date was probably between 62 and 66 AD. There is no indication where Paul was when he wrote the letter to Titus who was on the island of Crete, but the letter was probably sent between 62 and 66 AD. 2 Timothy was written from prison in Rome no later than 67 AD.

1 Timothy

In many ways, 1 Timothy is a letter from an older minister teaching a younger minister how to fulfill his calling. He warned Timothy about false teachers, instructed him on matters of worship, church leadership, and ministry to widows. He personally encouraged Timothy to hold faithfully to his calling, and he warned him about the dangers of falling in love with money.

Titus

Titus is not mentioned in Acts, but Paul mentioned him in Galatians 2.1-3. Paul led the young man to Christ, and this Gentile convert became a test case for the issue of circumcision and salvation (Galatians 2.3-5). He ministered with Paul in Ephesus on the third missionary journey. In 2 Corinthians, Titus was described by Paul as a trusted co-worker. He was even sent on important missions by Paul to Corinth. It was Titus' good report on the conditions at Corinth that prompted the writing of 2 Corinthians.

The few references to Titus provide the picture that he was a trusted servant with Paul and was sent on important missions on several occasions to strengthen faltering churches. This letter found Titus on the island of Crete, presumably on the same kind of mission. The letter to Titus was an encouragement to live the pure Christian life in the midst of an impure culture. When Paul wrote this letter is a matter of conjecture, but the best guess is 63 AD.

2 Timothy

This is most likely the last letter written by Paul before his death. He gave his final words to Timothy, his beloved partner in the faith. He warned against false teachers and spoke about the last days. He closed his letter writing ministry with these words: "The Lord be with your spirit. Grace be with you" (2 Timothy 4.22).

General Letters

Hebrews

The book of Hebrews defies the categorization as an epistle. It lacks a typical epistolary introduction, it lacks an addressee, and it fails to mention the author. However, the content of the book does illustrate that the author is addressing a small, definite, and known group of people.

As the title suggests, the letter was written to Jews, most likely Christian Jews. The book moves within the orbit of Old Testament Scriptures, speaks extensively about the tabernacle, sacrifices, and the priestly office.

The author of Hebrews is known only to God. As the early church father, Origen, wrote, "Who wrote the epistle? God only knows the truth." Scholars have suggested Barnabas, Apollos, and Priscilla as possible authors but without convincing proof. The authorship remains a mystery.

There is little evidence to help with the dating of the book. Timothy is mentioned but without enough historical reference to provide a date. The recipients have "not yet resisted to the point of the shedding of your blood" (Hebrews 12.4), so the date is most likely before the widespread persecution of the church. But that does little to narrow down the date.

The most telling evidence is the failure of the book to mention the destruction of the Temple in 70 AD. Since the author's purpose was to argue that Christianity superseded Judaism, the destruction of the Temple would have naturally been the crowning argument. But the fall of the Temple was not used by the author as proof of the old covenant being abolished. Of course, this is an argument from silence, but it points to a date of composition before 70 AD.

The book of Hebrews is the New Testament commentary on the book of Leviticus. It describes in great detail how the sacrifices and priestly office of the old covenant have been replaced by something far superior.

> And every priest stands daily at his service, offering repeatedly the same sacrifices, which can never take away sins. But when Christ had offered for all time a single sacrifice for sins, he sat down at the right hand of God, waiting from that time until his enemies should be made a footstool for his feet. (Hebrews 10.11-13)

There are two prominent sections in Hebrews that deal with other subjects besides the superiority of Christ to the Old Covenant. The first is the roll call of faith found in Hebrews 11. The author beautifully described the lives of the saints who had lived by faith in obedience to God.

The second is more difficult to interpret. There are five warning passages in Hebrews that describe the danger of falling away from the faith. They are found in Hebrews 2.1-4, 3.7-4.13, 5.11-6.20, 10.26-39, and 12.14-29. These are very difficult to interpret because they seem to imply that it is possible to drift away from salvation (Hebrews 2.1), to fall short of the promised rest (Hebrews 4.1), and to fall away (Hebrews 6.6). Moreover, they imply that those who wander away cannot return to the faith because no sacrifice for sins remains (Hebrews 10.26), and it is impossible for them to be brought back to repentance (Hebrews 6.6).

To understand these difficult teachings, we must consider them in context with other biblical teachings. For instance, many places in Scripture describe salvation with conditional terms. For instance,

> *Now I would remind you, brothers, of the gospel I preached to you, which you received, in which you stand, and by which you are being saved, if you hold fast to the word I preached to you—unless you believed in vain. (1 Corinthians 15.1-2)*

The conditionality of salvation does not depend upon our good works to hold our salvation secure. Instead, the biblical picture is that genuine salvation or saving faith is demonstrated through fruit and perseverance.

Whether or not the warning passages in Hebrews describe a person without saving faith who went out from the church because they never were redeemed in the first place (see I John 2.19) or they describe a person who abandoned the faith (see 1 Timothy 4.1) is a matter of more discussion. Regardless, these warning passages deserve our attention.

James

James was a common name in the first century, and there are four men with that name mentioned in the New Testament. Only two of these are possible candidates for the author of this book. James, the son of Zebedee, brother of John, and one of the apostles was martyred too early (44 AD) to have been the author (Acts 12.1-2). Therefore, James, the brother of Jesus (Mark 6.3) is most likely the author. Origen, Jerome, and Eusebius are just a few of the early church fathers who held this position. According to Josephus, James was martyred in 62 AD, so the book must have been written prior to that.

However, the internal evidence suggests an earlier date of composition. For instance, the book fails to mention the Judaizers or even Gentile Christians, the organization of the church was simpler with just teachers and elders, and James referred to the synagogue as the meeting place of the church pointing to a period when the church was still confined within Jewish circles. A suggested date of composition is between 45 and 50 AD.

The letter was written to Jewish Christians, but their location was not stated. However, they were most likely the Christians scattered abroad by the persecution mentioned in Acts 8.1 because the letter was addressed to "the twelve tribes in the dispersion" (James 1.1).

James wrote the letter to these Christians who were living outside of Jerusalem because they no longer had access to the apostle's teachings. So, as the leader of the Jerusalem church, James instructed them about key issues regarding their faith.

Many scholars have noted the similarities between the book of James and the Sermon on the Mount.

> But above all, my brothers, do not swear, either by heaven or by earth or by any other oath, but let your "yes" be yes and your "no" be no, so that you may not fall under condemnation. (James 5.12)

> But I say to you, Do not take an oath at all, either by heaven, for it is the throne of God, or by the earth, for it is his footstool, or by Jerusalem, for it is the city of the great King. And do not take an oath by your head, for you cannot make one hair white or black. Let what you say be simply 'Yes' or 'No'; anything more than this comes from evil. (Matthew 5.34-37)

Another parallel with the book of James is the book of Proverbs. For instance, James 4.6 (But he gives more grace. Therefore it says, "God opposes the proud, but gives grace to the humble") is a direct quotation of Proverbs 3.34.

James is one of the most practical and least theological books in the entire New Testament. It deals with relevant issues like trials, favoritism, taming the tongue, pride, and wealth.

1 and 2 Peter

Peter's leadership in the church was not matched by his literary output. Only two letters in the New Testament bear his name, and one of those is seriously in question.

The first letter claims to be from Peter, an apostle of Jesus Christ. This is none other than the Simon called by Jesus and turned into the fisher of men. He wrote the letter from "Babylon," most likely a code name for Rome. The letter was probably written shortly before the great persecution of Nero broke out against the church in 64 AD, so a date around 62 AD is a good suggestion.

The recipients are "Those who are elect exiles of the dispersion in Pontus, Galatia, Cappadocia, Asia, and Bithynia" (1 Peter 1.1). These were all cities in northern Asia Minor or present day Turkey. The Christians probably outnumbered the Jews in these regions, but the pagans still outnumbered them both. Peter wrote this letter to encourage the church to live for God in the midst of a society and culture that was ignorant of the one true God.

Regarding the second letter, its Petrine authorship has been seriously questioned by scholars. One commentary lists eleven arguments against Petrine authorship, but all of these can be substantially countered. For instance, some believe that 2 Peter's reference to Paul's letters must have been written by a later author after they had been collected by the church. However, the author does not refer to a corpus of letters but to a few letters. Surely, these were in circulation in the churches of Galatia in at least some form during the life of Peter. Without taking the time to delineate all of the arguments against Petrine authorship, suffice it to say that it remains in debate among scholars. But this author holds that the apostle Peter wrote the second letter as well as the first.

The letter was written after the first letter but before Peter's death, sometime around 64 to 68 AD. There is no evidence, internal or otherwise, that indicates the origination of the letter, and the same is true of the destination.

The purpose of the letter was to encourage the church to endure difficult times and false teachers as the day of the Lord was quickly approaching.

1, 2, and 3 John

Whereas the book of Acts supplies the background for the Pauline epistles, we have nothing similar for the letters written by the apostle John. There is almost no information to supply the background for these letters. What understanding we have comes from the content of the letters themselves.

The author of 1 John, and in fact of all three letters and the gospel bearing his name, never identifies himself in the epistle. He must have been so well know to his "children" that he did not need to identify himself. For those who recognize the common authorship for the gospel and the epistles, it is possible through a process of elimination to identify the beloved disciple as John, the son of Zebedee. The universal witness from the early church agrees with this identification.

Scholars believe that Johannine community migrated to Asia Minor to escape hostility from the Jews sometime before 70 AD. A very successful mission to the Gentiles followed. John wrote the gospel as a missionary document so that "You might believe that Jesus is the Christ" (John 20.31). During the next decade, a heretical faction developed that splintered off from the group. This group denied Jesus as the Christ and Son of God, that Christ had come in the flesh, the authority of Jesus' commands, and even their own sinfulness.

The first letter of John was written in response to this crisis sometime around 85 to 90 AD.

The short letter of second John was written shortly thereafter to warn the church not to welcome false teachers.

The third letter was addressed to a group of house churches most of which were doing well in the faith. However, one leader, Demetrius, needed correction. The date was probably around 90 AD.

The value of 1 John is that it paints a clear picture of what a true believer looks like and gives the church some basic criteria so that they might know they have eternal life. According to John, Christians can know that they have eternal life because they obey the Lord's commands and they are not burdensome (1 John

2.3), they accept Jesus as the Son of God (1 John 2.23), they do not continue in sin (1 John 3.9), they have the internal witness of the indwelling Spirit of God (1 John 3.24), and they love one another (1 John 4.7).

Jude

The author of Jude described himself as the brother of James. Since James the apostle was killed very early, it is most likely that Jude was the brother of James, the half brother of Jesus. So, Jude was the half brother of Jesus, too. If so, then he probably did not believe in Jesus as the Messiah until after the resurrection (John 7.5 and Acts 1.14). This explains the humility with which he introduces himself as a "servant of Christ." The letter was probably written between 60 to 65 AD, but there is little evidence to indicate a precise date. The letter gives no indication of its origination nor its destination.

The purpose of the letter was to contend for the faith since false teachers had slipped into the church. The exact identification of the false teachers is difficult, but they lived sexually immoral lives, denied the sovereignty of Jesus, and followed ungodly desires.

Revelation

The book of Revelation is a class of Scripture all to its own. It belongs to the apocalyptic genre, which means "to uncover." It is uniquely both prophetic and pastoral, both a warning and an encouragement.

The author of the gospel and the three letters of John is also the author of the last book of the New Testament.

Two dates have been suggested for the time of writing, neither of which carry any more evidence than the other. The revelation was either written down shortly after the reign of Nero when the persecution of the Christians was extremely intense (68 AD) or at the close of Domitians' reign (96 AD) as witnessed to by Irenaeus in 185 AD. Ultimately, the question must be left open.

The book contains the record of a vision that came to John while he was in the Spirit while on the island of Patmos. John was to write down what he saw and send it to the seven churches of Asia Minor.

> *Write therefore the things that you have seen, those that are and those that are to take place after this (Revelation 1.19)*

In chapters 2-3, John recorded specific words for each of the seven churches. They were words of affirmation and correction and were both specific for those seven churches and applicable to the church today. Like the first six chapters of Daniel, these are the easier parts of the book of Revelation to understand. The vision of what was to come in chapters 4-22 continue to challenge readers of the Bible.

There are four primary ways of understanding the visions of Revelation. In the Futurist view, all of the visions relate to a period immediately preceding and following the second coming of Jesus at the end of time.

In the Historicist view, the visions centered on the historical events of John's day and its immediate continuity. In other words, Babylon was both pagan Rome and papal Rome. Many with this view see the anti-Christ as connected to both Rome and the papacy.

In the Preterist view, all of the visions related to events that happened during the life of the author. The book was a "tract for the times" to encourage faithfulness during intense persecution.

Finally, in the Idealist view, the visions are understood to be poetic and symbolic in nature. They are not to be identified with any specific future events but teach principles of the timeless battle between good and evil, God and Satan.

Great caution must be used when studying and applying the book of Revelation. The student of the Bible must be careful not to develop extensive theological positions regarding end time events based upon unclear portions of Revelation. The words of Jesus should be obeyed: "It is not for you to know times or seasons that the Father has fixed by his own authority" (Acts 1.7). If we read Revelation as a textbook looking to unlock the dates of the end times, then we have missed the point. Broad strokes are painted, and the student of the Bible must look at the big picture and not the minute detail.

That being said, the best way to read Revelation is that the visions relate to the things that were during the days of John and the things that are still yet to come (see Revelation 1.19)

Making It Profitable

Daily Bible Readings

Obviously, there is no way to do any justice to these 22 books of the New Testament in only one week of daily Bible reading. Instead of suggesting daily readings from a variety of books, I am suggesting that you focus on reading and understanding one entire book of the New Testament this week. The following daily readings will guide you to read the entire book of Ephesians.

Remember as you read to continue the spiritual discipline of meditating on the Word of God. Each day, take the time to write down one or two verses that grab your attention. Write out what you observed about those chapters. Pray about why the God of all creation is having you read this chapter on this particular day of your life. And slow down enough to talk to God about what you read.

Read. Understand. Meditate. Pray.

Suggested Memory verses

For all have sinned and fall short of the glory of God (Romans 3.23)

For the wages of sin is death, but the free gift of God is eternal life in Christ Jesus our Lord. (Romans 6.23)

If you confess with your mouth that Jesus is Lord and believe in your heart that God raised him from the dead, you will be saved. (Romans 10.9)

But God, being rich in mercy, because of the great love with which he loved us, even when we were dead in our trespasses, made us alive together with Christ—by grace you have been saved—and raised us up with him and seated us with him in the heavenly places in Christ Jesus. (Ephesians 2.4-6)

For we are his workmanship, created in Christ Jesus for good works, which God prepared beforehand, that we should walk in them. (Ephesians 2.10)

But the fruit of the Spirit is love, joy, peace, patience, kindness, goodness, faithfulness, gentleness, self-control; against such things there is no law. (Galatians 5.22-23)

Put on the whole armor of God, that you may be able to stand against the schemes of the devil. For we do not wrestle against flesh and blood, but against the rulers, against the authorities, against the cosmic powers over this present darkness, against the spiritual forces of evil in the heavenly places. (Ephesians 6.11-12)

And I am sure of this, that he who began a good work in you will bring it to completion at the day of Jesus Christ. (Philippians 1.6)

Have this mind among yourselves, which is yours in Christ Jesus, who, though he was in the form of God, did not count equality with God a thing to be grasped, but made himself nothing, taking the form of a servant, being born in the likeness of men. (Philippians 2.5-7)

Finally, brothers, whatever is true, whatever is honorable, whatever is just, whatever is pure, whatever is lovely, whatever is commendable, if there is any excellence, if there is anything worthy of praise, think about these things. (Philippians 4.8)

If then you have been raised with Christ, seek the things that are above, where Christ is, seated at the right hand of God. Set your minds on things that are above, not on things that are on earth. For you have died, and your life is hidden with Christ in God. (Colossians 3.1-3)

If we confess our sins, he is faithful and just to forgive us our sins and to cleanse us from all unrighteousness. (1 John 1.9)

All Scripture is breathed out by God and profitable for teaching, for reproof, for correction, and for training in righteousness, that the man of God may be competent, equipped for every good work. (2 Timothy 3.16)

Be sober-minded; be watchful. Your adversary the devil prowls around like a roaring lion, seeking someone to devour. (1 Peter 5.8)

And my God will supply every need of yours according to his riches in glory in Christ Jesus. (Philippians 4.19)

Day One: Ephesians 1

_S:_

_O:_

_A:_

_P:_

Day Two: Ephesians 2

S:

O:

A:

P:

Day Three: Ephesians 3

_S:_
_____
_____
_____
_____
_____
_____
_____
_____

_O:_
_____
_____
_____
_____
_____
_____
_____

_A:_
_____
_____
_____
_____
_____
_____

_P:_
_____
_____
_____
_____
_____
_____
_____

Day Four: Ephesians 4

_S:_ _____
_____
_____
_____
_____
_____
_____

_O:_ _____
_____
_____
_____
_____
_____
_____

_A:_ _____
_____
_____
_____
_____
_____
_____

_P:_ _____
_____
_____
_____
_____
_____
_____

Day Five: Ephesians 5

S:

_____
_____
_____
_____
_____
_____
_____

O:

_____
_____
_____
_____
_____
_____

A:

_____
_____
_____
_____
_____
_____

P:

_____
_____
_____
_____
_____
_____

Day Six: Ephesians 6

S: _____

_____

_____

_____

_____

_____

_____

O: _____

_____

_____

_____

_____

_____

_____

A: _____

_____

_____

_____

_____

_____

_____

P: _____

_____

_____

_____

_____

_____

_____

13 | TEN PRINCIPLES OF INTERPRETATION

Reading and understanding the story of the Bible is one thing, but interpreting and applying the truths of the Bible to our life situation is something different. This is why the Bible encourages us to go beyond just reading the Word.

> *Do your best to present yourself to God as one approved, a worker who has no need to be ashamed, rightly handling the word of truth. (2 Timothy 2.15)*

The Greek word translated "rightly handling" is a word that means "to cut straight" or "to handle correctly" (*Thayer's*). It is also translated as "rightly explaining" (NRSV), "correctly handles" (NIV), or "accurately handling" (NASB) the word of truth.

The implication is that the word of truth can be incorrectly handled or wrongly explained. Since you have put your time into reading this book, I am sure that your heart's desire is to handle the Scriptures correctly.

To help towards this end, allow me to discuss a few foundational principles regarding the science of interpreting the Scriptures, otherwise known as hermeneutics.

1. Our View of Inspiration Will Determine Our Interpretation

The first principle in hermeneutics is to remember that our view of inspiration guides the manner in which we interpret the Scriptures. If we hold to a theory of inspiration that divorces the Word of God from the text of the Bible, then our interpretation of the Scriptures will be free to distance itself from the words of the Bible, too.

However, we have already studied that any view of inspiration must correspond to how Jesus interpreted the Scriptures. In John 10.34-35, Jesus linked the "word of God" which came to the writer of the Scriptures to the text of the Scripture. Furthermore, He linked it to the plurality of one word in His argument with the Jews. So, we regard the text of the Scriptures to be inspired by the Spirit of God. As a result, any interpretation must deal faithfully with the text.

2. The Plain, Literal Meaning

With this assumption about the nature of inspiration, it forces our interpretation of Scripture to deal faithfully with the text itself. This leads us to the second hermeneutical principle: we must deal with the plain literal meaning of the text. In other words, the words on the page mean something, and whatever they mean must be connected with the words on the page. We are not free to abandon the text in our creative attempt to develop an interpretation of Scripture. We must face the plain, literal meaning of the text.

The phrase most often associated with this principle is the grammatico-historical method. This principle focuses our attention on the literary forms, grammatical constructions, and historical contexts out of which the Scripture was written (Sproul, 56). Words have meanings and sentence structure helps to convey that meaning. Furthermore, understanding the historical setting in which the texts were written will aid us in understanding their meaning.

Of course, endorsing the plain, literal meaning of the text does not ignore the obviously symbolic sections of the Bible. But, it does state that the text itself determines whether or not the text is to be taken literally or figuratively. It prevents the reader from creating extensive allegories that actually avoid the simple meaning of the text.

Interpreting the Bible within the framework of the plain, literal meaning does not disregard the impact of differing genres, either. It simply locates the power of interpretation in the text instead of in the reader. A few scholars suggest that the text has no meaning itself, and the meaning is only provided by the reader as he or she responds to the text. But as the Scriptures proclaim, the Word of God came to the writers through the power of the Spirit, and it is the Spirit that gives those words meaning.

3. Context, Context, Context

The third interpretive principle focuses on context. The meaning of any portion of Scripture is determined by its context.

I remember a phrase from my seminary days: "A text without a context is a pretext." A pretext is a "purpose or motive alleged or an appearance assumed in order to cloak the real intention or state of affairs" (*Merriam-Webster*). In other words, any text removed from its context can be used to validate any preconceived understanding of the text. Outside agendas are easily forced upon a phrase or verse from the Bible. Simply put, if we are creative enough, we can make any verse in the Bible mean anything we want it to.

A simple example is take a phrase out of context from Psalm 14.1. Did you know that the Bible says, "There is no god"? A foolish Bible reader might develop a complete doctrine on the unreality of the divine from this one phrase. However, if we read the phrase in context, the meaning totally changes. Psalm 14.1 reads, "The fool says in his heart, 'there is no god.'" Here, the context of the full sentence gives a completely different interpretation to the phrase. Context always determines meaning.

Context has a variety of levels. Every word in Scripture is in several contexts: the sentence in which it is found, the paragraph in which the sentence is located, the chapter of the book which contains the paragraph, the book which contains the paragraph, the testament that contains the book, and ultimately the location within the context of the entire canon. A correct understanding of every word must take into account all of these contexts.

4. Authorial Intent

As I stated earlier, some scholars insist that the Scriptures have no meaning in and of themselves. Meaning, they say, only develops as a reader responds to the text. This is called "Reader Response Criticism."

However, if the Spirit brought the Word of God to the writer, and led the writer to the exact words to be used, then the intended meaning of the Spirit can be found in those words.

A very closely related principle of interpretation is the principle of authorial intent. This means that the author of Scripture wrote with a purpose. It might have been to teach, to correct, or to tell the story. The key is that the meaning of Scripture for us today is connected to the author's original intent. This is why I put so much emphasis on trying to understand the situation behind the various New Testament letters. It helps us come to an understanding of what God is saying to us today as we learn what God was saying to the original readers.

As we apply this principle, we must understand two important truths. First, there are often two levels of meaning in Scriptures. This is most often found among the prophetic writings. While the prophets were speaking to those who lived in Judah or Israel, the words of the prophet had meaning that transcended just that historical situation.

For example, consider the words of Isaiah 7. In this historical context, the prophet was giving a sign to the king to demonstrate that God's promise would come true. The promise in question was that God would deliver the city of Jerusalem from the invading army of Assyria. The prophet said to the king,

> *Therefore the Lord himself will give you a sign. Behold, the virgin shall conceive and bear a son, and shall call his name Immanuel. (Isaiah 7.14)*

In this setting, the word meant that before a young woman known to the king would give birth, the promise would be fulfilled.

But the meaning of this prophecy extended beyond the days of Isaiah. The gospel writer Matthew quoted this very prophecy in reference to the birth of the Messiah.

> *All this took place to fulfill what the Lord had spoken by the prophet: "Behold, the virgin shall conceive and bear a son, and they shall call his name Immanuel." (Matthew 1.22-23)*

So, even as we consider the intent of the author, we must keep in mind that the Spirit who inspired the author might have a fuller meaning than just the historical context of the author.

Second, the new covenant reader will often have to translate the intent of the author into either a new covenant period or into a new historical situation. The old covenant Scriptures have to be interpreted through the lens of the new covenant, and even the words of the apostles must be interpreted from one historical context to another.

5. Separate the Truth from the Cultural Expression

Another hermeneutic principle is to understand the difference between biblical truth and the cultural expression of that truth.

For example, consider Paul's statement in 1 Thessalonians 5.26, "Greet all the brothers with a holy kiss." Is this a command for men in all cultures to greet each other with a kiss? Of course not. The biblical truth is to greet one another with affection and love. In kissing cultures, like Italy or South America, this might be expressed with a kiss. However, in non-kissing cultures like North America, this greeting is contained in a firm handshake or a warm embrace. The biblical principle is expressed in different ways in different cultures.

However, most of the cultural issues in the Bible are not this clearly understood. The problem is exacerbated when we realize that not only is the Bible culturally conditioned, but the reader is, too. So, a few principles might guide us along the way.

First, we need to distinguish between a biblical principle and a specific application of a principle.

Second, distinguish between what the New Testament sees as inherently moral and what is not. Morality transcends culture but its expressions might change from culture to culture. For instance, the sin lists of the New Testament never contain cultural items.

Third, we must observe where the New Testament has a uniform and consistent witness and where it reflects differences. At times, the witness of the church is universal: murder and homosexuality are always sinful. However, at other times, the New Testament witness is divided. For example, how does Paul's statements about not allowing a woman to excercise authority over a man (1 Timothy 2.12) compare with his description of two females, Phoebe and Junia, as a deacon and an apostle, respectively (Romans 16.1-7)? When the biblical witness is not uniform, it calls us to look out for a cultural or situational difference where a universal truth is applied in different settings.

In the end, we must depend upon the Spirit to guide our understanding and to act in love with others who may come to a different interpretation over non-essentials. The common rule of faith must prevail: in essential, unity; in non-essentials, liberty.

6. Recognize the Power of Presuppositions

This brings up another principle in hermeneutics: we must recognize and pay attention to the power of presuppositions.

To presuppose is "to suppose beforehand" or "to hold as an opinion beforehand" (*Merriam-Webster*). As much as we try to prevent this, we all bring certain presuppositions to the text before we read it. These are a collection of all the "truths" was have picked up along the way from various sources. These sources might be our grandparents, our friends, movies, preachers, or books we have read. Together, these from a prism through which we read the Bible, whether we realize it or not. As a result, when we come to consider what the Bible might say, our presuppositions will often overpower the text. We will massage the text so that it fits with our presuppositions.

The problem is that most of our presuppositions are not even known to ourselves. They lie hidden, deep within our minds, and they can be very hard to uncover. Therefore, we must question everything that we think we know to be true. With every theological position, we must answer the question, "How do I know this to be true?" In trying to answer that question, we will often realize that we lack scriptural foundation for some of the things we believe to be true.

7. The Spirit Guides Interpretation

Another principle of interpretation is that we need the help of the Spirit to understand spiritual things.

> *The natural person does not accept the things of the Spirit of God, for they are folly to him, and he is not able to understand them because they are spiritually discerned. (1 Corinthians 2.14)*

This means that without the aid of the Spirit, our interpretations will always miss the mark. However, we must be careful about how we apply this principle.

Let's examine what it does not mean. The Spirit's ministry in Bible interpretation does not mean that He gives new revelation. The work of the Spirit is to illuminate the revelation contained in Scripture.

Second, it does not mean that one's interpretations are infallible because they are "revealed by the Spirit." We must work to make sure that we are understanding the Spirit. This is what Paul was writing about in 1 Corinthians when he said the church is to weigh what is said by the prophets (see 1 Corinthians 14.29). Just because a prophet claims to have a revelation from the Lord does not mean that the church is to accept it uncritically. The same is true when we think we receive insight from the Spirit.

Third, it does not mean that He gives the ability to see truths that have not been evident to any other dedicated Bible reader. We must be careful about finding hidden meanings that have alluded Bible scholars for two thousand years.

Fourth, the work of the Spirit is not a substitute for diligent study. The Bible commands that we work to become accurate handlers of the truth. This means that the Spirit's work does not rule out the use of study aids and helps like commentaries and Bible dictionaries (Zuck, 120-130).

The role of the Spirit in Bible interpretation is to reveal truth to the soul of the seeker of truth. For those who seek the truth through diligent prayer and study, the Spirit will illumine the mind so that they might apprehend the truth.

8. The Clear Guides the Unclear

The eighth principle of biblical hermeneutics is that the clear passages ought to guide the unclear.

One of the frustrating facts about Bible study is that the meaning of certain passages of the Bible are unclear and remain unclear to even the most studied theologian. For instance, take Paul's words to the church in Corinth about baptism.

> Otherwise, what do people mean by being baptized on behalf of the dead? If the dead are not raised at all, why are people baptized on their behalf? (1 Corinthians 15.29)

This is the only biblical passage that has any reference to baptism for the dead, and it is extremely unclear. Is Paul affirming the practice or simply using it as an illustration much like the altar to the unknown god in Acts 17.23? The only way to know the answer to these questions is to examine what the Bible *clearly* teaches about baptism.

When we study the biblical teachings about baptism, there is nothing that encourages one person to be baptized for another, much less for a deceased person. Baptism is always a testimony to one's own profession of faith in Jesus as Savior and Lord. So, the clear teachings about baptism inform the unclear instead of allowing the unclear to muddy the clear waters of biblical teaching. We are left with the unsatisfactory realization that we may never know what Paul was talking about in 1 Corinthians 15.29.

The corollary to this principle is that no doctrine ought to be developed on an unclear, obscure verse of the Bible. For instance, some religious groups practice baptism for the dead. While their defense for the practice probably lies outside of the a dependence upon 1 Corinthians 15.29, we do not want to make the mistake of accepting a complete theology of baptism for the dead because of an obscure reference to it in one verse of the Bible. We must allow what the Bible clearly teaches to set the parameters for what the Bible does not clearly teach.

9. Historical Narratives Should Be Interpreted by the Didactic

Another area where a lack of clarity often pervades the Bible is the historical narratives. What we must remember about the historical narratives is that they recount for the reader what happened. They often do not evaluate what happened or even attempt to answer the question of whether or not we should emulate the actions within the story.

Even the most notable biblical characters are presented to the reader with warts and all. While David was a man after God's own heart, he was also a man of many mistakes. Many chapters of the second book of Samuel focus on the poor decisions of his life. They are not written down for us to emulate, but they are recorded to teach us about following God.

Some Bible scholars teach that we should not use Old Testament narratives simply to illustrate New Testament principles. I agree that there is more to the Old Testament than just sermon illustrations for Paul's teachings. However, there is a reason why we look to the teaching portions of the Bible to guide our understanding of the narratives of the Bible, so many of which are in the Old Testament. The only biblical criteria for knowing the meaning or application behind a narrative is the clear didactic (or teaching) parts of the Bible. This is another example of allowing the clear to guide the unclear.

Another section of Scripture where this principle is extremely important is in the book of Acts, particularly in the movement of the Spirit in the narrative. The narrative tells us what happened, but it does not necessarily prescribe that event to continue to happen. This is particularly important to remember when studying the relevant passages about speaking in tongues, baptism in the Spirit, or casting out demons. These few passages simply tell what happened; it is the didactic portions of the New Testament that help us understand why it happened and what we should continue to expect in our experience with Christ.

10. Consider the Genre

Special attention is needed when studying particular genres of literature. These literature types often cause Bible students to stumble because of their unique features.

Parables

Generally speaking, the parables of Jesus are not to be treated as allegories. An allegory is a story where each element of the story represents something else. Unless there is something in the text that indicates an allegorical reading, this practice has demonstrated itself through church history to be very misleading. Extensive allegories often take the reader away from the reason Jesus told the story in the first place. In other words, allegories usually betray their context. Most of Jesus' parables are linked to a context that demonstrates the reason behind the parable. So, the best way to read the parables is to identify the one point of the parable. Parables usually answer the simple question, "Why did Jesus tell this story?"

Hebrew Poetry

The book of Psalms is a collection of poems, and poetry is found in many books of the Bible. It is helpful to remember three types of parallelism used by Hebrew poets when studying the Psalms and other poetic verses.

First, synonymous parallelism occurs when different lines of a poem express the same idea in a different way. For instance, "A false witness will not go unpunished, and he who breathes out lies will not escape" (Proverbs 19.5).

Antithetic parallelism is when two lines are set in contrast to each other. An example of antithetic parallelism is found in Proverbs 10.4: "A slack hand causes poverty, but the hand of the diligent makes rich."

Synthetic parallelism occurs when the second part of a passage completes the first part in a progressive movement. For example, "Ask, and it will be given to you; seek, and you will find; knock, and it will be opened to you" (Matthew 7.7).

Often, confusing passages will gain clarity when we take the time to realize the parallelism used by the author.

Law

The unique genre of law has been discussed, but we will take the time to repeat the primary principles here. The Old Testament law consisted of moral law, civil law, and ceremonial law. The ceremonial law has been fulfilled in Christ, so we no longer offer sacrifices for sins. The civil law was given to a theocratic state governed by the presence of God for a particular time. The moral law is the portion that continues to be effective for God's people today. Some of these moral laws were contained in both case law and even in ceremonial law, but it is the moral law that remains in effect today. Therefore, the hard interpretive work of reading the Old Testament is to identify the type of law in each case.

Proverbs

The flip side to the law is the proverb genre. Proverbs are practical truisms stated in catchy phrases. They are generally true, but do not reflect moral laws that can be applied absolutely to every life situation with guaranteed results. While it is generally true that if you bring up a child in the way he or she should go, they will not depart from it, this proverb does not carry a money back guarantee. The proverb does not override the free will of each person to accept or reject the path of life. However, there is truth in the proverb, and parents would do well to heed it.

Apocalyptic

The hardest parts of the Bible to interpret are the apocalyptic portions, most notably the books of Revelation and Daniel. These books are best faced after studying the rest of the Bible. However, many Bible students want to tackle them first because of their interest in last things. The key to understanding these portions is to accept one's limitations and to seek the wisdom of others scholars.

14 | FINAL WORD

We have journeyed together through the pages of Scripture for the purpose of handling it accurately so that the word of God could speak more powerfully to us. It is my hope and trust that you will continue to explore with more detail and passion the pages of the Bible. I can only hope that this brief introduction has whetted your appetite in such a way that it can only be satisfied with further reading and study.

These principles of interpretation are only of value to the person who pursues hearing the voice of God today. Many are content to leave the Bible on the shelf, nothing more than a religious relic of the past. Others take it to church so they can follow along with the preacher. Still others open it sporadically at moments of crisis hoping to find words of hope.

But the Bible is God's gift to us, profitable for teaching, correction, training in righteousness, and equipping us for the good works He has created us to do. These principles come to life as each believer exercises the disciplines of regular Bible reading, meditation, Scripture memory, and prayer. And as we read the Bible, seeking to hear God's voice to us each day, these principles will guide us and help us to clarify the voice of the Spirit.

15 | RESOURCES

Sources Cited

Boa, Ken and Larry Moody. *I'm Glad You Asked.* Wheaton: Victor Books, 1982.

Brown-Driver-Briggs, *Hebrew and English Lexicon.* Peabody: Hendrickson, 1979.

Erickson, Millard. *Christian Theology.* Grand Rapids: Baker Books, 1985.

Ewert, David. *From Ancient Tablets to Modern Translations.* Grand Rapids: Zondervan, 1983.

Foster, Richard. *Celebration of Discipline.* San Francisco: Harper Collins, 1998.

Harrison, Everett. *Introduction to the New Testament.* Grand Rapids: Eerdmans Publishing Company, 1971.

Lewis, Jack. *The English Bible from KJV to NIV.* Grand Rapids: Baker Books, 1981.

Merriam-Webster Online Dictionary.

Metzger, Bruce. *The Expositor's Bible Commentary*, ed. Frank Gaebelein, *Volume 1.* Grand Rapids: Zondervan, 1979.

Sproul, R.C. and Robert Wolgemuth. *What's in the Bible?* Nashville: W Publishing Group, 2000.

Thayer, Joseph Henry. *Greek-English Lexicon.* Grand Rapids: Baker Books, 1977.

Thomas, Robert L. *How to Choose a Bible Translation.* Fearn: Mentor, 2000.

Zuck, Roy. "The Role of the Holy Spirit in Hermeneutics," *Bibliotheca Sacra,* April-June, 1984.

Bible Reading Plans

www.bibleplan.org

www.youversion.com

www.biblegateway.com

www.gnpcb.org/esv/devotions/

www.bhpublishinggroup.com/readthebible/

Scripture Memory Plans

www.fighterverses.com

Helps to Understanding the Bible

Stott, John. *Understanding the Bible.* Grand Rapids: Zondervan, 1999.

Anders, Max. *30 Days to Understanding the Bible.* Nashville: Thomas Neslon, 2004.

Sproul, R.C. *Knowing Scripture.* Downers Grove: Intervarsity Press, 2009.

Fee, Gordon and Douglas Stewart. *How To Read the Bible for All Its Worth.* Grand Rapids: Zondervan, 1993.

Dr. Todd Pylant is the Senior Pastor of the First Baptist Church of Benbrook, Texas. He holds degrees from Baylor University, Southwestern Baptist Theological Seminary, and Bethel University. In 23 years of ministry, he has served churches in both Texas and Georgia. He and his wife, Kelli, live in Fort Worth, Texas with their three children.

Books, sermons, and other articles can be accessed at www.toddpylant.com.

Made in the USA
Charleston, SC
01 December 2011